HERMENEUTICS
FOR
PREACHING

Approaches to Contemporary
Interpretation of Scripture

HERMENEUTICS FOR PREACHING

Approaches to Contemporary Interpretations of Scripture

Raymond Bailey
Contributing Editor

BROADMAN PRESS
NASHVILLE, TENNESSEE

4210-16
ISBN: 0-8054-1016-3

Dewey Decimal Classification: 251
Subject Heading: PREACHING
Library of Congress Catalog Number: 92-6336
Printed in the United States of America

Unless otherwise indicated, Scripture quotations are from the King James Version.

Scripture quotations marked AT are that chapter's author's translations.

Scripture quotations marked GNB are from the *Good News Bible*, the Bible in Today's English Version. Old Testament: Copyright © American Bible Society 1976; New Testament: Copyright © American Bible Society 1966, 1971, 1976. Used by permission.

Scripture quotations marked RSV are from the *Revised Standard Version of the Bible*, copyrighted 1946, 1952, © 1971, 1973 by the National Council of the Churches of Christ in the U.S.A., and used by permission.

Scripture quotations marked NEB are from *The New English Bible*. Copyright © The Delegates of the Oxford University Press and the Syndics of the Cambridge University Press, 1961, 1970. Reprinted by permission.

Scripture quotations marked NRSV are from the *New Revised Standard Version of the Bible*, copyrighted © 1989 by the National Council of the Churches of Christ in the U.S.A., and used by permission.

Scripture quotations marked NASB are from the *New American Standard Bible*. © The Lockman Foundation, 1960, 1962, 1963, 1968, 1971, 1972, 1973, 1975, 1977. Used by permission.

Scripture quotations marked NIV are from the Holy Bible, *New International Version*, copyright © 1973, 1978, 1984 by International Bible Society.

Library of Congress Cataloging-in-Publication Data

Hermeneutics for preaching: approaches to contemporary interpretation
of scripture / Raymond Bailey, editor, contributor.
p. c m.
Includes bibliographical references.
ISBN 0-8054-1016-3
1. Bible—Homiletical use. 2. Bible—Hermeneutics. I. Bailey,
Raymond, 1938-
BS534.5.H47 1993
220.6 01—dc20   92-6336
                                                                        CIP

CONTENTS

INTRODUCTION
HERMENEUTICS: A NECESSARY ART

Raymond Bailey

You are a hermeneut. Every person is a hermeneut of sorts because each of us is called upon to make important decisions about interpretation every day. Have you not thought about a statement someone has made, "What did he *mean* by that?" or interpreted for another explaining, "What she meant was. . . ." We interpret the news on television, radio, and in the print media. We make decisions about the meaning of statements heard and read. Acts of foreign individuals and governments are interpreted for us by reporters, analysts, and our own government and political leaders. When national and international figures speak there are analysts who tell us what they "really" mean. We examine our personal history, acts and words of others in the context of our ongoing or past experience with them, the history of our culture, and works of art, and interpret the implications for our present and future happiness and well-being. The question is not whether or not one is a hermeneut, but whether or not one is a self-conscious, informed, critical hermeneut.

Hermeneutics, in simplest terms the art or science of interpretation, is a practical, necessary endeavor for meaningful existence in a society. Those who are a part of a religious tradition, who believe that there is a residue of sacred knowledge, usually in the form of written documents, must have a theory of hermeneutics. It may be a theory formed from careful reflection or an intuitive one developed from practice and impulse; it may be a theory or practice uncritically accepted from others. A theist who believes in the existence of a divine being who is involved in the universe and in human history struggles for a key to discovering exactly what the role of that being is and how it may be understood. A Christian who affirms revelation, that is, that God has disclosed God's personal self to humanity, must seek to discover and interpret that revelation. If one speaks of "God's will," one is driven to search for means of deciphering that will and understanding it in order to know the implications for one's personal life. Every Christian who affirms that God has disclosed God's self through Jesus Christ and that the Bible is in any way inspired must have a theory of hermeneutics. Christians contend that their Scriptures are not merely records of past experiences with God but also resources providing insight into human thought, feelings and behavior, and a view of the future. Understanding correctly the message of the Scriptures leads to an understanding of what God is doing in the world and how one can be a Christian in the world. The principles which inform the practice of biblical and literary experts should benefit any Christian who desires to be a serious student of the Bible.

The preacher's vocation requires him or her to be as familiar with hermeneutics as a doctor must be with theories and techniques of diagnosis. The preacher has the responsibility of determining meaning not only for self, but also for others. Poor diagnosis by physicians can result in serious physical damage to those they attend; poor interpretation by ministers may result in emotional and spiritual damage to those in their care. Preachers must strive to determine the meanings of texts, consider the implications for a particular people in a particular culture at a particular time, and then communicate their findings to those people. Preachers have the dual responsibilities of understanding and explaining.

Hermeneutics: A Tool of Rhetoric

Hermeneutics is derived from the name of Hermes, the messenger of the Greek gods. Hermes invented language as the means of accomplishing his mission. He would not disclose the message to anyone except the one for whom it was intended; therefore, language had ambiguity enough for misunderstanding. The preacher is a messenger divinely charged with delivering the correct message to those for whom it was intended. As in any rhetorical situation, there are four elements involved in the process: messenger, message, person for whom the message is intended, and the medium or form of transmission. The preacher as hermeneut must seek to understand and interpret all four.

Three contemporary definitions, one by a theologian, one by a New Testament scholar, and one by an Old Testament scholar help to focus the issues. Carl Braaten defined hermeneutics as "the science of reflecting on how a word or an event in a past time and culture may be understood and become existentially meaningful in our present situation."[1] I would prefer the term *art* to that of *science*, but either can suggest a skill whereby a fact or truth may be discovered or demonstrated. Braaten raised the critical issue of distance, distance in time and distance in culture. A function of biblical hermeneutics is to bridge that distance. The purpose of this bridge is to bring an idea or experience that has value into the present. Later, we will take note of how the purpose may be to generate an experience rather than to report or describe one. The purpose of hermeneutics is to discover meaning in the past that will affect, perhaps effect, existence in the present.

The world of the Bible was different from our world. The language sounds strange (even when translated). The lives of the people were unlike ours. Time, people, and events moved more slowly. People lived in a world without modern conveniences; there were no telephones, automobiles, or airplanes. The everyday concerns were different, yet there were striking similarities. Human motives, conflicts, and ultimate concerns were astoundingly like our own. I see in the behavior of those ancient people, in the laments of the psalmist, in the anguish of the victim, and in the guilt of the perpetrator of the pain a reflection of myself. I learned long ago that the Scriptures interpret me and my life.

Alice, the young heroine in Lewis Carroll's *Through the Looking Glass*, slipped through the "silvery mist" of the mirror over the fireplace and landed in the "looking-glass house." The world was a strange one filled with odd characters. It was a fantasy land unlike any on the earth, and yet the adventure there revealed much to her about herself and her world. The text of Holy Scripture is the looking-glass house where we see ourselves reflected as no real mirror can. Hermeneutics is the passageway through which we slide into a strange world where truth is larger than fiction or reality.

Bible		Message
Biblical	Hermeneutics	Our
Word		World

The revelation is about us and interprets our existence in such a way as to make our lives "existentially meaningful."

The preacher seeks to be the hermeneutical bridge for listeners ready to experience the biblical message. Preachers must move from understanding to explaining. According to Leander Keck this process occurs in three stages:

> On the simplest level, it is a matter of explaining terms and concepts... On another level, the interpreter seeks modern equivalents for biblical terms.... On the third level, the interpreter engages in... demythologizing. Here one asks for the religious/existential meaning that is expressed in mythological language.[2]

More is required than translating words from one language to another. If that were all that was required, preaching would be unnecessary. Any ancient document can only be properly understood in the context of the cultural milieu in which described events occurred or where stories and myths were created. The preaching hermeneut seeks to interpret and understand Scripture in order to explain the meaning of texts toand for others.

J. A. Sanders assigned two essential tasks to the hermeneut: "Determining valid modes of seeking the meaning of a biblical text in its own setting, and then determining a valid mode of expression of that meaning in contemporary settings."[3] Sanders' description of the hermeneutical task implies the rhetorical dimension. First, there is the sense that the message is written for the purpose of shaping society. Second, the interpreter intentionally exegetes the passage in order to explain its meaning in the context of a community that has a purpose for existence.

Sanders is a canonical critic who would address a passage in the setting in the canon, but that is in itself a hermeneutical decision. One might ask of a particular passage the setting of the event in history or salvation history, in the life of Jesus, in the life of the early church, or in the plan of an author who has arranged materials according to a literary or rhetorical plan. Once meaning is determined, the task becomes one of expressing it in such a way that it may be appropriated by the contemporary listener. Sanders went on to point out that for Western Christians, this means finding appropriate symbols to transform Eastern first-century ideas and images into modern philosophical thought patterns.

Modern discussions of hermeneutics have focused on the issues of understanding and explanation. The difficult task of communication is complicated by the distance. Even when two people talk face-to-face it is uncertain how one can really "know" what the other thinks. Can we ever be sure that what we heard was what another said? To reinterpret to a third party what was exchanged between two persons in personal encounter is a monumental task. The problems are manyfold when people with different fields of experience, different languages, and separated by hundreds of years try to communicate. Written discourse is already a step removed from oral discourse that includes vocal force and inflection, body language, and an opportunity for dialogue. When the original speaker/writer was attempting to explain the will of God and was thus already an intermediary, understanding and explanation are even more difficult. It may be easier to ascertain the original meaning of a text than to determine implications for the present, and easier to accomplish both those tasks than to communicate either or both to a contemporary audience.

Discovering modern equivalents is not an easy task, and word-for-word, sentence-for-sentence translations will not assure transference of meaning or understanding. J. A. Sanders offered some rules for interpretation including what he called "dynamic analogy." Dynamic analogy calls for individual and social identification. Like Alice in the looking-glass house, the hermeneut must go through the veil and into the world of the Bible for a sojourn. The interpreter must ask if he or she is an Egyptian or a Hebrew, a false prophet or true one. The church leaders of today must acknowledge that the Pharisees represented the most respected leaders of their day. "It [the Bible] should not be read to identify false prophets and Pharisees with another group or someone else, but with one's own group and with oneself, in order to perceive the right text in the right context."[4] When one reads the opening verses of Exodus, is there a sense of oneness with an oppressed minority or a common experience of fearing another group which threatens what one owns or wants? Preachers must read the text for self and others with honesty. "Most biblical texts must be read, not by looking in them for models for morality, but by looking in them for mirrors for identity."[5] We find ourselves in the world of the text and return to our world bringing with us the truths which we have discerned about ourselves and our world for others.

The remainder of this chapter is devoted to an overview of the major trends in hermeneutic theory and practice from the biblical period to the present. The limits of space constrain me to a rather cursory examination. I have chosen theorists and ideas which I believe to be the major ones and representative of subgroups and adaptations. Some thinkers whom others would view as important, perhaps even the most important, are not included. I hope that what is presented will stimulate the reader to seek and read lengthier, more thorough histories of interpretation.

The Hermeneutic Legacy of Judeo-Christian Tradition

Interpretation of events and experiences and records of those events and experiences are not peculiar to our age or even a concern of recent vintage. Examples of interpretation are woven into biblical hermeneutics, the fabric of the Bible itself.

Sanders pointed out that the covenant promise to Abraham was treated differently by various prophets according to their rhetorical purposes in particular moments and situations. He cited the example of Ezekiel who chided those who had broken the covenant for expecting God to give them possession of the land. The false prophets gave assurance that if God promised the land to one, He would not take it away from the many descendants of that one; but Ezekiel declared that Israel's apostasy had negated any right they had to possess the land (Ezek. 33:23-26). Isaiah, on the other hand, reinterpreted the promise of the land to Abraham to comfort the exiles (Isa. 51:1-3). Isaiah, in effect, used the text for hope that Ezekiel used for judgment. The later prophet seems to contradict the earlier one; but if the tradition is a living one with variant meanings to persons in different circumstances, then each is true to the text for particular people in a particular situation at a particular time.

A great deal of the New Testament is presented as interpretation of the Old. The Old Testament was the authoritative text for the earliest church. Jesus apparently established a model for interpretation for the New Testament writers. Examples of His interpretation can be found in the Sermon on the Mount. His method is demonstrated in Matthew 5:17-48. He began by establishing the principles of fulfillment. Following His example, the early church interpreted Jesus' life as the fulfillment of Old Testament prophecy (see 1 Pet. 1:10-12).

Jesus dealt with the spirit and purpose of the text, apparently looking behind or ahead of the words. He refused to be bound by a rabbinic tradition of interpretation and did not hesitate to say, "You have heard . . . , but I say. . . ." In Matthew 5:21-48, Jesus demonstrated His contextual and rhetorical approach. He asked why the commandment was given, what its intention was, and then moved to how that intention could be realized. The same pattern is presented by Mark in dealing with the issue of divorce because of the "hardness of hearts" (10:1-12). Mark's Gospel presents Jesus as shifting from the law to the broken relationships and attitudes that provoked the legal principle.

The hermeneutic of Jesus may have provoked His first opposition, at least as Luke's Gospel tells the story. His home synagogue at Nazareth provided the setting (4:16-27) for Jesus' interpretation of Isaiah 61:1. First, He declared that He was the fulfillment of the prophecy. If this was not bad enough, He proceeded to indict His neighbors for their failure to receive Him. He proceeded to interpret a number of Old Testament incidents (1 Kings 17:1; 17:8-9; 2 Kings 5:1-14) as evidence that the good news of Isaiah 61:1 was not limited in application to Israelites. It was the interpretation that the work of the Anointed One also applied to Gentiles that enraged His listeners. Later the disciples would be confused by His reinterpretation of Messiah in terms of the Suffering Servant of Isaiah as opposed to the triumphant Son of Man in Daniel 7.

The importance of hermeneutics may be nowhere clearer than its impact on Jesus' self-consciousness and His way of living in the world and carrying out His perceived mission. He built His community of followers on His understanding of and explanation of the people of God. He reinterpreted law and prophecy.

Paul used a variety of interpretative techniques including allegory (Gal. 4:21-31) and typology (Col. 2:13-17). Paul operated from some important assumptions about the function of Scripture that informed his use of it. He believed that the Old Testament was essentially the church's book (Rom. 15:4-6). It was intended to instruct and inspire the church to the end that the people would be "of the same mind with one another according to Christ Jesus " (NASB). A second important principle in Paul's exegesis had to do with the Spirit. Paul had much to say about the gift of discernment and claimed that authentic interpretation was a result of the liberating power of the Spirit of the Lord (1 Cor. 2:12-16). Paul also adopted the rabbinic practice of using Scripture to interpret Scripture (Rom. 10:5-13).

Jesus and Paul both operated from dominant theological perspectives that colored their thoughts. Jesus understood His mission and God's working in the world in relationship to the kingdom of God. Anthropology and ethics were by-products of the rule of God which had begun with Jesus' coming. Paul's understanding of the Old Testament, including his beloved "law," was seen through the lens of Christology and resurrection. Nearly every spiritual reference was used to explain Christ and the resurrection, and life was to be ordered according to this revelation.

The Hermeneutics of the Early Church

Allegory and typology dominated the hermeneutics of the early church. The master of allegory was the brilliant Origen. Origen worked in the early part of the third century. Allegory ("to speak other") seeks a meaning other than the surface or literal meaning of words and stories. The allegorist assumes that everything stands for something else. Origen believed that God inspired His word in such a way that levels of meaning would be revealed to the reader or learner according to the ability of each to receive and appropriate the message. Higher truths are hidden from those unworthy to receive them. He believed that Scripture has a plain meaning and a higher one. His scheme involved three levels of meaning: the plain or literal, the moral, and the mystical. Origen was convinced that God made the Scriptures hard to understand because God wanted us to have to dig for the meaning. He argued that the hermeneutical process itself was purposeful in shaping the believer. The problem is, of course, that each interpreter can find the meaning which best serves his or her interest. Final meaning would have to be determined by majority vote of the church.

Typology is a controlled form of analogy not to be confused with allegory. Typology assumes intentional correspondence, connection between people and events in the Old Testament and in the New. Typology identifies implicit ideas in the Old Testament that become explicit in the New. Joseph is said to be a "type" of Christ. The writer of Hebrews wrote that the law "has only a shadow of the good things to come" (10:1, NASB). In Colossians, Paul wrote that the old festivals and ceremonies were only a shadow of what was to come with

Christ (2:16-17). Care must be taken in typology to demonstrate significant similarity. Surface similarity may not represent similarity of essence. Moreover, any analogy may be pressed too far.

Over against the followers of Origen was the school of Antioch led by Theophilus who insisted on full literal exegesis. Grammar and linguistics were the tools of these interpreters. Disciples of Theophilus like Theodore of Mopsuestia and John Chrysostom were less rigid than their teacher and allowed for metaphor and extensive use of typology. This approach avoided the excesses of allegorical interpretation while allowing for symbolism, figures of speech, and apocalyptic literature within the canon.

Jerome and Augustine were the finest fruits of the earliest schools of hermeneutics. Jerome was converted from being a disciple of Origen and allegory to a literal approach. He was a careful student of the original languages who refused to disregard the letter. Augustine remained a modified allegorist. He followed Origen in stressing the process and insisting that God intended for access to the deep meaning of Scripture to be difficult and limited. Augustine, however, introduced a new principle for biblical interpretation. Theology, as interpreted by the church, was declared superior to the text. The rule of faith, the doctrine of the church, was to be the final arbiter in determining the meaning of questionable passages. Augustine also had an overarching theological criterion as he declared that any interpretation that did not lead to love of God and love of neighbor was incorrect.

Reformation Hermeneutics

Medieval thinkers continued the debate between allegory and literal interpretations, between a plain meaning and a spiritual one. The debate centered more and more on the issue of historicity. The development of scholasticism produced a rational literalism. Thomas Aquinas asserted that God had inspired not only the words of Scripture but also the things signified by those words. He insisted though that doctrines had to be based on the literal sense of the text.

The Reformation was founded upon a new understanding of the Bible. Luther's personal transformation was rooted in his careful study of the Scriptures. Luther put the Bible in the hands of the people because he believed that the Bible could be understood by common people. The Bible pointed beyond itself to Christ, who was the subject of the Scriptures and the One who stood in judgment over Scripture and those who interpreted it. Luther believed that meaning could be understood from the grammatical sense of the text. He believed that study of the historical context, knowledge of the language, and proper use of grammatical tools would reveal the "one clear, definite, and true sense"[6] of each passage. Difficult passages could be understood by examining them in the light of other passages. He believed that only the person of faith guided by the Holy Spirit could understand the Scriptures.

Modern Hermeneutics

The rise of rationalism, the experimental method, and modern science changed the course of biblical studies. Critical methodology applied to hermeneutic and scientific studies was soon utilized in the study of the origin of texts, the process of canonization, and the historical and literary questions about the content and form of the Bible. The tests of reason and empirical verification were applied to the message, and concerns about truth yielded to the issue of factuality. Theology was subjected to the test of historicity. Interpreters were challenged to examine texts with scientific objectivity. The biblical interpreter was urged to put aside faith commitments and examine the text as a linguist would scrutinize an ancient pagan work or as a scientist would study a bit of matter. The best exegete was considered the one who questioned every theological assumption, every jot and tittle. The witness of the Bible was a secondary concern to a scientific understanding of its history. The nature of the documents was far more important than the message they contained. The higher criticism of the nineteenth century focused on dating of manuscripts, techniques of transmission, authorship, and historicity.

Friedrich Schleiermacher and Wilhelm Dilthey moved the

hermeneutical focus from scientism to understanding. Historical circumstances were to be taken seriously as the context of literary creation but not as the final standard of determining meaning. Meaning lay in the mind of the author; intuition and creative imagination were to be used to project the reader into the author's social and, hopefully, mental framework. Language was understood as the symbolic representation of the life moment of the author. This approach assured that the language of the text served to link two human minds and that meaning was derived from human experience rather than objective knowledge. The unknown might be acquired only when related to the known. The purpose of religious rhetoric was to bring to consciousness what is ontologically present in a human being. The end of the process was to recognize the intention of the author by making author and reader of one mind. Schleiermacher, in the romantic spirit of his time, believed that feeling was superior to reason and that religion is essentially feeling. Dilthey said that the potential for understanding is limited to possible experiences which the author and interpreter have in common. Schleiermacher substituted psychological hermeneutics for grammatical-historical interpretation. His hermeneutic required penetration of language to inner connections between the reader's (or learner's) mind and the author's mind. Schleiermacher shifted the emphasis from objective verification to subjective understanding. The goal was self-understanding which is possible because of pre-understanding common to all humans:

> Schleiermacher ranks as a central figure for two reasons: one, he complemented grammatical exegesis with psychological interpretation, which he referred to as "divinatory." Hermeneutics is as much art as it is science; it endeavors to reconstruct the original creative act—"how it really was." Two, it is with Schleiermacher that we encounter the first attempt to analyze the process of understanding and inquire into the possibilities and limits of it.[7]

Rudolf Bultmann moved away from the particularism of author and reader to the universal consciousness of humanity.

Bultmann believed that meaning is rooted in human consciousness and experience rather than language or event. The subject of the Scriptures, according to Bultmann, is human existence. He believed that message and medium must be separated. He argued that the Bible is replete with myths that obscure the meaning of revelation. Modern science, he contended, will not permit the contemporary reader to accept the biblical cosmology. The form of the message becomes a barrier to the experience Scripture was intended to evoke.

Bultmann has become a lightning rod among Christians. His hermeneutical presuppositions and methodology sharply divided the Christian community. Bultmann discounted the supernatural and ignored the issue of historicity. The message of the Bible, in Bultmann's opinion, had nothing to do with science, and arguments over miracles he considered moot. The church's preoccupation with historical events and scriptural myths, Bultmann believed, hindered the experience of the gospel and thus confused modern minds and thwarted the purpose of the revelation. "It is impossible to use electric light...to avail ourselves of modern medical and surgical discoveries, and at the same time to believe in the New Testament world."[8] Belief in the New Testament was not the point of Jesus' life. Bultmann said that what really happened was so distorted by cultural accretions that we can't know it, and even if we could, we might miss the point of the gospel. He asserted that the purpose of Scripture was to generate an experience of faith resulting in an appropriation of self-revelation for meaningful existence. He rejected ancient historic modes ("husks") of presenting existential truths (myths) in order to discover the existential dimension (the kerygmatic kernel).

Bultmann used the method of form criticism to strip away the cultural accretions. As form critic he worked back through the conditions that have given a text its final structures to seek the life situation in which the words were spoken or repeated. He asked what was original about the gospel stories; he assumed that the simplest form was the oldest, and the oldest was the best or true form. Bultmann wanted to separate form and essence. In the tradition of Schleiermacher, the most important task of the hermeneut is understanding, and understanding is possible because of a universal preunderstanding. Understanding is in subjective experience. Language is not objective but a means of evoking experience. Understanding is prior to and more authentic than attempts to symbolize existential truth in language.

Bultmann placed great emphasis on preaching. His thought seemed to give greater importance to the preaching event than to the word that is proclaimed: "The redemptive event is only present in the word of preaching, the word of address and claim and promise. . . . Faith is faith in the Word of God which encounters me through the preaching of it."[9] Preaching opens the way to the experience of "the eschatalogical [sic] event that has its origin in Jesus."[10] The emphasis is not on past event but on present experience.

Gerhard Ebeling and Ernst Fuchs were followers of Bultmann who focused on the role of languages in generating experience. The language of Scripture is not everyday language but is the language of being (Heidegger). Language is a means of evoking a saving event. Ebeling believed that hermeneutics was theology because it was the means of divine-human encounter. The words of Scripture provoke new words which give birth to a dynamic experience of revelation.

Ebeling and Fuchs (influenced by Heidegger and Bultmann) stressed the performative power of language. The gospel is perceived as a language event that is regenerated in another language event, the Bible, which is a collection of word events: "Word of God . . . seeks to be understood as a word event that does not go out of date but constantly renews itself, does not create closed areas of special interest but opens up the world, does not enforce uniformity but is linguistically creative."[11] The interpreter becomes a translator who recognized that "the word of Holy Scripture discloses that which on a thousand occasions man may experience as his situation."[12] No longer can one be content to ask only what words "mean." One must now seek to understand what language "does." The concept of performative language demands a whole new attitude toward the media of revelation.

Recent Developments

The most influential individual in post-Bultmannian contemporary hermeneutics has been Hans-Georg Gadamer. Gadamer, a philosopher, addressed the issue of truth and its apprehension. His interest in hermeneutics had to do with how truth is discovered and transmitted. He developed a hermeneutical circle that takes seriously history, language, and preunderstanding. Gadamer viewed the problems of temporal and cultural distance in historical consciousness as potentially positive in the quest for meaning. Preunderstanding, he believed, could interact with history to shape thought. The Enlightenment positivists had advocated the suppression of bias in order to achieve a pure objective view. Schleiermacher and Dilthey argued that such objectivity was humanly impossible. Indeed, they believed it counterproductive to the hermeneutical task. Gadamer agreed with Schleiermacher, Dilthey, and Bultmann that preunderstanding was a key to meaning. Moreover, he concluded that one could not insulate self from the historical stream in which humans are submerged.

Gadamer thought that the temporal, cultural distance factor could be an impetus to the interpreter to see the differences between the world of the text and the present age. Awareness of this gap should open the reader to new possibilities. One is prodded to move beyond preunderstanding to a new synthesis:

> Gadamer takes the knower's boundness to his present horizons and the temporal gulf separating him from his object to be the productive ground of all understanding rather than negative factors of impediments to be overcome.[13]

Prejudices (prejudgments) are not necessarily erroneous and may be a gateway rather than an obstacle to truth:

> In fact, the historicity of our existence entails that prejudices, in the literal sense of the word, constitute the initial directed-

ness of our whole ability to experience. Prejudices are biases of our openness to the world. They are simply conditions whereby we experience something—whereby what we encounter says something to us.[14]

The questions with which the interpreter begins study of the text are reshaped by the message of the text. The meaning of the text emerges between the interplay of text and interpreter.

A key element of Gadamer's method is conversation. There is movement between interpreter and text. The prejudice of the interpreter is formed out of the whole of social experience. The interpreter's preunderstanding has been shaped by the tradition and conventions of time and culture. This view has tremendous implications for the preacher.[15] The preacher may profitably understand his or her function as engagement in a three-sided conversation with self, text, and congregation. Gadamer used the metaphor of horizon as his paradigm. The purpose of hermeneutics is the fusion of the horizon of the text and the horizon of the interpreter. Gadamer affirmed material importance for preunderstanding, language, and the life situation expressed in language.

Gadamer has had a profound effect on the more recent hermeneuts. Paul Ricoeur has developed a hermeneutic of correlation that places the text in the role of mediator between general and specific revelation. He contended that direct self-knowledge is impossible and that the only way one can understand the self in the world is by moving through signs, linguistically perceived. When the events contained in a text are interpreted, new events occur. Understanding is rooted in human experience that is expressed in language. Ricoeur placed primary emphasis on the text that reveals the God who is within us. Ricoeur brought hermeneutics back to the text. The mind and life of the author could be neither reconstructed nor penetrated. The narrative of the text takes on a life of its own.

Hermeneutics is tuned to comprehending genres, signs, and

symbols. "Interpretation," Ricoeur said, "is the work of thought which consists in deciphering the hidden meaning in the apparent meaning, in unfolding the levels of meaning implied in the literal meaning."[16] The text contains the revelation and allows for multiple meanings but is limited to the potential of the symbols. The text sets a course which the reader follows to fulfill the purpose of the passage. Ricoeur applied the techniques of secular literary critics, noting that religious revelation is ordinary poetics taken to the extreme. The ordinary language conveys an extraordinary message because of the extravagance of the claim of religious texts. Ricoeur insisted that revelation is in the text.

Locus of Meaning

The hermeneutical question is that of the location of meaning and understanding. This precedes and dictates how meaning is explained. The Christian expositor must decide if meaning lies behind the text, in the text, in a world universal consciousness, in the listener, or somewhere in the interaction of these points. Is truth behind, within, or in front of the text?

REVELATION
Writer   Work   World
Audience

Theological and philosophical decisions are made before one approaches the text. What is the nature of God and revelation? How does God speak, or does God speak at all? Is God involved in the world or only an absentee Creator? Did the Holy Spirit inspire the writers? If so, to what degree were they inspired: thoughts, images, experience, words? Does the Holy Spirit inspire the reader? If so, is meaning vested in the response of the reader to the text rather than in the text itself? How does God work in relationship to human thought, feeling, and experience?

Philosophically, the interpreter is concerned with the nature of knowledge and learning. How do we *know* anything?

Are there different kinds of knowledge? How do we learn? How is knowledge passed on between individuals and cultures? Is there such a thing as objective knowledge? What is truth? How does time affect relationships? Are there moral absolutes, or are all morals culturally conditioned? What is the nature of language? How are thought and language related?

The hermeneut's task is not an easy one, but it is a necessary one. Answers to the above questions—if answers exist—must inform the methodology of the preacher's hermeneutics. The preacher must exegete the biblical text, but he or she must also exegete self, culture, and audience.

The chapters which follow contain demonstrations of seven popular hermeneutical techniques. Each writer briefly introduces a hermeneutical theory and then practically applies the theory to a passage of Scripture. Hopefully, the reader will discern a method which implements the theory. The writer moves from theory to a sample analysis of a text to sermon. Each hermeneut derives meaning according to the writer's understanding and then seeks to explain the meaning in a way that the reader will understand. Think about the fact that each sample analysis and sermon has become a literary text for you to interpret.

Notes

1. Carl E. Braaten, *History and Hermeneutics*, vol. 2 in *New Directions in Theology Today* (Philadelphia: Westminster Press, 1966), 131.

2. Leander E. Keck, *The Bible in the Pulpit: The Renewal of Biblical Preaching* (Nashville: Abingdon Press, 1978), 112.

3. J. A. Sanders, "Hermeneutics," supplementary vol. in *Interpreters Dictionary of the Bible* (Nashville: Abingdon, 1976), 403.

4. Ibid., 406.

5. Ibid.

6. Duncan S. Ferguson, *Biblical Hermeneutics* (Atlanta: John Knox Press, 1986), 160.

7. Joseph Bleicher, *Contemporary Hermeneutics: Hermeneutics as Method, Philosophy, and Critique* (Boston: Routledge and Kegan Paul, 1980), 15.

8. Rudolf Bultmann, "New Testament and Mythology," in *Kerygma and Myth*, ed. Hans W. Bartsch and trans. Reginald H. Fuller (London: Society for Promoting Christian Knowledge, 1954), 5.

9. Rudolf Bultmann, quoted in Clyde Fant, *Preaching for Today* (New York: Harper and Row Publishers, 1975), 21.

10. Ibid.

11. Gerhard Ebeling, "God and Word" (1966), in *The Interpretation of Texts*, vol. 1 in *Hermeneutical Inquiry*, comp. David E. Klemm (Atlanta: Scholars Press, 1986), 218.

12. Ibid., 223.

13. Hans-Georg Gadamer, *Philosophical Hermeneutics*, ed. David E. Linge (Berkeley: University of California Press, 1976), xiv.

14. Ibid., 9.

15. For an in-depth discussion of Tracy's conversational model, see David M. Waters, "David Tracy and Theological Conversation: A Hermeneutic for Sermon Development in the Pastoral Context" (Ph.D. diss., The Southern Baptist Theological Seminary, 1991).

16. Paul Ricoeur, "Existence and Hermeneutics" (1965), in *The Interpretation of Existence*, vol. 2 in *Hermeneutical Inquiry*, comp. David E. Klemm (Atlanta: Scholars Press, 1986), 192.

1
A
HISTORICAL
MODEL

David S. Dockery

Biblical preaching is the task of bringing about an encounter between people of our times and the written Word of God, composed in another language, another time, another culture. Our goal in this chapter is to discover how to interpret the biblical text in its historical setting and expound its meaning and significance for the contemporary world. The task of interpretation focuses on discovering the historical meaning of the biblical text. The task of preaching relates the ancient text to the people to whom the preached word is now spoken again, as a living word for them.[1] Like the other contributions in this book, I will offer an explanation of the hermeneutical model represented in this chapter. Then I will briefly analyze a passage from Paul's Letter to the Ephesians. Next, I will show how to move from text to sermon. Finally, I will suggest responsible uses of the New Testament for expository preaching.

An Author-Oriented Hermeneutical Model

The "father of modern hermeneutics," Friedrich D. E. Schleiermacher (1768-1834), argued that interpretation consisted of two categories: grammatical and psychological.[2] Prior to Schleiermacher, hermeneutics was understood as special hermeneutics *(hermeneutics sacra)* and general hermeneutics *(hermeneutica profana)*. Special hermeneutics was concerned with how the Bible ought to be interpreted, and general hermeneutics was for interpreting other kinds of literature. Schleiermacher, however, insisted the understanding of linguistic symbols, whether biblical, legal, or literary texts, should be derived from a consideration of how understanding in general takes place.

The Primacy of the Author

Schleiermacher saw that what was to be understood must, in a sense, be already known. Acknowledging that this appeared circular, he nevertheless maintained this very account of understanding remained true to the facts of everyday experience. This was stressed in his comment that "every child arrives at the meaning of a word only through hermeneutics."[3] The child must relate the new word to what is already known. If not, the word remains meaningless. On the other side, the child must assimilate something alien or universal that always signifies a resistance for the original vitality. To that extent it is an accomplishment of hermeneutic. Schleiermacher added that since understanding new subject matter depended on positive relations to the interpreter's own known horizons, lack of understanding was never completely removed. Therefore, interpretation or understanding constituted a progressive process, not simply an act that can be definitively completed.[4] Schleiermacher contended for a preunderstanding that must take place before interpretation can happen.[5] For Schleiermacher, interpretation was related to the author's intention.

The early Schleiermacher, in his section on grammatical interpretation, articulated some of the most incisive statements found in all hermeneutical literature on the principles for grasping what an author willed to communicate. His grammatical hermeneutics were largely dependent upon the work of Ernesti's *Institute Interpret's Novi Testament* (1761).[6] Ernesti's eleven rules included:

1. Master the *usus loquendi* (the use which speakers/writers made of their words).
2. The sense of words is regulated by usage.
3. The sense is not totally determined by standard linguistic conventions because each writer has personal style.
4. The interpreter needs to be immersed in the linguistic

usage of the writer's place and time, and then in the writer's own characteristics.

5. The aim is to establish the literal sense of the utterance, unless there are clear indications for nonliteral understanding.
6. The interpreter must be aware that the verbal sense is often ambiguous and may have to appeal to indirect evidence such as: (a) author's purpose, (b) analogies, and (c) common sense.
7. It should be remembered that the author has freedom in usage of words, but cannot stray too far from the conventional or it becomes unintelligible.
8. The interpreter must never begin anywhere other than with words of the text and with the attempt to establish their sense. The hermeneutical task ends when the verbal sense has been discovered.
9. Scripture cannot be understood theologically until it has been understood grammatically.
10. There are two requisites of the competent interpreter: (a) an acuteness of understanding *(subtilitas intelugendi)* to discern the sense of a passage, and (b) an acuteness of skill *(subtilitas explicandi)* to exhibit that sense to the public.
11. Hermeneutics is the science which teaches us to find in an accurate and judicious manner the meaning of an author and appropriately to explain it to others.

The grammatical meaning, however, was not enough for Schleiermacher. He argued that the theme of an author's text was a product of the author's nature. The ultimate aim, therefore, involved getting through to an author's unique individuality, a psychological interpretation. Understanding required a knowledge of grammatical concerns, but also a divinatory intuition through empathy with and imagination of the author's experience. The interpreter's goal focused on sharing a life relationship with the author. Understanding, then, involved more than rethinking what an author thought. It included reexperiencing what was in the life of the author who generated the thought. Schleiermacher contended that if this

reexperiencing could take place, the interpreter could understand the author's work as well as or even better than the
author.[7]

Author-Oriented Hermeneutics
in the Twentieth Century

The prominent approach to biblical studies in both Protestant and Roman Catholic schools of interpretation until the
middle of this century was an author-oriented approach in
line with the Schleiermacher tradition. This view has been
called the "literal-grammatical," "historical-contextual," or
"historical-critical" method of interpretation. Advocates of
this approach such as Krister Stendahl and John L. McKenzie, writing in the *Journal of Biblical Literature* (1958), defined interpretation as determining the meaning intended by
the human author and understood by the original readers.[8]
Followers of this approach considered the meaning of biblical
texts to be stable and univocal. They considered meaning to be
located in the historical situation. Stendahl defined the task
of interpretation as furnishing the original, reconstructing
the transaction of the author to the original audience by way
of the text.[9]

In an early edition of *A Short History of the Interpretation of
the Bible* (1963), R. M. Grant affirmed a very similar position.
He did this even while recognizing the shifts toward existential hermeneutics under the widespread influence of Martin
Heidegger and Rudolf Bultmann. Grant maintained: "It
would appear the primary task of the modern interpreter is
historical, in the sense that what he is endeavoring to discover
is what the texts and contexts he is interpreting meant to
their authors in their relationships with their readers."[10]

In 1967, a University of Virginia literary scholar, Eric D.
Hirsch, Jr., published a major work—*Validity in Interpretation*—advocating an author-oriented, normative hermeneutic.
He followed this work in 1976 with *The Aims of Interpretation*.[11] Working within the Schleiermacher tradition of general
hermeneutics, Hirsch called for a grammatical and historical
interpretation that attempts to grasp the meaning an author

intended to convey in what was written. His influence in biblical interpretation is praised by many scholars of diverse theological traditions.[12]

Hirsch distanced himself from the Schleiermacher tradition, however, by maintaining that it was not the task of the interpreter to have access to the mental process by which an author produced a work. He affirmed that the author's verbal meanings can be grasped because the interpretation of texts is concerned with shareable meanings. Hirsch contended that authors choose language conventions that will bring to readers' minds the things they are attempting to communicate, so the readers can also know what the authors wanted to share with their audience by words.[13] Language is efficient in transmitting these meanings because it consists of conventions, of elements that the society using that language has agreed should stand for all its various aspects of common experience. Thus, "an author's verbal meaning is limited by linguistic possibilities but is determined by his actualizing and specifying some of these possibilities."[14] The meaning of words is thus limited by a context that has been determined by the author. Interpreters cannot, then, understand what writers meant except by what they have actually written. With reference to biblical studies, G. B. Caird has summarized:

> We have no access to the mind of Jeremiah or Paul except through their recorded words. *A fortiori*, we have no access to the Word of God in the Bible except through the words and the minds of those who claim to speak in his name. We may disbelieve them, that is our right; but if we try, without evidence, to penetrate to a meaning more ultimate than the one the writers intended, that is our meaning, not theirs or God's.[15]

To summarize Hirsch's position concerning an author-oriented interpretation, we can note he claimed the task of the interpreter is to understand what an author meant at the time of the writing. This is possible because the text's meaning is controlled by language conventions that exist between

the speaker and hearer or author and reader. Hirsch acknowledged that interpretation takes the form of process, a process
that takes the form of a guess, and there are no rules for
making good guesses. There are, however, methods for vali-
dating guesses as Hirsch elucidated:

> The act of understanding is at first a genial (or a mistaken)
> guess and there are no methods for making guesses, no rules
> for generating insights; the methodological activity of inter-
> pretation commences when we begin to test and criticize our
> guesses.[16]

Paul Ricoeur, agreeing with Hirsch, has likewise observed:

> As concerns the procedures of validation by which we test our
> guesses, I agree with Hirsch that they are closer to a logic of
> probability than a logic of empirical verification. To show that
> an interpretation is more probable in light of what is known is
> something other than showing that a conclusion is true. In this
> sense, validation is not verification. Validation is an argumen-
> tative discipline comparable to the juridical procedures of legal
> interpretation. It is a logic of uncertainty and of qualitative
> probability. . . . A text is a quasi-individual, the validation of an
> interpretation applied to it may be said, with complete legiti-
> macy, to give a scientific knowledge of the text.[17]

The most important contribution Hirsch's theory has made
to biblical studies is the distinction between "meaning" and
"significance." *Meaning* is what the writer meant when
addressing the original readers. Hirsch emphasized that there
is one primary normative meaning—that which the author
intended. However, he suggested the more important or meaningful a text is, the greater the possibility of deeper, fuller
meanings. The *significance* of the text includes all the various
ways a text can be read and applied beyond the author's
intention.

I would like to suggest that exegesis focuses on the primary
normative meaning of the biblical text. Preaching entails
expounding the fuller meaning or significance of the biblical

text in line with the way the early church read Scripture through the vehicles of typological and allegorical interpretation, plus the developments of *sensus plenior* (the fuller meaning of the text) and the analogy of faith since the second century.[18]

The goal, then, of interpretation is not to psychologize an author but to determine the author's purpose as revealed in the linguistical structure of the text. In other words, the goal of interpretation concerns itself with what the author achieved. Ricoeur has stressed that, generally, when one reads a text, the author is not present to be questioned about any ambiguous meaning in the text. This is certainly the case with the human authors of the biblical text.[19]

Ricoeur, like Hirsch, maintained a text's meaning is intelligible across historical and cultural distance. Because of the nature of writing, the text opens a possible world to the interpreter (the text world); the interpreter may enter into that world and appropriate the possibilities it offers. When that occurs, the meaning of the text is actualized in the interpreter's understanding. What is understood or appropriated, then, is the text itself, the result of the author's writing.[20] Let us now examine our text from this hermeneutical perspective.

Analysis of Ephesians 5:21-33

The initial chapters of Ephesians describe the church's spiritual blessings in Christ (1:3-14), her life in Christ (2:1-10), and the new community of Jews and Gentiles and their common union with Christ (2:11—3:13). After Paul showed how God brought believing Jews and Gentiles together into a new relationship in Christ, Paul emphasized the unity, variety, maturity, and purity of the church (4:1—5:21). At this transitional point in the letter Paul showed how believers, enabled by the Spirit, can live together in a practical way in new relationships. We can outline the epistle this way:

A. Introduction (1:1-2)
B. New Life (1:3—2:10)
C. New Community (2:11—3:21)
D. New Principles (4:1—5:20)

    E. New Relationships (5:21— 6:9)
    F. New Challenges (6:10-20)
    G. Conclusion (6:21-24)

The section on new relationships is characterized by the basic principle of submissiveness. Social relationships are similar to those that govern the community life. In 5:18-21, with the use of four participles, Paul listed for the church several results of being filled with the Spirit: (1) speaking to one another with psalms, hymns, and spiritual songs (v. 19); (2) singing and making music in your heart to the Lord (v. 19); (3) giving thanks for everything (v. 20); and (4) mutually submitting one to another out of reverence for Christ (v. 21). The apostle then applied the principle of mutual submissiveness to relationships between wives and husbands (5:22-33), children and parents (6:1-4), and servants and masters (6:5-9). Our analysis will focus on Paul's words for wives and husbands.

A General Principle (5:21)

Verse 21 serves as a hinge to connect what is prior with what follows. Grammatically, the participle phrase in verse 21 goes with 5:18-20. The content of 5:22-28, however, is dependent on the principle of submission in 5:21.[21] Paul built his argument for the household code on the idea that each family member should yield his or her own rights for the good of the other. This means no one is to coerce the other; each voluntarily accepts this discipline. Family members should not think of themselves more highly than they ought (compare Phil. 2:1-4). Delusions of superiority are dissipated.[22] The gospel places these relationships on a revolutionary new footing, since all are submissive to the lordship of Christ.

Applied to Wives (5:22-24)

While the household code is introduced by a plea for mutual submissiveness, the submissiveness enjoined in the code itself is not mutual.[23] Similar to the parallel code in Colossians 3:18— 4-1, wives are specifically directed to be submissive to their *(idios)* husbands.[24] The distinctive feature in Ephesians is that the relationship between husband and wife is treated as analogical to that between Christ and the church.

No verb is expressed in verse 22. The imperative *submit* is understood from verse 21. Wives are addressed first. They are to be submissive to their husbands.[25] The exclusiveness of the marriage relationship is emphasized. The verb (adopted from v. 21) is in the middle voice meaning that wives are to submit voluntarily to their husbands. No external coercion is found here.

The implied imperative is governed by the phrase "as unto the Lord" (v. 22). The submission of Christian wives to their husbands is one aspect of their obedience to Christ.

Verse 23 paints the marriage relationship as a reflection of Christ and the church. Verse 24 fixes our attention on the special point of immediate interest since verse 25 resumes the thought of verses 22-23.[26] The church as the bride of Christ is to acknowledge Christ's authority and seek to please Him in every respect. When marriage is viewed in light of Christ and His church, wives are able to understand their submission to their husbands as an aspect of their common obligation to the Lord (see vv. 32-33).

Though other household codes in the Greco-Roman world would have required wives to submit to their husbands, Paul explained the Christian relationship in terms of their "common union" in the Lord. Wives are to live out their commitment to Christ in their relationships with their husbands. The exhortation to be submissive means to be humble and unselfish. It means to yield one's own rights and consider the needs of others first. Submission is not the same thing as obedience. The word *obey* is found in 6:1 (children are to "obey" parents) and 6:5 (servants are to "obey" masters), but it is not found in 5:22-24.[27]

Applied to Husbands (5:25-33)

Paul then turned to the reciprocal duties of husbands.[28] The vocative *(andres)* identifies the shift in Paul's thought. The Greco-Roman society in which Paul was writing recognized the duties of wives to husbands but not of husbands to wives.

As in Colossians 3:19, husbands were exhorted to love their wives, but the self-sacrificing love of Christ for the church is set forth as the pattern for the husband's love for his wife. What a radical difference between Paul's command and his contemporary culture! As mentioned above, the ancient world was primarily a man's world. This was most apparent in the home.

Among the Jews the wife was often little more than chattel. The Greeks generally restricted the women to their own quarters and often separated the men from the women at mealtimes. Paul's instructions were in striking contrast to all of this.[29]

Husbands, like Christ for the church, must continually love their wives (note the present tense imperative). *Love* is more than family affection or sexual passion. Rather, it is the reciprocal responsibility of submission. It is a deliberate attitude, leading to action, that concerns itself with the well-being of another. A husband should love his wife: (1) as Christ loved the church (vv. 25-27); (2) as his own body (vv. 28-30); and (3) with a love transcending all other human relationships (vv. 31-33).[30]

Paul indicated this love is sacrificial like Christ's. Christ's love for the church is a self-sacrificing love, and the same love is implied to be true of a husband's love for his wife. The context, not necessarily the word itself (*agape*), informs us of the sacrificial nature of the husband's love.[31]

Verses 26-27 explain more fully the result of Christ's atonement for the church: to make the church holy and pure. The purpose of Christ's giving Himself up for the church is said to be her sanctification and cleansing with water. The Hebrew verb "to sanctify" in certain contexts is used in the sense of betrothal (to set apart for oneself as a wife). It is quite possible that Paul adopted such an idea here with the meaning, "He gave himself up for her in order to betroth her to himself."[32]

An old Jewish wedding custom calls for the groom to say to the bride as he gives the ring to her: "Behold, you are sanctified to me."[33] As the church is to the Lord, so the wife is to the husband (compare Rev. 21:9-11). While some try to find an-

cient rituals of the fertility cults or some gnostic schemes as
the background for Paul's words, the Old Testament portrayal
of Israel as the bride of Yahweh provides all the background
necessary.

Paul turned to his second comparison *(kathos)* in verse 28.
Husbands ought *(opheilō)* to love their wives as being one
flesh with themselves. The Greek phase points to their moral
obligation. So intimate is the relationship between husband
and wife that they are fused into a single entity. The language
is based on the previous imagery.

For a husband to love his wife is to love himself. She is not to
be treated as a piece of property, as was the custom in Paul's
day. She is to be regarded as an extension of the husband's
personality, as part of himself—"no one ever hated *(emisesen)*
his own body" (v. 29, NIV); the phrase expresses something
characteristically true. The analogy is applied further in
verses 29 and 30. The context indicates the apostle's thought
remains focused on the deeper one of the intimacy of the
Christian's relationship with Christ. In the divine purpose, a
wife becomes part of the very life of her husband; and the
husband nourishes and cherishes his wife. Similarly, as a wife
becomes a part of her husband, so members of the church
become a part of the Lord, part of His own life that He has
joined to Himself.[34] The closeness of this relationship is
stressed, similar to the relationship of branches to a vine (see
John 15).

The final comparison in verses 31-33 portrays a love that
transcends all other human relationships. Paul picked up
Genesis 2:24 which is God's initial statement in Scripture
regarding marriage. The Old Testament appeal substantiated
the apostle's argument from Scripture and shaped his thought
throughout the section.[35] The marriage commitment takes
precedence over every other human relationship and for this
reason is regarded as inviolable.

The "two will become one flesh" (Gen. 2:24, NIV) means
closely joined. It hallows the biblical standard of marital relations and excludes polygamy and adultery. What is primarily

a divine ordinance is graciously and lovingly designed for mutual satisfaction and delight.[36]

Paul, in verse 32, appeals to the fuller meaning of Genesis 2:24. Startlingly, he said this mystery (mysterion, wrapped up in Gen. 2:24), was realized when Christ came to win His bride, the church, by giving Himself for her on the cross. It is the likeness of the marital union to this higher spiritual relationship that gives marriage its deepest significance. This mystery refers to the relationship between Christ and the church, a mystery to which Paul had been given divine insight (compare Eph. 3:3,9).[37] Throughout the passage, Paul had been calling on husbands to measure up to the ideal of Christ in His love for the church and to wives to measure up to the church in her devotion to Christ.

Verse 33 concludes Paul's discussion of marriage. The final word is a practical and summary one. The *Good News Bible* emphasizes the practical nature of Paul's conclusion translating, "But it [Gen. 2:24] also applies to you." The husband's responsibility is to love (agapato) his wife (as described in the previous verses). The wife's responsibility is to respect (phobetai) her husband. Such respect is self-initiated (middle voice), conditioned by and expressive of reverence for Christ. It also assumes that the husband will so love his wife as to be worthy of such respect.

Now we will trace the steps involved in moving from text to sermon.

From Text to Sermon: A Method

The hermeneutical models and presuppositions outlined in the first section of each chapter will probably evidence numerous differences. The process, however, of moving from text to sermon will most likely find much more common ground. Here, I would like to identify seven steps (see chart) and appropriate questions involved in this text-to-sermon process. The first four steps are preliminary steps. The final three steps make up the heart of the process. The previous section, "Analysis of Ephesians 5:21-33," focused on step five. Steps one through four were followed carefully, though not as clearly evident.

Step 1. Introduction

The sermonic process begins with prayer. God's direction and enablement must be sought at each step. Then we bring our questions to the text at hand. Three questions help us deal with introduction issues. First and foremost we must ask, "What presuppositions do we bring to the biblical text?" Our basic assumptions pertain to the nature of the biblical text and hermeneutical models undergirding the interpretive process. Our basic assumption is that Scriptures are fully inspired and constitute a truly truthful, divine-human book. The hermeneutical model has been described in the previous section of this chapter. The next two questions focus on matters related to the historical situation and cultural context of the final form (or canonical shape) of the text. We must seek to determine, "What is the historical situation behind the author?" and "What is the cultural context out of which the author wrote?"

Step 2. Observation

As we observe the text being considered, we ask: "What are the limits of the text?" We must look for keys or structural signals (such as conjunctions, particles, etc.) in the text. While the basic unit for consideration is the paragraph, we must pay attention to sentences and word meanings as well. Much that is identified as interpretation is little more than word studies. Seeing the text's structure in paragraph units will enable us to see the major idea being communicated by the author.

Step 3. Translation

Here we ask, "What is the text?" Through textual criticism and comparison of various translations, we establish the text from which we will work. It is likely that most preachers will work from one basic, favorite translation (KJV, NIV, NRSV, NASB, etc.) and do minimal comparisons with other translations. We would encourage them to compare translations and

Introduction	Observation	Translation	Basic Exegesis	Interpretation	Theology	Proclamation
Step 1	Step 2	Step 3	Step 4	Step 5	Step 6	Step 7
Ask: What presuppositions do I have when I approach this text?	Ask: What are the limits of the text?	Ask: What is the text?	Ask: What kind of text (genre) is this?	Ask: What does the text mean in its context?	Ask: What does the text mean to the contemporary reader?	Ask: How can the historical meaning and contemporary significance be communicated?
What is the historical situation?	Basic translation	Establish the text	Advanced observation	Why was it said this way? What is its canonical meaning?	What cultural factors need to be contextualized?	How will the text be heard and understood?
What is the cultural context?	Observe the structure: • paragraph • sentence • words		Lexical exegesis What does the text say? • macro-structure • plot	Study commentaries Survey the history of the text's interpretation	What is its theological significance?	

study commentaries before simply accepting one translation. Learning and using the original languages is even more helpful.

Step 4. Basic Exegesis

Before moving to our primary steps, we need to ask, "What kind (genre) of text are we interpreting?" Is it poetry, narrative, prophetic, parabolic, gospel, epistolary, or apocalyptic? Then we can begin to do basic work with Bible dictionaries, concordances, and grammars. Diagramming a sentence flow at this point can be extremely helpful for seeing the major emphases of the text. Gordon Fee's step-by-step instructions for analyzing the text with the use of sentence flow charts will be most helpful in this process.[38] For certain genres, discovering the plot or macrostructure of the text will be necessary at this point.

Step 5. Interpretation

This is the most important step in seeking the textual meaning from an author-oriented perspective. We bring the question: What did the text mean in its historical setting to the initial readers? Here the question moves from *what* to *why*. We move beyond asking "What does the text say?" to: "Why was it said in this way?" Now we must examine commentaries, trace the history of interpretation of our passage, and move toward seeing the meaning of the text in its literary and canonical context.

Step 6. Theology

Three important questions will help us seek the theological significance of the passage. First, "What did the text mean to the contemporary reader?" Second, "What cultural factors need to be contextualized or retranslated?" Third, "What is the theological significance of the passage?"

Step 7. Proclamation

Finally, we must raise two questions, "How can the historical meaning and contemporary significance be communicated to our contemporary world?" and, "How will the text be heard

and understood today?" The final step of the exposition includes applications, illustration, and motivation as well
(which will generally be absent from my sermonic section). I
would like to address these final two steps in greater detail
before interpreting the text and developing the sermon.

An Interlude

Preaching, as the means of expressing Christian truth in
the modern world, stands between two worlds: "the then" and
"the now."[39] What are the forces at work in contemporary
culture that are of particular relevance to the role of preaching? Peter Berger has identified three dominant sociological
streams or trends that characterize the modern world: (1)
secularization, (2) pluralization, and (3) privatization.[40] These
diverse trends, coupled with gaps in time, culture, and language between the biblical world and ours, demand that
preachers exegete our world as well as the biblical text.

Clearly, recognizing some of these differences will be helpful. Likewise, learning the historical-cultural background of
the biblical passage is needful. Yet, we must recognize that
life cycles of birth and death and customs relating to family
and certain institutions are common for our world and the
ancient world. Similarly, human feelings and experiences can
enable us to bridge the gap between ourselves and the people
of the Bible. Even though there are many contextual and
cultural differences that might call for the biblical message to
be contextualized or resignified, we must recognize aspects of
the human condition that have not changed.

Even with all of our sophisticated technological progress,
our relationship to God remains unchanged. Even the advanc-
ing wisdom and knowledge of the world cannot help men and
women in the spiritual aspects of life. The basic problem of
how sinful humans are to approach a holy God and how these
persons are to live in relationship to the life-giving Spirit of
God and with another is the same for all ages. The needs are
similar, but we need preaching that awakens twentieth-
century readers to an awareness that the Bible still speaks in
a relevant way to contemporary needs.

Exposition in Our World

Now we will attempt to discover the biblical author's message for *our* day concerning Christian marriage from Ephesians 5:21-33, based on the analysis of the text in section two and consistent with our model in section one. I conclude this chapter by developing an exegetical or expositional sermon.

The Sermon

Yield Right of Way: Primary Responsibilities in Christian Marriages

Text: Ephesians 5:21-33

One of the most difficult and complex transitions of life is marriage. The new couple, friends, and family want to see it as a happy, joyful time. The new bride and groom may see their marriage as a solution to the problem of loneliness or family hassles. Their parents may respond: "Finally, he's settled down," or, "Now she has someone else to take care of her." Marriages face challenges that many people are not prepared to face. The statistics indicate that these challenges are often overwhelming. Many people today think the last couple who lived happily ever after was in a Walt Disney film. What we need are men and women who can move beyond wishfulness, fantasies, and unrealistic expectations to realize their mutual responsibilities in marriage. Let us look at Paul's words in Ephesians 5:21-33 to see: (1) The Responsibility of Christian Wives, (2) The Responsibility of Christian Husbands, and (3) Contemporary Implications.[41]

I. The Responsibility of Christian Wives (Eph. 5:21-24,33)

Paul has been outlining the standards that God expects of his new society, the church, especially in terms of its unity and purity. These two qualities are indispensable to a life that is worthy of the calling of the people of God (4:1). This section has a direct bearing on the main theme of the epistle. God's purpose is to reconcile all things in Christ, to create a new community of faith, the church. Within the divine plan, the church is the vehicle through which the ministry of reconciliation takes place. Here Paul brings this theme to a particular focus.

A. A General Principle (5:21)

Verse 21, a hinge verse in Paul's letter, reveals that submitting "to one another out of reverence" for God is a distinct mark of the new society. This general principle forms the foundation for understanding the different responsibilities of Christian husbands and wives. Underlying this general principle are other important themes:
1. The dignity and worth of all members of the new community
2. The equality of all members of the new community
3. The unity of all believers
4. The need for mutual submission among all believers

B. The Principle Applied to Wives (5:22-24,31)

If we can get beyond certain "buzz" words in this passage, we can see God's beautiful model for wives in contemporary Christian marriages. These "buzz" words are *submission* and *headship*. The meaning of these words becomes clear in light of Paul's general principle (5:21) and the command for husbands to love their wives (5:25).

First, we need to remind ourselves that the wife's responsibility cannot be understood apart from the mutual submission called for in verse 21. The verbal imperative in verse 22 is not present in the Greek text and is implied from verse 21. Before focusing on the meaning of submission for today, let us first look at what submission is not:
1. What submission is not:
a. *One modern view.* Within the modern world, Paul is often seen as an oppressor who championed the status quo, subservient position of women. Those advocating this view reject any idea of submission because they think it magnifies chauvinism and reduces the status of women; but Paul's meaning, understood in its context, points us in a different direction.

b. *An unbiblical view.* Within the Christian community are
some who stress the subordinate role of women in the Christian home. These wish to establish a "chain-of-command" in
which husbands have absolute authority over wives. Often,
under the guise of submission, women within such a system
fall into manipulation of their husbands. Others submit out-
wardly in appearance only without really giving themselves
totally to their husbands. Both of these views fail to produce
the partnership God desires in Christian marriages.
2. What submission is:

Submission means to yield your own personal rights and
lose yourself for another. This is patterned after Christ Himself (Phil. 2:5-8) and reflects the essence of the gospel. Our
world is receptive to terms like *self-assertion* and *self-
actualization.* We cower from terms like *submission* and
self-denial because we tend to be self-seeking and self-serving
people. Yet Paul's words, like those of Jesus in Mark 8:34-35,
affirm that self-fulfillment comes through giving ourselves up
for another, considering the needs of others above our own
self-interests. The apostle calls for a wife's submission in a
setting where the world of all persons is valued, and the needs
and interests of one's husband are more important than getting one's own way.

Submission is an ethical emphasis throughout the New
Testament. It is a cross-type life of service to which the entire
church is called. Paul particularly appealed to wives to follow
the Lord in their relationship to their husbands. The verbal
form indicates an earnest inner appeal that cannot be exter-
nally coerced. Paul restated his appeal in verse 33, calling for
wives to respect their husbands. This is the essence of the
significance of Paul's message for contemporary marriages.

Wives are to submit to their husbands, not because it
fulfills the status quo but because submission distinguishes
the life-style of all Christians. When wives live this way, the
"status quo" is deprived of its divine sanction and its inherent permanence. In its place is mutual respect, affirmation,
and service. There are no high or low positions in Christian
marriages. In the new society created by the reconciling

work of Christ, a new order has been born in which all participants regard themselves as servants of one Lord, Jesus Christ,
and yield themselves to one another because of Him. Now let's
see how this relates to the responsibilities of Christian husbands.

II. The Responsibility of Christian Husbands (5:25-33)

Christian husbands "yield right of way" by loving their wives.
We often speak about marrying the person we love. Couples
sometimes consider divorce because they are "no longer in
love" with one another. Nowhere in Scripture are we com-
canded to marry the person we love. Granted, cultural differences exist. Today we choose whom we want to marry after
times of dating and courtship. Yet the biblical principle
crosses this gap of time and culture; the Bible calls for us to
love the person we marry.

In Paul's time, submission was status quo for women, but
husbands had few reciprocal duties. The Greco-Roman society
in which Paul was writing recognized the duties of wives
to husbands, but not of husbands to wives. The command for
husbands to love the wives was unheard of—a revolutionary
approach. A husband's love is more than family affection; it is
a Calvary-type love. It requires work, commitment, and
sacrifice.

Paul calls for husbands to move beyond selfishness and
unconcern. Marriage is demanding, and we must be willing to
invest ourselves in the relationship to grow an exciting,
enriching, effective marriage. Husbands are to love their
wives: (1) as Christ loved the church; (2) as their own bodies;
and (3) with a love transcending all other human relationships.

A. Love as Christ Loved the Church.

When husbands love their wives as Christ loved the church,
they give up their personal rights for the good of their wives.
This sacrificial love provides security and freedom for a
marriage. It is a solemn picture of covenant love.

Christ loved the church and will one day present her beautiful, glorious, holy, and without blemish. It is to this construc-

tive end that Christ has been working and is working. The bride (the church) does not make herself presentable; it is the Bridegroom who beautifies her in order to present her to Himself. Christ's love for the church, His cleansing and sanctifying of her, are all designed for her liberation and perfection.

Here we see the implications of Christ's loving headship. Christ does not crush the church. He sacrificed Himself to serve her. In the same way, a husband should never exercise his leadership to stifle his wife or frustrate her from being herself. Rather his love for her will lead him in another direction. He will give himself up for her so that she may develop her full potential under God and thus become more fully herself, the kind of person and wife God wants her to be. As John Calvin noted years ago, leadership does not imply kingship but companionship.

B. Love as You Love Your Own Body.

On first sight Paul seems to descend from the lofty standard of Christ's love to the low standard of self-love, but Paul reminds Christian couples of their oneness, their "one flesh" relationship. For this reason the obligation for a husband to cherish his wife as he does his own body is more than a helpful guide for daily living. He does so as a symbol and expression of the sacred marital union. When a husband and wife have this spiritual, emotional, and physical oneness with each other, true love is evidenced.

C. Love with a Transcending Love.

In conclusion, the apostle said this permanent, intimate love transcends all other human relationships. Unfortunately, husbands often mistake infatuation for true love and offer inadequate substitutes for love. We must realize that love grows and that growth takes time. Infatuation may be attracted to one characteristic in a person while love grows out of an appraisal of the total personality. Infatuation is self-centered. Love is other-centered and concerned with the total well-being of the other. Love offers true identification with the other person.

Husbands sometimes offer substitutes in the place of authentic, sacrificial love called for by the apostle. In our day we are accustomed to substitutes. We have artificial flavoring, substitute foods, formica instead of wood, vinyl in the place of leather, and the list goes on. However, substitutes in the marriage relationship are inadequate and unacceptable.

A husband's love that transcends all other human relationships will not be satisfied with merely providing his wife's physical and material needs. He will instead share his very life with her. He will not substitute intimidation for leadership. He will not smother her but will honor her and appreciate her. The ultimate responsibility of the husband then is to love his wife with a Christlike love.

III. Contemporary Implications

Let us now see the implications of this for our own lives. We know that men and women have the basic psychological and emotional needs of *security* and *significance*. Wives who respect their husbands and choose to give themselves up for the other provide their husbands with needed significance. Likewise, husbands who choose to give themselves up for their wives with a loving, caring concern provide their wives with needed security. So submission means a choice to give oneself up for the other. Sacrificial love means giving oneself up for the other. It means wives must be willing to live for their husbands; husbands must be willing to die for their wives. The result is family strength characterized by commitment, communication, and appreciation.

When husbands and wives take their responsibilities seriously in obedience to God, it creates opportunities for shared ministry and spiritual friendship. When marriages and homes are strengthened, churches are strengthened and ministry is enhanced. May God give us faithful, loving, caring Christian marriages.

Conclusion

I have offered a hermeneutical model that grounds the meaning of the biblical text in the author's purpose or result. Sometimes hermeneutics is prized in philosophy or theology but neglected in preaching. Preaching deals with both the construction and communication of sermons. Too often preaching is only concerned with communication, but preaching should primarily focus on the message.

If we regard the Bible as God's Word through which He addresses people in history, then it follows that preaching must be based on the Bible. Expository preaching emerges then not merely as one type of sermon but as a consistent outgrowth of a hermeneutical model, affirming a high view of biblical inspiration and an author-oriented view of hermeneutics.

Declaring to a congregation that the Bible is God's Word does not necessarily mean it has been expounded. Often in our churches, the biblical text read and the sermon preached are like strangers passing in the night. I have tried to move away from such faulty preaching so we can see how a sermon should be based on a contextual analysis of the biblical text.

This chapter has offered a hermeneutical model and method that moves us from biblical text to expositional sermon. Sermons are derived from and transmitted through a study of a passage in context. Preaching involves faithful exegesis of the grammar, history, genre, and the cultural literary setting of the text. Preaching is more than effective communication. It is bringing out the contemporary significance of the normative, historical meaning of Scripture.[42] When this is done, we can uphold the purity of God's Word and can faithfully proclaim the whole counsel of God's Word.

Notes

1. Gordon D. Fee, *New Testament Exegesis: A Handbook for Students and Pastors* (Philadelphia: Westminster Press, 1983), 118.

2. Friedrich D. E. Schleiermacher, *Hermeneutics: The Handwritten Manuscripts*, ed. H. Kimmerle and trans. J. Duke and H. J. Forstman (Missoula, Mont.: Scholars Press, 1977), 66-68.

3. Ibid., 40.

4. Ibid., 141.

5. Anthony Thiselton, *The Two Horizons* (Grand Rapids: Wm. B. Eerdmans Publishing Co., 1980), 103-06.

6. Ernesti's work was translated by Moses Stuart (*Elements of Interpretation* [1822]) and noted in Stuart's, "Are the Same Principles of Interpretation to Be Applied to the Scripture as to Other Books?" *The Biblical Repository* (1832):124-37; cited by Walter C. Kaiser, Jr., in "Legitimate Hermeneutics," *Inerrancy*, ed. Norman L. Geisler (Grand Rapids: Zondervan Publishing House, 1979), 117-47.

7. Richard E. Palmer, *Hermeneutics: Interpretation Theory in Schleiermacher, Dilthey, Heidegger and Gadamer* (Evanston: Northwestern University Press, 1969), 84-97.

8. Krister Stendahl, "Implications of Form Criticism and Tradition Criticism for Biblical Interpretation," *Journal of Biblical Literature* 77 (1958): 33-38; John L. McKenzie, "Problems of Hermeneutics in Roman Catholic Exegesis," *Journal of Biblical Literature* 77 (1958):197-204.

9. Krister Stendahl, "Contemporary Biblical Theology," vol. 1 in *Interpreter's Dictionary of the Bible* (Nashville: Abingdon Press, 1976), 419-20. Here he distinguished between what a text meant and what it means.

10. Robert M. Grant, *A Short History of the Interpretation of the Bible* (New York: Macmillan Publishing Co., 1963), 186.

11. See Eric D. Hirsch, *Validity in Interpretation* (New Haven, Conn.: Yale University Press, 1973); idem, *The Aims of Interpretation* (Chicago: University of Chicago Press, 1978).

12. See H. C. Kee, *Community of the New Age* (Philadelphia: Westminster Press, 1977); G. Osborne, *Meaning and Significance* (Downers Grove, Ill.: Inter-Varsity Press, 1991); Peter Cotterell and Max Turner, *Linguistics and Biblical Interpretation* (Downers Grove, Ill.: Inter-Varsity Press, 1989).

13. Hirsch, *Validity in Interpretation*, 17-18,47.

14. Ibid., 48; compare also Walter C. Kaiser, Jr., *Toward an Exegetical Theology* (Grand Rapids: Baker Books, 1981).

15. G. B. Caird, *The Language and Imagery of the Bible* (Philadelphia: Westminster Press, 1980), 61. Caird has discussed the concept of "meaning" and discovering "meaning" in Scripture as carefully as anyone (see pp. 32-61). He distinguishes between meaning R (referent), meaning S (sense), meaning V (value), meaning E (entailment), and meaning I (intention).

16. Hirsch, *Validity in Interpretation*, 25. Hirsch does not argue that the interpreter can know the author's meaning better than the author as was posited by Schleiermacher.

17. Paul Ricoeur, *Hermeneutics and the Human Sciences*, trans. and ed. J. B. Thompson (New York: Cambridge University Press, 1981), 212.

18. See David S. Dockery, *Biblical Interpretation Then and Now* (Grand Rapids: Baker Books, 1992); also idem, "Author? Reader? Text? Toward a Hermeneutical Synthesis" *Theological Educator* 38 (1988):7-16.

19. Ricoeur, *Hermeneutics and the Human Sciences*, 131-44, 182-93; compare also Paul Ricoeur, *Interpretation Theory: Discourse and the Surplus of*

Meaning (Fort Worth: Texas Christian University Press, 1976); idem, *Essays on Biblical Interpretation* (Philadelphia: Fortress Press, 1980).

20. Paul Ricoeur, *The Conflict of Interpretations: Essays on Hermeneutics*, ed. D. Ihde (Evanston: Northwestern University Press, 1974), 142-50.

21. Contemporary translations show the ambiguity of the construction:
1. The NRSV treats verse 21 as a complete sentence and a separate paragraph. The editors have placed the section heading between verse 20 and verse 21.
2. The NASB treats verse 21 as a dependent clause, the conclusion of the sentence that began at verse 18. The paragraph is divided between verse 21 and verse 22.
3. The NIV (1973) treats verse 21 exactly like the NRSV. The *NIV Study Bible* (1985), however, treats verse 21 as a complete sentence and a separate paragraph, but the subject heading is placed between verse 21 and verse 22.

We are following the structure of the NIV (1973).

22. A. Skevington Wood, "Ephesians," vol. 11, in *Expositor's Bible Commentary*, ed. Frank E. Gaebelein (Grand Rapids: Zondervan Publishing House, 1978), 75.

23. J. Paul Sampley, *"And the Two Shall Become One Flesh": A Study of Traditions in Ephesians 5:21-33* (New York: Cambridge University Press, 1971), 104.

24. Compare Richard R. Melick, Jr., *Philippians, Colossians, Philemon*, vol. 32 in *New American Commentary* (Nashville: Broadman Press, 1991), 307-20.

25. The text says *nothing* about women in general being submissive to men, but only wives to their own husbands.

26. The conjunction does not have the full adversative force. It should be translated "now" instead of "but."

27. Diana R. and David E. Garland, *Marriage for Better or for Worse* (Nashville: Broadman Press, 1989), 90-91.

28. H. C. G. Moule, *Studies in Ephesians* (New York: Cambridge University Press, 1893), 139. Moule observed that each party is reminded not of rights but of duties.

29. Curtis A. Vaughan, *Ephesians: A Study Guide Commentary* (Grand Rapids: Zondervan Publishing House, 1977), 117; see also W. K. Lacy, *The Family in Classical Greek* (London: Thames and Hudson, 1972).

30. Vaughan, *Ephesians,* 118.

31. I agree with F. F. Bruce's comment: "There is much uninformed opinion on the allegedly superior quality of *agapao* and *agape* as such over other kinds of love." See Bruce, *The Epistles to the Colossians, to Philemon, and to the Ephesians* in *New International Commentary on the New Testament* (Grand Rapids: Wm. B. Eerdmans Publishing Co., 1984), 387.

32. Sampley, *"And the Two Shall Become One,"* 42-43; compare Jeremiah 2:2; Ezekiel 16:6-14; and Hosea 2:14-15.

33. Cited by Wood, "Ephesians," 76. See Markus Barth, *Ephesians*, vol. 2 in *Anchor Bible* (Garden City, N.Y.: Doubleday & Co., 1974), 691.

34. Francis Foulkes, *The Epistle of Paul to the Ephesians* in *Tyndale Bible Commentary* (Grand Rapids: Wm. B. Eerdmans Publishing Co., 1963), 160-61.

35. The words "of his flesh, and of his bones" in KJV are probably not original but may have been added due to the influence of Genesis 2.

36. Wood, "Ephesians," 78.

37. See F. F. Bruce, *Biblical Exegesis in the Qumran Texts* (Grand Rapids: Wm. B. Eerdmans Publishing Co., 1960), 7-11. See also David S. Dockery, "Typological Exegesis: Beyond Abuse and Neglect" in *Reclaiming the Prophetic Mantle: Preaching the Old Testament Faithfully*, ed. George L. Klein (Nashville: Broadman Press, 1992).

38. See Fee, *New Testament Exegesis*, 60-77.

39. See David Hesselgrave, *Communicating Christ Cross-Culturally* (Grand Rapids: Zondervan Publishing House, 1978); Ernest Best, *From Text to Sermon* (Edinburgh: T and T Clark, 1988); Margaret Parker, *Unlocking the Power of God's Word* (Downers Grove, Ill.: Inter-Varsity Press, 1991); and James E. White, "Contemporary Culture and Old Testament Preaching" in *Reclaiming the Prophetic Mantle*.

40. See Peter L. Berger, *Facing Up to Modernity* (New York: Basic Books, 1977); also see John R. W. Stott, *Between Two Worlds: The Art of Preaching in the Twentieth Century* (Grand Rapids: Wm. B. Eerdmans Publishing Co., 1982); and Kenneth A. Myers, *All God's Children and Blue Suede Shoes: Christians and Popular Culture* (Westchester, Ill.: Crossway Books, 1989).

41. In addition to the commentaries noted in the analysis section, I have been helped in preparing this sermon by several sources. Particularly useful were: Paul Stevens, *Marriage Spirituality* (Downers Grove, Ill.: Inter-Varsity Press, 1989); H. Norman Wright, *Seasons of a Marriage* (Ventura, Calif.: Regal Books, 1982); Lawrence J. Crabb, Jr., *Effective Biblical Counseling* (Grand Rapids: Zondervan Publishing House, 1977); idem, *Men and Women* (Grand Rapids: Zondervan Publishing House, 1991); John R. W. Stott, *God's New Society: The Message of Ephesians* in *The Bible Speaks Today Series* (Downers Grove, Ill.: Inter-Varsity Press, 1979); Maxie D. Dunnam, *Galatians, Ephesians, Philippians, Colossians, Philemon* in *A Textual Commentary on the Greek New Testament* (Waco: Word, Inc., 1982); Diana R. and David E. Garland, *Beyond Companionship: Christians in Marriage* (Philadelphia: Westminster Press, 1986); Ronald Allen, *Liberated Traditionalism* (Portland: Multnomah Press, 1985); and Charles Swindoll, *Strike the Original Match* (Portland: Multnomah Press, 1980).

42. The view of expository preaching offered here has been informed by, among others, Haddon Robinson, *Biblical Preaching* (Grand Rapids: Baker Book House, 1980); Stott, *Between Two Worlds*; Walter Liefield, *New Testament Exposition* (Grand Rapids: Zondervan Publishing House, 1985); and Joel C. Gregory, "Interpretation in Preaching," *Southwestern Journal of Theology* 27 (1985):8-18.

2
A CANONICAL MODEL

John D. W. Watts

The current interest in biblical authority and biblical preaching has focused major attention on a renewed interest in the Bible as canon. This has led to renewed historical investigation of the process by which the Old and New Testaments came to be the Bible, that is, the canon, of the synagogue and the Christian church.[1]

A second direction that scholarly interest has taken is recognition that the canon emerged from a historical process. "Canon is process, and the results of process; it is not simply a time-bound ecclesiastical pronouncement."[2] B. S. Childs led in such discussion,[3] followed soon after by J. A. Sanders.[4] Their studies have taken two directions. Sanders and his followers have worked to open up "the historical and theological dynamics of canonical process—the collection, selection, interpretative sifting and application of traditions, a process which finally produced the body of writings now designated as canonical."[5] The other direction, espoused by Childs, has focused on the final shape of the books and on their interpretation within the church.[6] These directions have profound implications for preaching.[7]

Walter Brueggemann has made extensive use of canonical methodology in his writings. He takes seriously the theological implications of canon as shown in his recent study of Wisdom literature.[8]

This chapter provides an example of the use of canonical interpretation for preaching and examines the techniques inherent in the process.

Text Analysis of Habakkuk 2:4
and its New Testament Citations

Habakkuk 2:4 is cited three times in the New Testament, each time with a slightly different emphasis. It became the text for Luther's Reformation, again with a different emphasis. This chapter proposes to look at these citations as a model of the way a text can be reinterpreted (resignified) within a canonical context and explore the possibilities for preaching that this suggests.

First, we will take a careful look at the Hebrew verse in context, followed by an analysis of the way the LXX[9] translated the verse. Then we will look at each of the New Testament references (Rom. 1:17; Gal. 3:11; and Heb. 10:38); finally, we will trace the way the verse has been used in the exegesis of the Christian church, especially by Martin Luther.

The Hebrew text says: "Behold, [as for] one puffed up, his soul is not upright in him, but a righteous one in his faithfulness will live" (AT).

The context is established by the first chapter of Habakkuk in which the prophet prayed to God in the midst of great crisis for the people, asking, "How long, O Lord?" (1:2, NIV). The first words of chapter 2 indicated his determination to wait before the Lord until he received an answer. The Lord promised to provide a vision which the prophet would record and transmit to the people.

Verse 4 is the expected word from God.[10] It is partly a word of judgment and partly a message of hope. The two halves of the verse deserve separate consideration, and each word is important.

The English translations are instructive of the possibilities in the verse:

> **KJV** Behold, his soul which is lifted up is not upright in him: but the just shall live by his faith.

> **ASV** Behold, his soul is puffed up, it is not upright in him; but the righteous shall live by his faith.

> **RSV** Behold, he whose soul is not upright
> in him shall fail,
>   but the righteous shall live by his faith.

NIV   See, he is puffed up;
> his desires are not upright—
> but the righteous will live by his faith.

NEB   The reckless will be unsure of himself,
> while the righteous man will live by being
> faithful.

WBC   Behold, (the oppressor) is puffed up,
> his soul is not upright in him,
> but the righteous shall live by his faithfulness
> (Word Bible Commentary).[11]

NICOT Behold! The proud—his soul is not upright in him;
> but the justified—by his steadfast trust he shall
> live (New International Commentary on the Old
> Testament).[12]

The verse contrasts two persons. The first is probably representative of the oppressing conquerors, or of those in Israel who sought to use this situation to their advantage. The kind of persons they are, the state of their spiritual attitude, and their fate is contrasted with the second type of person, "the righteous." The kind of persons they both are is stated in ambiguous terms; their spiritual attitude and their fate are not.

The variety of translations above reflects the ambiguity of the first word, *'uppela*. It is variously understood from the root BDB I: "bloated," "puffed up," or "tumorous."[13] The *New English Bible* translates the root according to BDB II: "the reckless." Another way to translate this would be "an audacious one" (AT).[14] Others suggest that two Hebrew letters *p* and *l* have been reversed or transposed to form an original *'alaph* which in Isaiah 51:20 and Ezekiel 31:15 seems to mean one who has fainted or lost his senses (AT). The next words are direct: "His spirit (or soul) is not straight (level, or upright) in himself" (AT).

Contrast this oblique word with *zaddiq*, "a righteous one." There is no doubt about the meaning of the word, but the reference is less clear. Perhaps the reading "one who is in the right" (AT) is clearer. This is joined to "by his faithfulness."

This word is often rendered "by faith," as we shall see. The final contrast is between "shall live" and the implied death of the first person.

The verse clearly contrasts the fate of the seemingly triumphant and boastful conqueror with that of the conquered to the advantage of the latter who is called a righteous one.

Canonical interpretation begins by noting that the key words for "righteous" and "faithfulness" occur also in Genesis 15:6. Thus two key Old Testament texts relate "being in the right" with God and the idea of "faithfulness." By "faithfulness" they mean to be firmly in God and in His ways. They connote trust and fidelity. In both texts, life is being threatened. Life is promised to those who trust in God and thus are "in the right" with Him.

The Septuagint's Translation

The first step toward understanding the New Testament usages of Habakkuk 2:4 is found in the Septuagint (abbreviated LXX): "If he should draw back, my soul has no pleasure in him: but the just shall live by my faith."[15]

The Greek translator read the first line very differently than the Masoretes. One decisive change was making the first person pronouns in both lines third person. It is God's soul and God's faith that is described while the Hebrew speaks of the soul and the faithfulness of two persons. The Hebrew makes no mention of God in the verse while the Greek draws Him in decisively.

A second example of change is that the Greek translator read the Hebrew noun "one puffed up" as a verb from the root *'lph*.[16] This root word may mean something like "be faint" or "swoon." If this is taken literally, the verb should be feminine and probably have "soul" as a subject: "Behold, his soul shall be faint in him, it will not be upright" (AT).

A third decision by the Greek translator was to read *hinneh*, "behold," as a particle introducing a conditional clause, "if." This is possible in Hebrew, but not necessary.

A fourth and key change occurred when the Greek substituted for the Hebrew word "faithfulness" the word *pistis*, "faith." In the Greek, this connotes God's faith while the Hebrew speaks of a righteous one's faithfulness.

The New Testament usage of the verse drew on the Greek's choice of *pistis* ("faith") to translate *'emunah* ("faithfulness"). However it ignored the pronouns in two of the three uses and changed a pronoun's position in the third.

The New Testament's Use

The New Testament picks up the verse three times, each time with a different emphasis. The decisive changes in meaning each time are evidenced by each verse's context.

Romans 1:17

"The righteous will live by faith" (AT).

The *mou* ("my") of the LXX is left out, but the first part of the verse makes it clear that Paul thought in the terms of the LXX. The emphasis in Romans is on the first word, "the righteous." The LXX had already added the definite articles, turning "a righteous one" into "the righteous." Here Paul emphasized: "the righteous who is righteous through his faith will live" (AT). Whereas the Hebrew Old Testament presumed that the one spoken about is already righteous and simply described his reactions to events and their outcomes, Paul was concerned with the process by which the righteousness of God can become an attribute of a believing person. The gospel proclaims salvation by faith because in it the righteousness of God is revealed "through faith and for faith" (Rom. 1:16-17, AT).

Galatians 3:11

"The righteous will live by faith" (AT).

This passage emphasizes "faith." The Septuagint had already made the change from the Hebrew "faithfulness" to the Greek *pistis*, "faith" or "believing". Yet the word is properly understood in both senses: faith that is faithful, and faith that produces right living and holds fast to God. It is not through the law, said Paul, but through this faith that is faithful that the righteous have hope for salvation.

The essence of religious understanding is no different for us than for Paul. Our focus of attention is not on the law but on God. The key to stability and vitality is holding fast to God, believing His faithfulness to fulfill the good news of Jesus in bringing life, freedom, and acceptance by God. In this we have both the promise and the fulfillment of that promise.

Hebrews 10:38

"But my righteous one will live by faith;
And if he shrinks back my soul will not be pleased with him"
(AT).

This reading follows the LXX more closely than either of the Pauline texts and also quotes both lines, not just the second; but it makes a decisive shift of the pronoun *mou* ("my") in the first line from "my faith" to "my righteous one." It also reverses the order of the two lines.

Here the emphasis is on *life*—not destruction—but life as the lot of God's own who remains faithful in his beliefs.

The variations in the pronouns are remarkable. The Hebrew has three third person masculine pronouns: "his soul," "in him," and "his faithfulness." The LXX keeps "in him," but changes the other two into first person: "my soul" and "my faith."

The New Testament references in Romans and Galatians drop all pronouns but make "the righteous" definite (the Hebrew means, "a righteous one"). The Book of Hebrews has the third person pronoun, "with him," and two first person pronouns, "my righteous one" and "my soul."

Explanation of the Technique

What we have been doing is looking at a particular, important text, first in terms of its meaning in its historical and literary context, and then assessing the influence of this text on other writings in the Bible, specifically in the New Testament. This text is fairly easy to follow because it is clearly quoted three times in the New Testament.

Chart of the Translations

Hebrew	LXX	Romans 1:17	Galatians 3:11	Hebrews 10:38
Behold	If			And if
noun	verb			verb
puffed up	he should draw back			he should draw back
is not upright	has no pleasure			has no pleasure
his soul	my soul			my soul
in him	in him			in him
But a righteous	but the righteous	but the righteous	the righteous	but my righteous
by his faithfulness	by my faith	by faith	by faith	by faith
will live	will live	will live	will live	will live

In this process we have also kept in mind that the Old Testament used by the apostles and the early church was the Greek translation known as the Septuagint. Therefore, the effect of translating this text into Greek was also drawn into the equation.

A third step was noting the importance of the theological ideas of the text which related "righteousness" and "faith." There is one other text in the Old Testament which explicitly relates these two themes, Genesis 15:6, so it was also drawn into the discussion.

Homiletic Use

Homiletic exploitation of the observations above concerning the canonical use of Habakkuk 2:4 may take several routes. The most extensive could preach a series of sermons on these texts.

The first sermon could concentrate on the Habakkuk text. The verse would be placed in the context of 2:1—3:19, almost as an aside during the lengthy tirade against the tyrant who is oppressing Israel. The thrust of its meaning would be: the tyrant by his tyranny may appear to be great. In fact, he is "puffed up" or "a swollen tumor" whose end is near and certain; but in these troubled times a righteous person, simply by continuing to be faithful to God—to God's Word and covenant—*will live.*

A second sermon could take the Septuagint's understanding of the verse. It also would be set in the context of Habakkuk 2—3 and in the historical circumstances implied by the book's opening verse. Here both parts of the verse (2:4) refer to the Israelite and God's attitude and relation to him: "If he should draw back" (LXX), that is, be timid or abandon his faith, the Lord ("my soul") will not be pleased with him; but the one who is truly right with God will live by God's faith ("my faith"). This phrase, "God's faith," bears further exploration. Does it mean God's faith in the righteous one? Does it mean that God's faith has been implanted in those whose righteousness consisted in their faith in God, as Genesis 15:6 teaches? In either case the verse calls for a strong and bold faith for those troubled times, a faith that is "God's faith" or God's kind of faith. *Or does it mean "God's faithfulness to the righteous"*

The third sermon could deal with Romans 1:17 which defines the gospel Paul preached and believed. The emphasis would be on righteousness by faith. The passage should include verses 16-18. In verse 17, the term "the righteousness of God" is drawn from the LXX translation of Habakkuk 2:4 which introduced God into the verse by the personal pronoun "my." Whereas the LXX had spoken of God's soul and God's faith, Paul added God's possessive to "righteousness," continuing the tendency to read the verse as referring to God.

Paul then went on to relate the ideas of "righteousness" and "faith" as Hebrews 10:38 and Genesis 15:6 have done, citing Habakkuk 2:4b: "the righteous will live by faith" (AT). The citation has "the righteous" like the LXX instead of the Hebrew, "a righteous one." It uses the LXX's *pistis* ("faith") instead of the Hebrew's "faithfulness," but it omits the LXX's "my" or "my faith." It has not altered "righteousness" to read "my righteousness" (that is, "God's righteousness") in spite of the use of the idea at the beginning of the verse. The result is a quotation closer to the Hebrew but that owes the term "faith" to the Greek text.

The sermon should also note Paul's awareness of the context of Habakkuk 2:3 that is reflected in Romans 1:18. He picked up the picture of the believer who lives in an oppressive world of evil powers. The message of Habakkuk is these powers will be overcome and judged, and the believer will live.

The fourth sermon could use the text of Galatians 3:11. The contextual reading begins with 3:1 and continues through verse 14. Genesis 15:6 is cited in verse 6 and Habakkuk 2:4 in verse 11. The passage deals with the issue of whether one is saved by keeping the law or by believing the gospel (3:5). Paul answered the question first by turning to Genesis 15:6 and arguing that the children of Abraham are those who believe as Abraham believed God. Thus, Gentiles who believe share the blessing of Abraham.

He then argued that reliance on keeping the law for salvation is self-defeating: no one is justified before God by the law. At this point he introduced Habakkuk 2:4: "The righteous will live by faith" (AT). The words are exactly the same as in Romans 1:17, but the context has changed the emphasis. Here faith is contrasted with legal observance. The emphasis is on faith that is counted as righteousness. The passage ends by saying that Christ died in order that the blessings of Abraham might become available to everyone who believes and who then receives the promise of the Spirit.

The last sermon could deal with Hebrews 10:38. The context may begin with verse 35, or it may go all the way back to verse 19. It should continue through verse 39. It is dominated by a call for faithfulness through difficult times of persecution in view of the promised return of Christ.

Habakkuk 2:4 is cited as an example of how bold and continued faith is rewarded with life while apostasy (or shrinking back) is deplored. The context in Habakkuk is as important here as the verse itself.

The author of Hebrews defined the righteous one as "my righteous one." (Does this draw on the Dead Sea Scrolls' idea of the eschatological teacher of righteousness?[17]) He stressed the righteous one's relationship to God, but the greater emphasis is on "will live." The call for strong faith and faithfulness under persecution was undergirded by this Scriptural promise that these will be rewarded with life, while fearfully turning away will incur the displeasure of God. (This is the only New Testament reference that quotes the entire verse, and even here the two parts are reversed. The second line seems to be added only as an afterthought.)

Verse 39 closes the argument by identifying the congregation with believers, not those who shrink back and are destroyed. They are those who believe and are saved. Habakkuk's idea of reward as "life" is here interpreted in the New Testament sense as "saved," which of course means saved to eternal life.

In these sermons, the full richness of the range of ideas that can be related to "righteousness" and "faith/faithfulness" can be explored as the expositor follows the steps of the New Testament interpreters of this great Old Testament verse. A follow-up sermon might deal with the way Luther used the verse as a battle cry for the Reformation.

Another homiletic use of Habakkuk 2:4 and its canonical references might take the form of a single sermon titled, "Righteousness by Faith." Each of the parts of the sermon would deal with a scriptural passage:

1. Genesis 15:6: "Abraham believed God, and it was reckoned to him as righteousness" (AT).
2. Habakkuk 2:4 (Hebrew): "A righteous one by being faithful will live" (AT).
3. Habakkuk 2:4 (Greek): "The just shall live by my faith" (AT).
4. Romans 1:17: "The *righteous* will live by faith" (AT).
5. Galatians 3:11: "The righteous will live *by faith*" (AT).
6. Hebrews 10:38: "The righteous *will live* by faith" (AT).

The Method

Canonical interpretation for the preacher and teacher must be carried over into exegesis and interpretation in order to be useful or effective. This is precisely what is attempted here.

Three Principles

Three principles control this exegesis. The *first* is recognition of the value of each text. Each one is important in its own right; but we also recognize a kind of hierarchy in the relation of similar or related texts. This hierarchy may be one of several kinds.

There is a hierarchy of *substance*. The actual contents of the text show that text to be more substantial, more important, than other texts.

The hierarchy may be one of *influence*. One text has exercised a greater influence within the Bible, or beyond it, than the other texts. This is true in the present study where Habakkuk 2:4 is quoted in the three New Testament texts. Its influence is obvious. This is not true of its relation to Genesis 15:6. From a canonical point of view, the Torah text should be given priority, although its direct influence on Habakkuk cannot be shown.

The hierarchy may be one of *temporal priority*. This is evident in this study. Habakkuk 2:4 is obviously older than the New Testament texts, and they are clearly dependent upon it. Notice also that there is a kinship with other texts on the same subject. This is particularly true in Paul's extensive treatments of faith in Romans and Galatians. A further kinship may be recognized—although it cannot be followed up in this study—with texts on related subjects, such as righteousness established by covenant obedience or by sacrifice.

A *second* principle calls for keeping one exegetical goal in mind: to find biblical truth and to develop biblical doctrine. This leads to defining the specific doctrine to which the exegesis of these texts contributes. Beyond that, it calls for determining how this doctrine relates to the broader order of truth about God and about His relationship to His people and theirs to Him.

A *third* principle should apply. When dealing with a group of texts, it is proper to note their similarity (as called for above), but also to take note of their differences. Even small verbal differences may be significant.

In the texts before us, we have seen how a similar doctrine was expressed in Genesis, Habakkuk, and the New Testament. We have also seen how a basic text, Habakkuk 2:4, was used for several different purposes in the New Testament. There is a range of meaning derived from the first text that is legitimately applied in several different situations. This is a good example of the way a preacher may use a text to support a message, as well as its being a source for his message.

Canonical interpretation views Scripture as potentially authoritative, expecting to find in it direction for our lives, our faith, our teaching, and preaching. It does not automatically exclude any part of Scripture from this process. It does recognize that some Scriptures are not appropriate for some uses.

It is sensitive to precedents in finding some Scripture particularly meaningful. In the case at hand, Paul's repeated use of Habakkuk 2:4 obviously affects our willingness to give it an important place in our considerations. Sometimes these precedents come from the Church Fathers. Sometimes they come from theological systems or confessions of faith. The preacher who uses this text is the latest in a long line of interpreters who have done the same thing. We do well to take note of this by using commentaries.

However, it is the Scripture—its setting, context, and repetition—that is to be most appreciated and honored. Later usage is to be judged and critiqued by exegesis of the Scripture and the way Scripture uses the text.

The canonical interpreter is aware of a theological dimension in exegesis. How does the doctrine developed from this passage relate to the broader pattern of doctrine in Scripture? With what other doctrines is it compatible and supportive? With what others does it stand in tension or contradiction? If it is in tension, how does one resolve or recognize this tension?

In the case at hand, the doctrine of faith-righteousness, we need to determine how these passages relate to other passages about faith (especially in Romans and Galatians, but also in the Gospels). There is the tendency in them to stress that our relationship to God is primary to all other considerations, but we also need to ask: How does being righteous by faith or faithfulness relate to righteousness through obedience to covenant law, righteousness through practicing justice and mercy, or righteousness gained through sacrifice?

Canonical criticism is a broad foundation. It can effectively use insights gained from other methods. While it has been developed specifically as a replacement for historical criticism that seeks insight into how the literature came into being, canonical criticism may make use of insights gained from historical research. It recognizes the importance of understanding meaning in the historical setting attributed to it by its context.

It may also profitably use literary criticism. The canon is composed of many different kinds of books. Texts have meaning within the context of the book and genre in which they first appear.

Form and rhetorical criticism are also compatible with canonical criticism. The way words are used and the intended usage of the various forms of expressions can be effectively used in canonical interpretation. Insights into reader response are also useful because canonical interpretation is particularly concerned with making the texts meaningful to hearers or readers; but canonical interpretation insists that none of these with their particular concerns be allowed to overshadow the meaning of a text as a part of the Christian Bible. It seeks to understand the contribution each text makes to the larger whole of biblical truth and teaching.

Canonical interpretation will not allow the individual text to be lost in the larger whole, but it will also not allow it to be used without regard to the whole of Scripture. It will not allow it to be treated simply as a record of how an ancient people thought.

A summary of the steps used in this study of Habakkuk 2:4 would include:

I. A Careful Analysis of the Primary Text (Hab. 2:4)

The key words "righteous" and "faithfulness" were examined carefully, as well as the context of living and dying in

oppressed times, and the contrast to the "one puffed up."
The literal statement of the text was determined.

The context was examined to establish the probable historical setting and the contextual application and meaning.

An attempt was made to establish the truth that may have a broader application. A "righteous" one has his existence and destiny determined by his "faithfulness." Righteousness is often related to covenant, sacrifice, obedience, acts of justice, or morality. These are not excluded here, but the text looks behind them to motivation and to a characteristic attitude. This righteous one is defined not by the acts as such but by faithfulness toward God, toward covenant, and toward the people of God which these acts represented. Hebrews 11:6 later puts it succinctly: "Without faith it is impossible to please God" (NIV).

II. A Look Behind the Text

The Old Testament presumes that Torah, the Pentateuch, takes precedence over the Prophets, and was the foundation for their teaching as it is for all Judaism. Writers of the prophetic books often acknowledged this explicitly and implicitly.

There is a text in Torah that also speaks of righteousness derived from faith. It is found in Genesis 15:6. A canonical approach would examine the relationship between these two texts. This may be a diachronic relationship if the second text was derived from or expressly depended on the first, or it may be synchronic if the two texts are looked on as belonging to the same Bible, and the question of temporal priority is not considered relevant. The examination of the two texts will show that the ideas of Habakkuk 2:4 were not unique in Scripture. The Genesis reference helps to establish a broader base for the teaching.

III. The History of the Text

Habakkuk did not enter the Christian Bible in its original (Hebrew) form. It was first translated into Greek. Christian apostolic authors knew and used the Greek version of the Old Testament known as the Septuagint. A canonical approach recognizes this and traces the effect of new Greek words used to translate the Hebrew in the interpretation of the text.

It is instructive to weigh the effect that subsequent translating had on the ability of the text to convey its message. Each one brought nuances of meaning which are communicated to the readers.

IV. The Appearance of the Text in Later Writings

In the case of Habakkuk 2:4, not only are the ideas of the verse used, but the verse itself is quoted three times in the New Testament. The verse clearly influenced Paul and the author of Hebrews. Canonical interpretation takes this into account.

These quotations began the history of the interpretation of this verse as a Christian Scripture. They also developed nuances of its meaning which, in turn, have Scriptural authority.

V. Its Use in the Church

Canonical interpretation is concerned with the authority of the Scriptures in the church. This makes investigating the history of the interpretation of any particular verse appropriate and useful. In this study we have restricted this to noting Martin Luther's use of the verse as a motto for the Reformation.

Conclusion

The authoritative use of the whole Bible is the substance of canonical interpretation. The Old Testament is to be used for Christian direction and instruction, as well as the New.

No verse or passage is to be used alone. It is to be interpreted within the literary context and within the canonical context of the Bible. Old Testament verses are to be interpreted with due attention to New Testament teachings on the subjects they address. New Testament passages are to be understood with due attention to their Old Testament background.

The Scriptures are to be viewed as valid for establishing doctrines about God and about each worshiper's relationship to Him, and about the church, its thought and its life.

The Sermon

How to Live as One Who Is Right with God

Text: "The righteous will live by his faithfulness" (Hab. 2:4, AT).

This text has a vital message for every one of us. It has reverberated through the Scriptures as it has been applied to various situations. It has a message for you. Listen to it. Read it and decide what it says about your need today.

The original Hebrew text is composed of just three words. Each one is important. "Righteous" is a term used in the Bible to describe the person who is prepared to be in the presence of God, whether in the temple (that is, in church), or in the spirit (as in prayer), or in the life to come. How is one to *become* righteous? It is clear that no one is automatically right with God. Everyone is a sinner and is, for this reason, estranged from God.

The Bible speaks of several ways to gain the designation "righteous." One can bring a sacrifice in confession of sin and be pronounced fit to enter the temple for worship; one can keep the Law and thus be found in covenant with God and a part of His people. However, the kind of "righteousness" described here is a deeper kind and reflects an attitude that must precede both sacrifice and keeping the law for them to be valid. It speaks of the righteous person as one who is righteous because of "faith" and "faithfulness." Perhaps you are saying "faith" and "faithfulness" are not the same thing. Of course, you are right; however, in the Bible they are treated as two sides of the same coin. In Hebrew these two spiritual gifts are expressed by the same word, as we shall see.

The third word is "live." We assume everybody wants to live, to be alive, and to survive. People may have different ideas of what that entails, but every one of us wants to live. We need to affirm that God is very much involved with life. He created life in the beginning. He gives each of us the physical breath of life at birth; He yearns to also give the spiritual breath of life, His Holy Spirit, to all who believe in Jesus Christ and His promise of eternal life. This text is about all of that, but we are getting ahead of ourselves. Let us go back and look at the matter carefully and see where you and I fit into this.

Before Habakkuk, we can find another text that speaks of faith and being right with God. It also, in a sense, deals with being alive. The text is Genesis 15:6: "Abraham believed the Lord, and he credited it to him as righteousness" (NIV).

I. When the Future Seems Uncertain, Believe in God (Gen. 15:6).

Look at the story. Abraham had become discouraged after so much time had passed, and yet he and Sarah had no children to inherit the land and the promise God had given to them. Their lives and obedience seemed meaningless; so Abraham prayed to God repeatedly.

First, God met with Abraham. It is in meeting with God that faith can exist.

Then God gave Abraham assurance. He said:
"Do not be afraid.
I am your Shield.
I am your great reward" (Gen. 15:1, AT).
The attention is on God and what He is to Abraham. The primary issue in life for Abraham was his relationship to God. So it is for everyone who aspires to being right with God.

Abraham's problem was that he was childless. He assumed that God's blessing and His promise required a child to inherit that blessing, to be Abraham's link to that progeny more numerous than the grains of sand on the seashore (Gen. 22:17). God assures him that everything is on schedule, that he and Sarah will have children and children's children, as many as the stars. Then comes the key verse, verse 6. Abraham is not described as believing the promise; he believes God. "Abraham believed the Lord" (Gen. 12:6, NIV). The Hebrew word for "believe" is one we all know and use frequently, "Amen." It means "to be firm." What Abraham did was to confirm himself in relationship to the Lord. That is faith. When we are firm in the Lord, it does all sorts of things for our inner peace and well-being, as undoubtedly it did for Abraham.

The biblical text is more interested in what God thought of Abraham's response: "He credited righteousness to Abraham's account" (AT). When God saw Abraham's faith, He thought of that faith as righteousness. If God keeps books in heaven, He had the recording angel write "righteousness" in Abraham's ledger on that day.

Now we don't usually think about believing in those terms. However, if it is God in whom we believe, then every act of believing in God is more significant in our standing with God than any gift we bring, any sacrifice we make, or any obedience to covenant law we accomplish. Remember, any of these actions are good, if faith comes first. Without faith, they are meaningless. Hebrews 11:6 puts it concisely: "Without faith it is impossible to please God" (NIV).

So Abraham endured his long wait, was rewarded with a son, and came to be known as the father of the faithful.

Now turn again to the main text in Habakkuk 2:4: "When the arrogant cannot keep his soul straight within himself, a righteous one in his faithfulness will live"(AT).

II. When Threatened, Believers Survive, Although Others Fall Apart or Die.

The "arrogant" is one who is puffed up, who in bravado and ambition has made himself or herself out to be much more than they in fact are. You know the types who look so good, but in crisis fall apart.

Habakkuk was written against the historical background of the Babylonian invasions. For over a century, the heavy hand of Assyria had been on Palestine. The great prophets from Hosea and Amos through Isaiah and Micah had interpreted this as God's judgment on Israel for her sins. Now Assyria had begun to weaken, but Babylon was taking her place, more cruel and arrogant than Assyria ever was.

Habakkuk turned to God to ask for an interpretation of what this meant. This verse is the only answer he got. The "arrogant" may refer to the Babylonian tyrant, or it may refer to the opportunistic Israelites who tried to take advantage of the situation by working with the enemy. In such desperate times, the rewards for these persons looked extremely appealing; but God said that such persons would not be able to keep their souls pure or their heads on right. They would not be able to regulate their lives. God implied that such persons cannot survive.

On the other hand, the one who is right with God and with fellow believers will survive simply by being faithful in doing what he or she has always done in serving God, in keeping God's laws, and in seeking God's ways. In the words of Rudyard Kipling:

> If you can keep your head when all about you
> Are losing theirs and blaming it on you.[18]

As we face life and its problems, the question "Why?" is seldom answered. The prayer for help in going forward is never left unanswered. The one who is in the right with God by continuing to be faithful will survive, and more, will truly live.

Before we turn to the three New Testament uses of this verse, let us take a look at the Greek translation of this Old Testament text that the early Christian church used. Each translation draws upon some special potential in the original language that we often do not see.

This Greek translation has understood God as more closely involved with the righteous than the Hebrew text did, and has rendered several of the third person pronouns as first person. Its translators understood the word we translated "arrogant" to be a verb meaning "to be faint." "If he should draw back, my soul has no pleasure in him, but the righteous shall live by my faith" (AT). Our principle interest is in the second phrase.

III. When Courage Is Called for, One Right with God Lives Out of God's Faith (Hab. 2:4, LXX).

The idea of God having faith in us is not our usual thought when we think of faith. The translators of the Greek Old Testament lived in centuries when faith came hard. Jews were under political pressure from Greeks and then Romans. Attempts to revolt had not obtained long-term results. There were religious and intellectual pressures as well. Faith came hard. It was not easy to believe. (Is it ever easy?) Some felt they were unable to muster the strength to believe.

In such a time, this verse spoke to them of grace, of God's supplying what they were unable to give. Those who were faithful would live, not because of the strength of their own faith, but out of the fullness of God's faith. The New Testament cry—"I believe; help my unbelief!" (Mark 9:24, NRSV) —grows out of such a moment. We can all identify with that.

Something else should be noticed in this move from Hebrew to Greek. While a translation is never exactly the same as the original, the result of translation is not necessarily of less value than the original. It often enriches the meaning.

The Greek word for "righteous" does the work of two words in Hebrew. The Hebrew "righteous" is either a religious term for what is needed to enter the holy place or a reference to "justice," which speaks of what is expected in court. The Greek word covers both righteousness and justice. This has conditioned all Christian use of the term, especially Paul's use of it in the New Testament.

The Hebrew word for "faithfulness" also covers the idea of "believing," as we saw in Genesis. The Greek word is more specifically focused on faith, not in things or ideas, but in a person. It is less concerned with faithfulness. This is important when we begin to hear Paul's use of this verse. Three times in the New Testament Habakkuk 2:4b is quoted. Each of the instances focuses attention on a different word.

IV. Who Can Be Right with God (Rom. 1:17)?

"For in the gospel a righteousness from God is revealed, a righteousness that is by faith from first to last [from faith to faith, KJV], just as it is written: 'the righteous will live by faith'" (NIV).

Paul was concerned with defining "righteousness," so he focused here on the first key word in the text he quoted. He dropped the pronoun before the word "faith" (not "his faith" but simply "by faith"), which leaves open the possibility of using both the Hebrew "his (the righteous one's) faith" and the Greek "my faith" (God's faith). Perhaps that is what Paul meant by "from faith to faith" (KJV).

Paul answered the question "Who is right with God?" by quoting this verse to mean the believer: the one who lives according to faith. Not sacrifice nor meticulous obedience to law, but faith is that which saves a person from sin and creates a right relationship with God.

Do you want to be "right with God"? Believe the gospel. Believe in God who in Jesus Christ prepared a way of salvation for you. "Believe in the Lord Jesus, and you will be saved" (Acts 16:31, NIV). Then you will be counted among the righteous.

The second New Testament reference is also from Paul in Galatians 3:11, where his attention is focused on faith.

V. What Is Saving Faith (Gal. 3:11)?

"Clearly no one is justified before God by the law, because, 'The righteous will live by faith'" (NIV).

This passage distinguishes righteousness attained by obedience to law from true saving righteousness which can only come through faith. The passage emphasizes faith. The Greek translation had already changed the Hebrew "faithfulness" to a word which means "faith" or "believing." Yet the word is properly understood in both senses: a faith that is faithful. It is a faith that produces right living, but it is also a faith that holds on to God.

Our religious understanding conforms to Paul's emphasis. We must focus our faith on God, not on the law. If we want vitality and stability in our spirits and in our lives, we can have it by holding fast to God, believing He is faithful, and believing He will fulfill the good news of Jesus in bringing us life, freedom, and acceptance before God. In this we have both the promise and the fulfillment of the promise, just as Abraham had.

The third New Testament text is in Hebrews 10:38. Here the emphasis is on life.

VI. What Is Life with God (Heb. 10:38)?

"But my righteous one will live by faith. And if he shrinks back my soul will not be pleased with him" (AT).

This reading follows the Greek Old Testament more closely than Paul's references, but it makes two changes. This translation moves the pronoun "my" from "my faith" to "my righteous one." The order of the two lines is also reversed.

The setting here is in an appeal for believers to keep the faith, patiently expecting the return of Christ. God claims the believer as His own—"my righteous one"—and promises life on the basis of faith alone. He warns against apostasy (shrinking back). The next verse affirms: "But we are not of those who shrink back and are destroyed, but of those who believe and are saved" (Heb. 10:39, NIV).

This last quotation is close to the Old Testament settings. The threat of losing life—of being destroyed—is as real as in Genesis or Habakkuk. The promise is that life belongs to the one who is righteous by virtue of faith, life now and life eternally.

The true Christian life is one of faith-righteousness characterized by staying close to Jesus, by living expecting His coming, and by being assured of life from Him wherever we are.

Conclusion

This verse has had a tremendous impact on many people's lives and thoughts. You might say it has changed history. Paul read, "the righteous shall live by faith" (AT). The verse described what happened to him on the way to Damascus, when he met the Lord. That meeting changed his life, and he spent the rest of his life testifying to the effect of meeting the Lord Jesus. From being a legalistic rabbi who persecuted Christians, Paul became a flaming evangel of the gospel of God's grace. He had discovered the righteousness that comes from faith.

Martin Luther seized on this verse to break the oppressive hold of an errant church. He preached "the just shall live by faith," and the Reformation was born. This verse brought freedom and new life to those who believed its message. It can do the same for you.

What is binding you? Is it sin? Is it the legalistic demand of an impossible perfection? Is it guilt for sins that you think you must bear yourself?

Hear the good news! This mighty word from God says that you can be free. You can have the words "right with God" entered by your name. Believe in the Lord. Jesus offers forgiveness for sin. Believe Him. He promises new life and new direction to those who ask for it.

God looks at your heart and your intentions. He does not make impossible demands. Believe God, His promise, and His offer in Jesus Christ. And live!

Notes

1. See A. C. Sundberg, Jr., *The Old Testament in the Early Church*, vol. 20 in *Harvard Theological Studies* (Cambridge, Mass.: Harvard University Press, 1964); Sid Leiman, *Canonization of Hebrew Scripture: The Talmudic and Midrashic Evidence* (Hamden, Conn.: Shoe String Press, 1976); Joseph Blenkinsopp, *Prophecy and Canon: A Contribution to the Study of Jewish Origins* (Notre Dame: University of Notre Dame Press, 1977).

2. George W. Coats and Burke O. Long, eds. *Canon and Authority* (Philadelphia: Fortress Press, 1977), xi.

3. B. S. Childs, *Biblical Theology in Crisis* (Philadelphia: Westminster Press, 1970).

4. J. A. Sanders, *Torah and Canon*, 2d ed. (Philadelphia: Fortress Press, 1972).

5. Coats and Long, *Canon and Authority*, xi.

6. See particularly B. S. Childs, *The Book of Exodus: A Critical Theological Commentary* (Philadelphia: Westminster Press, 1974).

7. See J. A. Sanders, "Hermeneutics," supplementary vol. in *Interpreters Dictionary of the Bible* (Nashville: Abingdon Press, 1976), 402-407.

8. Walter Brueggemann, *In Man We Trust: The Neglected Side of Biblical Faith* (Richmond: John Knox Press, 1973).

9. LXX is an abbreviation for the Septuagint, the Greek translation of the Old Testament.

10. See my commentary in *The Books of Joel, Obadiah, Jonah, Nahum, Habakkuk and Zephaniah,* in *The Cambridge Bible Commentary on the New English Bible,* eds. P. R. Ackroyd, A. R. C. Leaney, and J. W. Packer (Cambridge: Cambridge University Press, 1975), 134-135.

11. Ralph L. Smith, *Micah-Malachi*, vol. 32 in *Word Biblical Commentary* (Waco, Texas: Word Books, Publisher, 1984), 105.

12. O. Palmer Robertson, *The Books of Nahum, Habakkuk, and Zephaniah,* in *The New International Commentary on the Old Testament*, ed. R. K. Harrison (Grand Rapids, Mich.: Wm. B. Eerdmans Publishing Company, 1990), 173-174.

13. Smith, *Micah-Malachi*, 105; and Robertson, *The Books of Nahum, Habakkuk, and Zephaniah*, 174.

14. See J.A. Emerton,, "The Textual and Linguistic Problems of Habakkuk II 4-5," *Journal of Theological Studies* (1977):1-18; he divided the word and translated "fly away" with the implication of dying.

15. Smith, *Micah-Malachi*, 107.

16. F. Brown, S.R. Driver, and C. A. Briggs, *Hebrew and English Lexicon of the Old Testament* (Oxford: Oxford University Press, 1907), 763.

17. The Dead Sea Scrolls are a group of manuscripts found near the Dead Sea in Palestine during the last half century that were written and hidden there near the time of Christ.

18. Rudyard Kipling, "If," in *The Best Loved Poems of the American People*, sel. Hazel Felleman (Garden City, N.Y.: Garden City Books, 1936), 65-66.

3
A
LITERARY
MODEL

R. Alan Culpepper

Those of us involved in biblical studies have witnessed exciting and unsettling developments in the last fifteen years. Many of the traditional methods and conclusions have been questioned. Their limitations have been exposed, and a variety of new approaches to the study of biblical texts has emerged. One of the most exciting developments is in the area of narrative criticism.

As with other methodological advances, narrative criticism is both a development from earlier methods and a response to their deficiencies. Antecedents can be found in the work of all biblical scholars who have been sensitive to the literary features of the biblical texts. More specifically, the first steps toward narrative criticism were taken by those who began to speak of "composition criticism" rather than redaction criticism,[1] since composition criticism focused on the composition of the entire text, not just those elements that could be assigned to the work of the redactor. During the early 1970s there was considerable interest in structuralism; this contributed to the development of narrative criticism by challenging us to set aside historical concerns to address structural features of the text.

During the mid-seventies, among specialists in the Gospel of Mark, a new direction began to be evident.[2] The concern of their work was not the historical setting of the Gospel, nor the history of the tradition contained in the Gospel, nor the theology or intention of the evangelist, but the Gospel itself as a coherent narrative text. They were concerned with what the Gospel is, not just what it is about. Rather than breaking the

Gospel up into its individual units, they began to look at it as a whole, an entire composition. That marked the beginning of narrative criticism.

In contrast to earlier methods, the aim of narrative criticism is to understand the intricacies of the narrative text and the ways it draws the reader into the process of conveying and receiving the story. The narrative critic is interested in both *what* the text says and *how* it says it. Whereas historical criticism puts historical questions to the text, narrative criticism asks what the text is as it is and how it functions as literature.

Narrative criticism is, therefore, based on a different understanding of the locus of meaning and the way in which a narrative text conveys meaning. Meaning is not latent in the text, waiting to be discovered by the reader. Neither can the meaning of a narrative text be separated from the text itself, as though one could state its meaning abstractly and have no further need for the text itself. Rather than vehicles conveying meanings to the reader, narrative texts should be viewed as strategies for evoking certain responses from the reader. This is particularly true of ancient heroic and epic texts that elicit wonder, loyalty, reverence, praise, and virtue from their readers. For too long, we have concentrated on the cognitive aspects of biblical texts, especially for theology and history, and neglected their affective qualities.

Over the past several decades, the aim of interpretation has moved from concentration on the author to concentration on the text to concentration on the reader. With the biblical texts, the authors can be known only from the texts themselves, so at best their intention can only be surmised from the texts. What narrative criticism seeks are readings that respond to the texts perceptively and faithfully, without neglecting or distorting significant features of the text.

To achieve such readings, we will continue to need to do historical research. The biblical texts are ancient texts, written in ancient languages. They assume ancient world views and ancient Near Eastern, Hebrew, Hellenistic, and Mediterranean social norms. Only when these are recognized can we hope to respond to the nuances, humor, irony, and scandals that the texts assume will be apparent to their readers. Work in philology, history, archaeology, and sociology will therefore continue to be essential for biblical studies; but the pursuit of such data is only preliminary to interpretation of the biblical texts.

We are not really interpreting the biblical text when we seek to understand its composition history, the historicity of the events it describes, or the theology that it implies. All of these are interesting pursuits that may follow after one has attempted to understand the text itself, but they are not interpretation. When we dissect the text in order to establish the history behind it or extract theological principles from it, even granting that these are historical narratives for which theology is important, we are using the text as a data base for information about issues we bring to the text. We have set goals other than understanding the text itself, and, implicitly, we have placed greater value on the historical reconstructions or systematic theology that we construct from the text. In the case of the Gospels, this means that the aim of interpretation is not to discover the historical Jesus, the teachings of Jesus, the *Sitz im Leben* of the Gospels, the process by which they were composed, or the theology of the evangelists.

Stated positively, the aim of interpretation should be a reading of the text which minimizes distortions due to lack of understanding of the text's language and implied cultural norms, bias on the part of the reader, or inattention to:

1. The text's language, tone, and structure
2. The levels of narrative communication: implied author, narrator, characters, and
3. The story's development of characters, conflicts, and settings.

The effort to interpret these features of the biblical narratives has meant that we have had to keep abreast of significant work being done by specialists in narrative theory and the study of narratives. This field is just as energetic and diverse as that of biblical studies, so one cannot speak of narrative criticism, or literary criticism, as though it were a static, unified phenomenon.[3]

How does one proceed in doing narrative criticism? Space will not permit a full review of the concepts and categories that have been defined by narrative critics, but handbooks are readily available for any who care to read further.[4]

First, it is necessary to distinguish between what the text says and how it says it. Seymour Chatman, as the title of his book indicates, distinguished the two levels of a narrative text as *story* and *discourse*.[5] Shlomith Rimmon-Kenan followed the lead of Gerard Genette, organizing her succinct handbook, *Narrative Fiction: Contemporary Poetics*, in three sections that treat the story, the text, and the narration.[6] Similarly, Robert W. Funk, in his *Poetics and the Narrative Text*, distinguished between the tale, what is told, and the telling: narrative as discourse, narrative as story, and narrative as performance.[7] The latter has generally been neglected in biblical studies that have been thoroughly text oriented. These distinctions allow us to examine both story and discourse with a methodological awareness and precision that is usually lacking in earlier studies.

The teller of the tale is the *narrator*. The voice of the narrator must be distinguished from both the *real author* (or authors) of the text and the *implied author*, which is the picture of the author that the reader infers from the various components of the text. Both the narrator and the implied author are features of the narrative text. The narrator is the voice that tells the story. The implied author, on the other hand, has no voice but becomes the mind and the artist sensed and inferred by the reader.

Similarly, the narrator tells the story to a *narratee* or *implied reader*, who may be distinguished from the *real reader*. The narratee is the one addressed by the narrator. Both narrator and narratee may be either characters in the story or merely constructs evoked by the narration. The implied reader is the reader created by the text, sometimes called the ideal or the intended reader, the reader who is able to make sense of and respond to all the nuances of the text. The implied reader fills gaps in the narration, perceives ironies, understands the symbolism, yet requires the explanations that are given. A portrait of the implied reader may, therefore, be constructed from the text, but the implied reader may not correspond to the actual first readers.

As the story is told, the narrator depicts a narrative world populated by characters, settings, and significant events. Again, one must be careful about assuming that the narrative world corresponds to any actual historical setting. In the case of the Gospel of John, the narrative world of the Gospel undoubtedly has points of contact with both the world of the ministry of Jesus and with the world of the Johannine community, but we cannot always be sure what those points of contact are. In places, the author may be deliberately lifting norms or conflicts out of their historical setting and placing them in a new context so that the reader will be forced to evaluate them in a new light. This narrative technique is called *defamiliarization*.[8]

Characters may be characterized explicitly, as in the characterization of the Baptist in John 1:6-8, or implicitly, as with Peter. With Peter, the reader sees what he does, hears what he says, and hears what others say about him, and in the process forms conclusions about the character. The narrator shows us the character but does not tell us who he is. Characters may be more or less fully developed, and they may be either static or change and develop.

Events evoke the characters, just as characters create events. Events also define the *plot*. The story usually moves from an initial *stasis* through a *process* to a *closure* or resolution of the conflicts. The conflicts in the story may be between characters, between characters and God or nature, or within characters. Some events are passed over, some are summarized, some are narrated in detail. Narration and dialogue, or reported speech, alternate to form the narrative. Scenes may then be clustered in episodes.

The point of view of the narrator or focalizer can also be analyzed. Boris Uspensky identified five planes of the narrator's point of view: the ideological (or evaluation norms), the

phraseological (speech patterns), the spatial (the location of
the narrator), the temporal (the time of the telling), and the
psychological (internal or external to the characters).[9] The
focalization can also change from time to time as the narrative progresses.

Commentary is another important feature of a narrative,
and commentary may be either explicit or implicit. At times
the narrator will turn aside from the story to offer the reader
an explanation, an aside, or a comment on the story. At other
times, the commentary is implicit. The implied author assumes that the implied reader will catch a discrepancy, sense
an incongruity, delight in an irony, or see the subtle symbolism that is present. If the reader misses these, an important
part of the reading experience is lost.

The narrator may not move systematically and smoothly
through the story from start to finish—that could make for a
dull narrative! Instead, the narrator spends more time on
some parts of the story while hurrying through others. Some
parts are told in sequence; at other times the narrator may
skip back and forth in the sequence of events. All of these are
aspects of narrative time: order, duration, and frequency.
Events may be foreshadowed, or gaps in the narrative may be
left for the reader to fill. Suspense and surprise can therefore
be created in various ways.

Detailed analysis of each of these features of a narrative
may not always be necessary, but attention to how the story is
told awakens a fresh sensitivity to the nuances of the text and
their effects on the reader—that is the goal of narrative
criticism.

Text Analysis

The exchange between Jesus and Nathanael occurs at the
end of the narrative introduction to the Gospel of John
(1:43-51), in the context of the calling of the first disciples.
Just as the Gospel of John seems to have two conclusions
(John 20:30-31 and 21:24-25, with John 21 serving as an
epilogue), so the Gospel begins with both a poetic prologue
(John 1:1-18) and a narrative introduction (John 1:19-51 or

1:19—2:11). The prologue sets the characterization of Jesus in the context of the incarnation of the preexistent *Logos*. It establishes the evaluative perspective of the narrative, introduces John the Baptist, and acquaints the reader with some of the themes that will be developed later.[10] John 1:19-51 presents the witness of John the Baptist: his response to the authorities, his description of Jesus' baptism, and his introduction of Jesus to his followers with the words: "Behold, the Lamb of God who takes away the sin of the world!" (1:29,36, NASB).

Verses 35-42 are significant for the interpretation of Jesus' encounter with Nathanael because they establish the pattern by which readers will judge the scene. In these verses, two of John's disciples begin to follow Jesus. The first words that Jesus speaks in the Gospel are addressed to them: "What do you seek?" (1:38, NASB). By this point, the readers' introduction to the narrative is nearly complete. The narrator has led the reader from the beginning of time in the prologue to the day John the Baptist pointed Jesus out to his disciples the second time. We are ready to begin to test what we have been *told* about Jesus against what we are about to be *shown*.

From the beginning, Jesus' words are open to more than one level of meaning. The question, "What do you seek?" can be read as either the response of one irritated because two men were following him or as a probing invitation to reflect on the deepest motives for their pursuits. Does the reader hear more in the question than the characters do? The two disciples respond, apparently naively, "Where do you abide?" Again, the question can mean no more than "Where are You staying?" (NASB), but ultimately Jesus will reveal to the disciples that He lives in them (John 14:23). To their question, Jesus responded with an invitation, "Come and see." Once more, Jesus may simply be inviting the two to see where He was lodging, but the reader suspects that this is an invitation to discipleship. Jesus' response focuses the theme of seeing and believing that will be important in the text where Philip will repeat the words of Jesus, "Come and see," and Jesus will say, "Because I said to you, I saw you under the fig tree, do you believe? You shall see greater things than these" (v. 50, RSV). Ultimately, of course, the theme of seeing and believing will culminate with Jesus' response to Thomas: "Have you believed because you have seen me? Blessed are those who have not seen and yet believe" (20:29, RSV).

One of the first two disciples, Andrew, brings his brother Simon to Jesus, and Jesus gives him a new name: *Cephas* (which is translated Peter). As readers, we are therefore alerted to the significance and meaning of names and to the pattern that we learn our true identity when we discover who Jesus is. Andrew had told Peter, " 'We have found the Messiah' (which means Christ)" (1:41, RSV)—the very confession for which Peter would be remembered in the Synoptic Gospels (compare Mark 8:29).

By now we are ready to read our text. The scene occurs "the next day" (compare 1:29,35) when Jesus called Philip. A new scene is therefore introduced by a temporal reference and the introduction of a new character. Jesus' words to Philip are familiar to a reader of the other Gospels: "Follow me" (v. 43). While this is the first use of this command in John (compare 12:26; 21:19), the term "follow" (*akolouthein*) was used three times in the previous scene (1:37,38,40); it has already been identified as a technical term for discipleship. Philip's origin from Bethsaida, which was also the hometown of Andrew and Peter, is reported by the narrator.

One could take John 1:43-51 as the textual unit, but a new scene is introduced in verse 45 with the person of Nathanael. Philip's action is reported using the formula of discovery and witness from the previous scene:

VERSE 41: He first *found* his brother Simon, *and said to him,* "*We have found* the Messiah."

VERSE 45: Philip *found* Nathanael, *and said to him,* "*We have found* him of whom Moses in the law and also the prophets wrote, Jesus of Nazareth, the son of Joseph" (RSV).

The repetition invites comparison and contrast with the previous scene. We are not told what Philip's relationship to Nathanael was. Neither are we told Nathanael's origin, or hometown. The roles of the disciples are defined at this early stage by the pattern of each one bringing another to Jesus. Similarly, the repetition of the pattern amplifies the designation "the Messiah" by means of the much longer and more specific identification: "him of whom Moses in the law and also the prophets wrote, Jesus of Nazareth, the son of Joseph" (RSV). While the extraordinary circumstances surrounding the birth of Jesus are alluded to later (John 7:42; 8:41), there is no narrative of the virgin birth in John.

Philip's identification of Jesus in verse 45 is the fifth of seven titles attributed to Jesus in this narrative introduction to the Gospel (1:19-51, RSV): (1) "the Lamb of God" (vv. 29,36); (2) "the son of God" (vv. 34,49); (3) "Rabbi" (v. 38); (4) "'the Messiah' (which means Christ)" (v. 41); (5) "him of whom Moses in the law and also the prophets wrote" (v. 45); (6) "the King of Israel" (v. 49); and (7) "the Son of man" (v. 51). In a remarkable way, therefore, many of the lofty titles that the church applied to Jesus are used in this first chapter in John. In Mark, by contrast, the disciples do not confess that Jesus is the Christ until Peter's confession at Caesarea Philippi (8:29), and no one confesses that Jesus is the Son of God until His death (15:39).

Nathanael's response, "Can anything good come out of Nazareth?" (v. 46, RSV) provides our first clue (aside from His name) to His character. The narrator used indirect characterization here. He did not tell us about Nathanael in advance but let us draw our own conclusions from what Nathanael said and did, and from what Jesus said to him. Nathanael's response signals provincial snobbery on one level, but also raises the question of Jesus' origin. Since so much attention has been given to Jesus' origin from God in the prologue, the reader cannot miss the contrast. We know who Jesus is because we know where He is from; Nathanael did not have the information given in the prologue. All he knew was what Philip told him: "Jesus of Nazareth, the son of Joseph." The gap between the reader's knowledge and the information available to the character allows the narrator to exploit the ironic potential of the narrative situation. The reader is drawn to the lofty heights of the narrator's perspective while watching the character fumble in ignorance. The choice between identifying with the narrator or Nathanael is easy: the reader will choose the narrator's view of Jesus over that of Nathanael. We know that Jesus did not actually come from Nazareth. The Christian reader probably knows that Jesus was born in Bethlehem, since the debate between Jesus and the authorities plays on this point later (7:42). The real point, of course, is that Jesus comes from above (3:31).

At this point the issue becomes how Philip will respond to such skepticism. Will he turn away from Nathanael as a hopeless skeptic? Will he debate the Scriptures or the merits of Nazareth as a prophet's hometown? With disarming simplicity, Philip repeated the invitation Jesus gave a few verses earlier: "Come and see" (v. 46; compare v. 39). Implied is a confidence that if Nathanael will only come to meet Jesus, he will see that what Philip has said is true: "We have found him of whom Moses in the law and also the prophets wrote" (v. 45, RSV). *Seeing* is full of potential for further insight, however. Like the blind man to whom Jesus will later give sight (ch. 9), Nathanael may discover much more than he could ever have imagined.

The narrator moves directly to Jesus' words to Nathanael. We are told nothing more about where Philip met Nathanael or how long it took them to find Jesus. Jesus announced Nathanael's coming even before he reached Him. His words tell us who Nathanael is, or at least who he can become: "an Israelite indeed, in whom there is no guile!" (v. 47, RSV). This is the first demonstration of Jesus' divine knowledge. As the incarnate Logos, He "needed no one to testify about anyone; for he himself knew what was in everyone" (2:25, NRSV). Two key terms in Jesus' announcement catch our attention: "Israelite" and "guile." This is the only reference to an "Israelite" in the Gospel of John, but note the references to "Israel" in 1:31,49; 3:10; and 12:13. *Israel,* of course, was the name given to Jacob and eventually to his descendants. Guile (or deceit), moreover, is the character trait with which Jacob is tagged in Genesis narratives:

> When Esau heard the words of his father, he cried out with an exceedingly great and bitter cry, and said to his father, "Bless me, even me also, O my father!" But he said, "Your brother came with *guile*, and he has taken away your *blessing*." Esau said, "*Is he not rightly named Jacob?*" (27:34-36, RSV; author's italics).

Jacob's name was later changed to Israel:

> Jacob was left alone; and a man wrestled with him until the breaking of the day. When the man saw that he did not prevail against Jacob, he touched the hollow of his thigh; and Jacob's thigh was put out of joint as he wrestled with him. Then he said, "Let me go, for the day is breaking." But Jacob said, "I will not let you go, unless you *bless* me." And he said to him, "What is your name?" And he said, "Jacob." Then he said, "Your name shall no more be called Jacob, but Israel, for you have striven with God and with men, and have prevailed." Then Jacob asked him, "Tell me, I pray, your name." But he said, "Why is it that you ask my name?" And there he *blessed* him (32:24-29, RSV; author's italics).

These passages not only show that Jesus' identification of Nathanael is meant to echo with a familiar passage from the Torah; they also introduce the issue of blessing. Isaac blessed Jacob (albeit by mistake), and the man with whom Jacob wrestled blessed him and gave him the name *Israel*. Jesus was now blessing Nathanael. He said that Nathanael was a true son of Israel, one in whom there was no guile. This identification set the expectation that those who are true Israelites will come to Jesus, while those who reject Him show that they are actually not of Israel. For this hostile response, John often used the term *Ioudaioi* ("the Jews," or "Judeans").[11]

Nathanael's question, "How do you know me?" (v. 48, RSV), underscores the wonder of what has just happened. Jesus has demonstrated that He does indeed know what is in the heart of each person (compare 2:25). Indirectly, His blessing of Nathanael confirmed Jesus' identity as the incarnate Logos, the creative Word. Jesus' response drove the point home. He saw Nathanael when the Israelite was under the fig tree, before Philip called him. Interpreters have debated the significance of this response. Does it fulfill a legal convention, identifying under what sort of tree an offense occurred? Does it evoke recognition that the fig tree was a conventional place for the study of Torah, or is it an allusion to what God said in Hosea 9:10?

> Like grapes in the wilderness,
>   I found Israel.
> Like the first fruit on the fig tree,
>   in its first season,
> I saw your fathers (RSV).

Alternatively, does Jesus' remark recall the vision of "every man under his vine and under his fig tree" (1 Kings 4:25; Mic. 4:4; Zech. 3:10, RSV)? Zechariah 3:8 voices the expectation of a messianic figure called "the Branch."[12] The passage concludes, "In that day, says the Lord of hosts, every one of you will invite his neighbor under his vine and under his fig tree" (Zech. 3:10, RSV). The "Branch" was understood as a royal, Davidic figure, and this passage had already been interpreted messianically in various Jewish sources (4Q Florilegium; 4QP Bless; 4Qp Isa. 8—10; *T. Judah* 24).[13] Craig Koester was on solid ground, therefore, when he concluded his study of these verses with this observation:

> The evangelist expected that readers able to recognize the role of Zech. 3.8 and 10 in this narrative would discover that what appears to be an obscure interchange is a subtle and engaging conversation, in which Nathanael identifies Jesus in royal terms appropriate to the messianic 'Branch', and Jesus identifies Nathanael in terms appropriate to Jacob or 'Israel', promising that Nathanael, like Jacob, would see God made manifest.[14]

The closing verses of John 1 contain Nathanael's confession and Jesus' promise. Nathanael's confession culminates the series of titles applied to Jesus in John 1: "Rabbi, you are the Son of God! You are the King of Israel!" (v. 49, RSV). The identification of Jesus as the Son of God echoes the words of the prologue: "We have beheld his glory, glory as of the only Son from the Father" (1:14, RSV). Jesus' relationship to God as Son to Father is one of the hallmarks of John's Christology (compare 5:19-27). In the Gospel of Mark, by contrast, no one confessed Jesus as the Son of God until the very end of the Gospel, after Jesus' death (Mark 15:39). At the end of the Gospel of John, the narrator explained that the Gospel was written to lead the reader to make the same confession that Nathanael made at the outset, that Jesus was the Son of God (20:30-31).

The title—"King of Israel"—sets up John's later development of the theme of Jesus' kingship. Whereas the Synoptic Gospels report Jesus' teaching on the kingdom of God, the Gospel of John gives far greater emphasis to Jesus' role as King (6:15). Jesus entered Jerusalem as the King of Israel (12:13-15). Pilate questioned Jesus' kingship (18:33,37-39), presented Jesus to the crowd as their King (19:3,12-15), and eventually fixed the title—"the King of the Jews"—over His cross (19:19-21). In contrast to Nathanael (the true "Israelite"), "the Jews" in John's Gospel ultimately confessed, "We have no king but Caesar" (19:15, RSV).

Jesus responded to Nathanael's confession with a question and a promise: "Because I said to you, I saw you under the fig tree, do you believe? You shall see greater things than these" (v. 50, RSV). The question probes the source and authenticity of Nathanael's belief. For the reader of the Gospel, it also raises for the first time the question: What constitutes authentic faith? Jesus seems to be elevating Nathanael as a worthy model for others, since he professed belief in response to what Jesus had said. All through the Gospel, the narrator will lift up first one response to Jesus, then another, encouraging the reader to compare and assess the various responses. The Gospel of John can therefore be viewed as a series of episodes, in each of which a different character meets Jesus and must decide how he or she will respond to Him.[15] Like John the Baptist, Nathanael serves as an early and exemplary response, in comparison with which other responses in subsequent chapters (Nicodemus, the man at the pool of

Bethesda, the crowds in Galilee) will be deficient, incomplete, or inauthentic.

In a play on the relationship between seeing and believing, Jesus assured Nathanael that because he has believed he will see even greater things. What these "greater things" are is not explained, but it is often surmised that it is a reference to the signs, the death, and the resurrection of Jesus, recorded later in the Gospel.

The scene concludes with Jesus' promise: "Truly, truly, I say to you, you will see heaven opened, and the angels of God ascending and descending upon the Son of man (v. 51, RSV). This is the first of twenty-five sayings in John that begin with the unprecedented use of the formula, "Amen, amen, I say to you."[16] The opening of the heavens was associated with the baptism of Jesus (Mark 1:10) in early Christian tradition. This saying, however, evokes another scene from the story of Jacob: his dream at Bethel of the ladder from heaven to earth and the angels descending and ascending (Gen. 28:12). The effect of this allusion to Scripture is to affirm that Jesus is the new Bethel, the new meeting place between heaven and earth. Yet another of Israel's hopes for the future, the coming of the Son of man, has been fulfilled in Jesus.

Explanation of Technique

The distinctive feature of narrative sermons is that they keep the biblical narrative primary. The preacher does not draw "points" out of the text, or seek to organize it into a logical, argumentative, or alliterative outline. Instead, the sermon retells the story in such a way that the hearer is drawn into it; connections are made in passing with the life situations of the hearers. This intent means that nothing should be allowed to intrude or distract from the retelling of the story. Illustrations, asides, and background information need to be handled briefly so that attention can be focused throughout on the story line of the text.[17]

In such a sermon, the preacher becomes a partner and alter ego to the narrator of the text, alternatively assuming the role of the narrator by telling the story and standing apart from the narrator in the text by commenting on the way the story is told. A variation on the narrative sermon is the dramatic monologue in which the preacher assumes the role of one of the characters (sometimes in costume). The narrative sermon need not be a dramatic presentation, but good storytelling skills are important.

Even if the congregation is accustomed to this style of sermon, some introduction is necessary. The function of the introduction is to gain attention and shift the focus of interest from other concerns to the text at hand. In the course of the introduction, the preacher needs to make clear that it is by entering the biblical story imaginatively that we experience God's grace and God's Word to us. The biblical story depicts a world under God filled with conflict, drama, grace, hope, and redemption. We participate in God's fellowship as we discover that the biblical world is, in fact, the world in which we live.

Because the narrative sermon follows the movement of the story, the introduction needs to bring the hearer to the starting point. It needs to set the context, the mood, and the problem that prevails at the beginning of the story. The hearer can thereby "get in step" with the story from the outset. This orientation of the congregation may be accomplished by characterizing briefly what the story is about or the need that it addresses. Invite the congregation to hear the story afresh.

As the central characters are introduced, they need to be presented as distinctive individuals so that we can respond to their individuality. On the other hand, some dimension of their character or experience needs to be universalized so that in them we each see something of ourselves and our own experience. Settings may be interpreted so that the hearer can identify comparable settings or situations today. The fig tree is an ordinary place, nothing special, where persons live out their days waiting for God to fulfill the promises of Scripture. It may also be a place of quiet despair or private frustration.

The biblical stories are significant because they sketch for us a vision of the biblical world in which God is active and trustworthy, full of grace beyond our wildest dreams. By entering into the biblical story, we are challenged to review our per-

spective on life and see that the biblical world view is truer
than the secular substitutes with which we live. As we hear
the biblical story, we rehearse the responses to God, to life,
and to others that God is calling us to make.

Because the biblical stories are revelatory, the preacher as
interpreter needs to be sensitive to the great themes that are
being played out in the particular events of the individual
stories. Unless we relate the mundane to the magnificent, we
will miss the impact of the story. Unless we relate the magnificent to the mundane, it never touches our lives. John 1:45-51
is the story of the most important event in Nathanael's life. It
was the turning point, the eureka moment, the *kairos* in
which he discovered the Christ in his everyday experience.

What are the major movements of the story? The changes of
time, setting, or characters mark off the major scenes. John
1:45-51 is divided into two scenes: Nathanael's conversation
with Philip and Nathanael's conversation with Jesus. Throughout, echoes of Jacob's experience can be heard. The second
part, likewise can be divided into two or three major movements: Jesus' blessing of Nathanael, Nathanael's confession,
and Jesus' promise. I have chosen to focus the major sections
of the sermon around Nathanael's experience of God's invitation, God's blessing, and God's promise. If some such abstrac-
tion from the story is used, it should focus motifs that draw
out features of the story rather than substitute for the story
line or plot of the story. The story itself provides the outline, or
better, charts the course for the sermon.

At points along the way, the preacher may need to supply
background information and answer questions that will occur
to the hearer and distract attention unless they are recognized. The preacher will also need to make connections with
current situations. This is all part of the art of the preacher as
interpreter. Humor should be injected where it is appropriate.
Anachronistic references can help bridge the gap between
then and now, biblical story and life. All the while, the sermon
remains focused on the story. As with all preaching, the tim-
ing, pace, inflection, metaphors, images, vivid descriptions,

word pictures, and the emotional involvement of the preacher are essential to the effectiveness of the sermon.

At the conclusion, hearers need to be invited and challenged to make appropriate responses to the story. Responses will vary with each hearer. Narrative preaching requires that the preacher open up the story to a variety of applications. On the other hand, the preacher must allow the story to speak for itself and be heard in a variety of ways. Some will have heard one part of the story; others will have heard the story very differently. The conclusion may focus on certain themes and invite a range of relevant responses.

Shall we try a sermon based on John 1:45-51? The result may not be a flawless example of the application of narrative theory to preaching, but it will offer a sample for further reflection.

The Sermon

Nathanael's Story: The Drama of Redemption

Text: Genesis 27:34-36a; 32:24-29; John 1:45-51

Have you been waiting for something special to happen? One of the fascinating things about the Gospel of John is that it shows how Jesus changed the lives of people with whom we can identify. Sometimes in just a few words it describes individual responses to Jesus in such a way that we can experience the work of God's power through the experience of these Bible personalities.

Nathanael is such a person. He is not mentioned in any of the other Gospels; and for that reason, he has sometimes been identified with Bartholomew. However, John tells us more than any of the other Gospels about many of the individuals around Jesus. Virtually all we know about Philip, Andrew, Thomas, Nicodemus, Lazarus, Mary, and Martha comes from John. Also, all we really know about Nathanael is this story of the turning point in his life. Would you hear his story and see if anything in it corresponds with your own experience?

Nathanael's story is a drama of invitation, blessing, and promise.

I. Invitation

In the first act Nathanael's friend, Philip, finds him and tells him that they have found the Messiah of Israel. For centuries Israel had been waiting for the coming of the Messiah, waiting for deliverance and blessing, waiting for the promise of a more blessed future. Prophets had prophesied. Seers had seen visions, and all the while Israel suffered from persecution and foreign oppression. Her present was not nearly as grand as her past in the days of Moses or David. Neither was it anything like the promises of the Age of the Messiah that every Israelite had heard from childhood.

Suddenly the period of waiting was over, but the invitation to Nathanael did not come from any king or prophet. Philip, his friend, came and reported a "eureka" experience. Philip, Simon, and Andrew had found the Messiah of whom Moses and the prophets wrote, Jesus of Nazareth, the son of Joseph. Who would have thought that a friend's sharing his discovery would be the way in which the announcement of the Messiah's coming would spread through Israel? What if Philip had been too embarrassed or too busy with other things to share his discovery with Nathanael? Nathanael might have gone on sitting under his fig trees, waiting, and missed the greatest experience of his life.

At first, Nathanael did not receive the good news with anything more than wary skepticism: "Oh yeah? How do you know this one's the Messiah? Who ever heard of anything good coming from Nazareth?" Nazareth was an insignificant town in Galilee. It is not even mentioned in the Old Testament, the writings of Josephus (the Jewish historian), or in the writings of the Jewish rabbis. No prophet had ever said the Messiah would come from Nazareth.

This is the first time in the Gospel—but not the last time—that someone misunderstood Jesus' origin and held it against Him. In Nathanael's eyes, Jesus came from the wrong side of the tracks, from a nothing place where one would not expect to find anything good. Prejudice is like that. It chains people to where they are from and never lets them become what they might be. Prejudices hurt us as well as others; here Nathanael's prejudice almost kept him from meeting Jesus.

A vivid memory I carry with me of visits to my grandparents' home in the early 1950's is that they had a contraption called a stereopticon. It had a lens for each eye, and at just the right focal distance one put matching postcards of two different views of the same scene. It held these views at just the right angle so that when one looked through the lens, one's eye merged the two perspectives and got a three-dimensional view of the scene. That was a high-tech novelty in the early fifties.

The Gospel of John insists that we cannot understand who Jesus is unless we see Him from the perspective of His origin and His destiny: He came from the Father, and He returned to the Father. Jesus Himself said in John 16:28, at the end of His ministry, "I came from the Father and have come into the world; again, I am leaving the world and going to the Father" (RSV).

Nathanael's difficulty was that he did not understand where Jesus was from. Until he discovered that Jesus had come from the Father, that He was the divine Word who had come into the world in human form, Nathanael would not know who Jesus was. In fact, Nathanael's misunderstanding was compounded. Jesus was not from Nazareth; He had been born in Bethlehem. Only Matthew and Luke contain the accounts of the birth of Jesus, but I am convinced that John knew more about the birth of Jesus than He ever tells us. In chapter 7 the people in Jerusalem debate among themselves. Some said, "Is the Christ to come from Galilee? Has not the scripture said that the Christ is descended from David, and comes from Bethlehem, the village where David was?" (vv. 41-42, RSV). John knew that Jesus had been born in Bethlehem, but more importantly, he knew that Jesus was the Son of God, who had come from above.

Philip did not seem to have been the brightest of the disciples. He was overshadowed by Andrew. In John 6, Jesus asked Philip how they would buy bread to feed the multitude. Philip was astounded; 200 denarii—almost a year's wages—would not be enough to feed that hungry crowd! In the twelfth chapter, the Greeks came wanting to see Jesus. Philip did not know what to do, so he went to Andrew, and Andrew told Jesus. Finally, Philip protested in exasperation, "Lord, show us the Father, and we shall be satisfied" (14:8, RSV). To which Jesus answered, "Have I been with you so long, and yet you do not know me, Philip?" (14:9, RSV). I tell my students that Philip failed his ministry test, his Greek test, and his theology test; but he was still a faithful disciple and effective evangelist. Look how he handled Nathanael's skepticism. He did not get into an argument with Nathanael about the Scriptures. He did not get sidetracked into a discussion about whether any good could come from Nazareth. He merely repeated the words that Jesus had used in His invitation to the first disciples a few verses earlier: "Come and see."

Nathanael had questions about Jesus. I suppose we all do. How can we accept a Messiah from Nazareth, a Messiah with a cross in His heart? But Jesus never ran from people who had questions. He allowed His disciples and His critics to question Him until the truth was plain for all who would receive it. To Nathanael's credit, he was willing to follow his questions until they led him to Jesus. Nathanael was willing to put his prejudices to the test, to go and see whether this Jesus from Nazareth could really be the Messiah of Israel.

The first step, therefore, regardless of how long or how desperately we have searched for something better in life, is to be willing to set aside our cynicism, our despair, and our stereotypes about religion and the church, then come and see for ourselves whether Jesus can be the answer to our quest for truth. Ask your questions. The invitation to discipleship is open and fearless. Jesus can help you deal with the past, set it once and for all behind you, and move ahead. The church can provide a community that befriends you and cares about you. Making Jesus the Lord of your life can also reorient your life and give it meaning, purpose, and hope; but you will have to be willing to throw off your skepticism and "come and see."

II. Blessing

The second act of the drama of redemption is the act of blessing. In the previous paragraph of our text, John the Baptist had introduced Jesus as the Redeemer, "the Lamb of God, who takes away the sin of the world!" (1:29,36, RSV). Traditionally, the church has emphasized God's work through redemption. In the exodus, and then in a definitive way through Jesus' death, God delivered His people. God redeemed them from the power of sin, but there is another side to God's work. God also blesses those He calls. When God called Abraham, He promised: "I will bless you, and make your name great, so that you will be a blessing. I will bless those who bless you, and him who curses you I will curse; and by you all the families of the earth shall bless themselves" (Gen. 12:2-3, RSV). The traditional blessing of Israel and the church is contained in these familiar words from Numbers:

"Thus you shall bless the people of Israel: you shall say to them,
The Lord bless you and keep you:
The Lord make his face to shine
    upon you, and be gracious to you:
The Lord lift up his countenance
    upon you, and give you peace.
"So shall they put my name upon the people of Israel, and I will bless them" (6:23-27, RSV).

Interestingly enough, the words of this blessing are written on the oldest fragment of a biblical text that we possess, an inscription in silver that was found in a tomb at Ketef Hinnom just south of Jerusalem. This fragment has been dated around 600 B.C.

We should not be surprised then that Jesus blessed Nathanael as soon as He met him. In fact, the Scripture says, "Jesus saw Nathanael coming to him" (v. 47, RSV). Jesus took the role of the Father who saw the prodigal son coming home and ran to meet him, calling for a robe, a ring, and shoes for the prodigal. Jesus exclaimed, "Behold, an Israelite indeed, in whom is no guile!" (v. 47, RSV).

Here the shadow of Jacob falls over the text. Jacob was the father of Israel, the rascal and trickster patriarch, who had cheated his brother out of his birthright and then taken most of his father-in-law's flock of sheep. "Guile," which means "deceitful cunning, or duplicity," stuck as Jacob's leading character trait. When Esau learned what his brother had done, he pleaded with his father, speaking some of the saddest words in all of Scripture: "'Bless me, even me also, O my father!' But [Isaac] said, 'Your brother came *with guile*, and he has taken away your blessing'" (Gen. 27:35, RSV; author's italics).

Other Old Testament passages in which the word *guile* appears shed further light on our text. Those who are blessed would be delivered from deceit. Psalm 32:12 states the blessing this way:

> Blessed is he whose transgression is forgiven,
>   whose sin is covered.
> Blessed is the man to whom the Lord imputes
>   no iniquity,
>   and in whose spirit there is no deceit (RSV).

Jesus did not hold Nathanael guilty. He blessed him. He recognized him as a true descendent of Jacob, who had been given the name *Israel* by the angel of the Lord. Jacob wrestled with the angel all night until the angel blessed him, and he carried this blessing in his bones the rest of his life. Jacob became the father of the twelve tribes of Israel. Zephaniah, the prophet, said of the remnant of Israel centuries later:

> Those who are left in Israel;
> they shall do no wrong
>   and utter no lies,
> nor shall there be found in their mouth
>   a deceitful tongue (3:13, RSV).

Jesus declared that Nathanael was a true Israelite. This is the only reference to Israel in the Gospel of John, which instead speaks of "the Jews." Jesus came to His own, to Israel, but His own received him not (John 1:11). Here, though, was a true Israelite, one who was willing to come to Jesus.

This son of Jacob did not need to wrestle with God's servant to receive a blessing. Jesus blessed him freely. This son of Jacob did not have to resort to guile or deception to get what he wanted. Instead, he discovered that God was more ready to bless him than he was to receive God's blessing. He was Nathanael, a name which in Hebrew is a compound of two words, *Nathan*, which means "he gave" and *el* which means God. In this experience Nathanael learned the meaning of his name: "God has given."

Now a question: Did Jesus simply recognize who Nathanael already was, or did He bless Nathanael with a blessing the disciple could live up to? I don't guess there is any way to know for sure; but in the previous paragraph, when Andrew brought his brother Simon to Jesus, Jesus gave Simon a new name— *Peter*—which means rock. Peter was certainly not a rock from the beginning, but Jesus recognized what Simon could become. The pattern may hold in the case of Nathanael also. He had expressed doubt and cynicism, "Can anything good come out of Nazareth?" Nevertheless, Jesus recognized that Nathanael was, or at least could become, a true Israelite in whom there was no guile. Jesus looks not just at who we are. He sees what we can become. He blesses us, and He enables us to attain the potential that we can achieve only with His blessing.

Nathanael was aghast: "How do you know me?" (v. 48, RSV). The good news is that the Lord knows you, too, just as surely as He knew Nathanael, telling him, "Before Philip called you...I saw you" (v. 48, RSV). Here we have not only the invitation to believe in Jesus, but the incredible news that God already believes in you. He is ready to receive you and bless you and help you grow in His grace to become all that you can be.

The appropriate response to blessing is confession and commitment. Nathanael answered him: "Rabbi, you are the Son of God! You are the King of Israel!" (v. 49, RSV). Nathanael had indeed seen who Jesus was. Here is a true Israelite recognizing the true King of Israel.

Recognizing that Jesus is our King requires that we make Him the Lord of our lives. It is hypocrisy to claim Jesus as Lord and then dismiss Him from our lives. As the people of God, we are to honor Him by upright and committed living. Discipleship extends to all areas of life. We study the Bible because there we find His Word to us. That means not only regular private study but also joining with others in Bible study and worship. Discipleship means we put aside guile and hypocrisy and we order our financial commitments so that we can support the Lord's work here and around the world. It means we take care of our personal and family relationships so they will be pleasing to God.

III. Promise

In the experience of Nathanael we have seen a drama of change that involved invitation and blessing. The third act of this drama is Jesus' promise to Nathanael. Jesus not only stands as our rear guard, defending us against the armies of guilt, anger, and grief that come at us from our past, but also He is the Lord of our present who blesses us and gives us hope for tomorrow.

Jesus said to Nathanael, "Because I said to you, I saw you under the fig tree, do you believe? You shall see greater things than these.... Truly, truly, I say to you, you will see heaven opened, and the angels of God ascending and descending upon the Son of man" (vv. 50-51, RSV). Here again we hear echoes of the experience of Jacob, who had a dream at Bethel in which he saw the heavens opened and angels descending and ascending. Have you ever sung: "We Are Climbing Jacob's Ladder"? Jesus declared that He was the new meeting point between heaven and earth. In Him we see the true character of God.

If we will follow Jesus, we will see even greater things than we have ever witnessed before. Has the Lord blessed you? That is just the beginning! Has He forgiven you and freed you from the past? That is just preparation for what you can do and what you can become! That may be the hardest part of His invitation: to believe that there is yet more, greater things than these; but these greater things we realize only in His fellowship, only as we follow Him and grow in His grace and love.

My challenge to you, therefore, is to reexamine your commitment to Christ. I challenge you:

1. To search out the things of Christ for yourself,
2. To search for an area in which you can make your own distinctively personal contribution to the life and work of the church,
3. And to say no to all who would bind you with preconceptions about where good or truth can or cannot be found.

When you hear the call of Christ, let nothing hold you back.

I challenge you to receive His blessing with glad and grateful hearts. No gift is more important to abundant life than the gift of knowing that God has given you His fatherly blessing. You don't need to strive to earn God's blessing. You are free now to use the gifts God has given you in the service of His kingdom.

Finally, I challenge you to set before the cynicism of the prophets of despair the promise that you will see even greater things than have been seen before. Believe and go on believing until the kingdom of our Lord is seen in all the earth.

The drama of redemption moves through three acts: invitation, blessing, and promise. Our response is confession and commitment. The invitation has been given, so it is time for the drama to begin.

Conclusion

Each text confronts the preacher with its own difficulties and its own potential. Johannine texts are rich in echoes, allusions, overtones, irony, and symbolism. As a text for a narrative sermon, this one is relatively brief. The story in two scenes is about as simple as any story can be. All the interest focuses, therefore, on the conversations, the exchanges between Nathanael and Philip, and Nathanael and Jesus. Each conversation provides insight into the characters. Longer, more complicated, and dramatic stories provide a wealth of material for narrative preaching. With such a short, simple story, the sermon naturally gravitated toward the richness of its Old Testament allusions, its development of Johannine motifs, and its leading theological themes. Be ready to follow the text where it leads you. Any method or technique needs to be adapted to the text because, ultimately, the text is primary, and the method is secondary.

Nevertheless, narrative preaching disciplines the preacher to keep the text primary, makes the inherently fascinating art of storytelling central to the sermon, and enables the sermon to be fundamentally biblical yet open to a whole range of human situations. No preacher should follow only one method or approach, but narrative sermons are a powerful and effective weapon in the arsenal of truth.

Notes

1. Ernst Haenchen, *The Acts of the Apostles: A Commentary* (Philadelphia: Westminster Press, 1971), 49. See also Paul Minear, *To Heal and to Reveal: The Prophetic Vocation According to Luke* (New York: Seabury Press, 1976), 83 ff.; and Charles Talbert, *Reading Luke: A Literary and Theological Commentary on the Third Gospel* (New York: Crossroad Books, 1982).

2. Robert C. Tannehill, "The Disciples in Mark: The Function of a Narrative Role," *Journal of Religion*, 57 (1977):386-405. Werner H. Kelber, *The Kingdom in Mark: A New Place and a New Time* (Philadelphia: Fortress Press, 1974). *Kingdom* is still thoroughly historically critical in its orientation but already showing signs of concern with the effect of the whole Gospel on its readers. Werner H. Kelber, ed., *The Passion in Mark* (Philadelphia: Fortress Press, 1976). Kelber argued that the Passion narrative, like the rest of Mark, was composed by the evangelist. Werner H. Kelber, *Mark's Story of Jesus* (Philadelphia: Fortress Press, 1979). This book treats the Gospel as a coherent narrative and traces its story line in a nontechnical fashion. See also Norman R. Petersen, *Literary Criticism for New Testament Critics* (Philadelphia: Fortress Press, 1978); "'Point of View' in Mark's Narrative," *Semeia* 12 (1978):97-121; Robert M. Fowler, *Loaves and Fishes: The Function of the Feeding Stories in the Gospel of Mark*, Society of Biblical Literature Dissertation Series 54 (Atlanta: Scholars Press, 1981); David Rhoads and Donald Michie, *Mark as Story: An Introduction to the Narrative of a Gospel* (Philadelphia: Fortress Press, 1982); David Rhoads, "Narrative Criticism and the Gospel of Mark," *Journal of the American Academy of Religion* 50 (1982):411-434; and Frank Kermode, *The Genesis of Secrecy: On the Interpretation of Narrative* (Cambridge, Mass.: Harvard University Press, 1979).

3. For introductions to the various schools of literary criticism, see Terry Eagleton, *Literary Theory: An Introduction* (Oxford: Basil Blackwell, 1983); Edgar V. McKnight, *The Bible and the Reader: An Introduction to Literary Criticism* (Philadelphia: Fortress Press, 1985); Wallace Martin, *Recent Theories of Narrative* (Ithaca: Cornell University Press, 1986); Jane P. Tompkins, ed., *Reader-Response Criticism: From Formalism to Post-Structuralism* (Baltimore: The Johns Hopkins University Press, 1980); and Raman Selden, *A Reader's Guide to Contemporary Literary Theory* (Lexington: The University of Kentucky Press, 1985).

4. See Mark Allan Powell, *What is Narrative Criticism?* Guides to Biblical Scholarship Series (Minneapolis: Augsburg Publishing House, 1990); Seymour Chatman, *Story and Discourse: Narrative Structure in Fiction and Film* (Ithaca: Cornell University Press, 1978); Northrop Frye, *The Great Code: The Bible and Literature* (New York: Harcourt Brace Jovanovich, 1982); Robert W. Funk, *Poetics and the Narrative Text* (Sonoma: Polebridge Press, 1992); Gerard Genette, *Narrative Discourse: An Essay in Method*, trans. Jane E. Lewin (Ithaca: Cornell University Press, 1979); Shlomith Rimmon-Kenan, *Narrative Fiction: Contemporary Poetics* (London: Methuen, 1983); Meir Sternberg, *The Poetics of Biblical Narrative: Ideological Literature and the Drama of Reading* (Bloomington: Indiana University Press, 1985); Tzvetan Todorov, *The Poetics of Prose* (Oxford: Basil Blackwell, 1977).

5. Chatman, *Story and Discourse*, 19-22.

6. Genette, *Narrative Discourse*, 27; Rimmon-Kenan, *Narrative Fiction*, 3.

7. Funk, *Poetics and the Narrative Text*, 1-2.

8. See James L. Resseguie, "Reader Response Criticism and the Synoptic Gospels," *Journal of the American Academy of Religion* 52 (1984):307-324.

9. Boris Uspensky, *The Poetics of Composition: Structure of the Poetic Text and the Typology of Compositional Forms*, trans. Valentina Zavarin and Susan Wittig (Berkeley: University of California Press, 1973).

10. See the essays in "How Gospels Begin," *Semeia* 52 (1990).

11. See my "The Gospel of John and the Jews," *Review and Expositor* 84 (Spring, 1987), 273-288.

12. This interpretation has been cogently stated by Craig R. Koester, "Messianic Exegesis and the Call of Nathanael (John 1:45-51)," *Journal for the Study of the New Testament* 39 (1990):23-34.

13. Ibid., 27-30.

14. Ibid., 30-31.

15. See my *Anatomy of the Fourth Gospel: A Study in Literary Design* (Philadelphia: Fortress Press, 1983), especially chapters 4 and 5.

16. See my essay, "The *Amen, Amen* Sayings in the Gospel of John," in *Perspectives on John*, eds. Robert Sloan and Mikeal Parsons (Macon, Ga.: Mercer University Press, forthcoming).

17. Throughout this section I am indebted to H. Stephen Shoemaker for stimulating conversations about the techniques of narrative preaching, for stirring experiences of his skill with this art, and for his discussion of the subject in his last chapter of *Retelling the Biblical Story: The Theology and Practice of Narrative Preaching* (Nashville: Broadman Press, 1985).

4
A RHETORICAL MODEL

Craig A. Loscalzo

Hermeneutics is the art and science of determining the meaning of a written text, with specific interest in the methods of interpretation. Hermeneutics for preaching is concerned not only with discovering meaning in a biblical text but with determining ways of effectively communicating meaning to contemporary hearers. Finding meaning falls within the confines of hermeneutics; effectively communicating meaning to modern hearers and having those hearers act upon what they have heard falls into the realm of rhetoric. Possible definitions of rhetoric include "the act of speaking and writing effectively," and "skill in the effective use of speech."[1] Rhetoric is also interested in the way the content of a work is organized for clear and persuasive communication. The province of rhetoric is the intentional use of language for a specific purpose. A rhetorical model of interpretation is related both to hermeneutics and rhetoric.

The rhetorical model presented in this essay is grounded in the work of the twentieth-century rhetorician, Kenneth Burke. Burke focused on the dynamic and dramatic way that written works engage readers and move them to a change of attitudes and behavior. Written works are never literature for literature's sake. All literature, according to Burke, has a rhetorical motive; that is, literature is designed to *do* something. Burke understood that literature is an answer to questions posed by the situation in which it was written. Therefore, as we examine Luke 24:13-35, we will attempt to discover what the passage is designed to do: What is its purpose, what

questions does the text answer, and what happens to readers
as they experience this text?

A key to Burke's work is his interest in persuasion through
identification. Luke creates identification between the characters in the story and the readers. We will note how this
happens and what effect it has in accomplishing the overall
goal of the passage. Burke also found that language plays a
key role in effectively realizing a rhetorical goal. Words are
rich symbols that often portray meanings deeper than a surface reading supposes. Burke called his study of the function
of language *logology*; that is, the study of words about words.

In this essay, we will analyze Luke 24:13-35 using Burke's
rhetorical approach. Our goal is to understand what the text
is trying to accomplish, and then to present a sermon that
attempts to do what the text does. Since our discussion centers
on a rhetorical model, we are concerned throughout the interpretation process with how we will preach this text. David
Buttrick has been selected as a conversation partner to dialogue with Burke. Buttrick's *Homiletic* has a major section on
hermeneutics that provides a theological perspective to the
inquiry. He asks key hermeneutical questions: (1) "How do
texts, clearly products of an earlier age and reflecting an
ancient world view, articulate today?"[2] (2) "How can words
written in an earlier age to a different people have *anything* to
say to us today in a twentieth-century time and place? How
can words bridge time?"[3] To shed light on the answers to these
questions, Buttrick has made the following hermeneutical
proposals:

1. "Biblical texts are addressed to communal consciousness."
2. "The consciousness which texts address is the 'double'
   consciousness of being-saved in the world."
3. "Speaking of God, the Bible tells stories and singles out
   symbols. Thus, the Bible must be interpreted within an
   interaction of symbol and story."[4]

Later, we will evaluate Burke's rhetorical method in light of
these proposals.

The following section is an analysis of Luke 24:13-35 using

the Burkean model described above. An explanation of the approach follows.

On the Road to Emmaus

As the passage in chapter 24:13-35 opens, Luke described the scene in terms of time, place, and persons. When did the event take place? Where did the event take place? Who were the characters in the event? These features provide a framework for the action presented in verses 13-35.[5] Luke set the time for the scene with the words "that same day" (vv. 1-13, NRSV). Most likely Luke was referring to more than just the first day of the week itself. Burke suggestes that language is charged with meaning and often points beyond the literal understanding of words and phrases. Luke implied that all the events of that day were pivotal for what was about to take place. Luke's statement is charged with possibilities: (1) It was the first day of the week. (2) It was the day when the women "found the stone rolled away from the tomb, but when they went in, they did not find the body" (vv. 2-3, NRSV). (3) It was the day that the two men in bright clothing asked the women, "Why do you look for the living among the dead? He is not here, but has risen. Remember how he told you, while he was still in Galilee, that the Son of Man must be handed over to sinners, and be crucified, and on the third day rise again" (vv. 4-7, NRSV). (4) It was the day the women returned from the tomb and told the eleven apostles all that had happened; but the women's words "seemed to them an idle tale, and they did not believe them" (vv. 8-11, NRSV). (5) It was the day for saying good-bye to hopes, dreams, and friends. (6) Finally, it was the day of unbelief. Though the Gospel of Luke only says "that same day," a review of the day's events and a consideration of the implications of those events is implied and has rhetorical significance. In other words, Luke was intentionally setting the stage, providing the reader with clues and cues for what was about to take place.

Luke then related that "two of them" were traveling to a village named Emmaus, about seven miles from Jerusalem (v. 13). Their names are not mentioned here, and there is no

comment about why they were going to Emmaus. Perhaps the
two lived there. The climactic scene appears to take place in a
home, possibly the home of the two. If this suggestion is
correct, then we can speculate on their reasons for returning
home. The passover had just ended. One might think that
much celebration would follow such an important event. Typi-
cally it would, but not for these two, not this day. They returned
home because there was no longer any reason to remain in
Jerusalem. Jesus had been crucified. They had hoped He was
the one to redeem Israel. Now their hope was gone. No reason
existed for them to remain in Jerusalem and be constantly
reminded of their shattered dreams. Emmaus was a place to
forget what had happened, a place to try to put confused lives
back together. Nevertheless, as much as we might speculate,
we are kept in suspense about the two and their reason for
going to Emmaus; the Gospel does not reveal anything too
soon.

Luke narrowed the focus by commenting that the two were
"talking with each other about all these things that had
happened" (v. 14, RSV). As when he said "that same day,"
Luke again used the rhetorical device of *review*; the reader is
keenly aware that Luke was referring to the events that had
taken place that day.[6]

Luke's narrative brings the reader into the opening scene
by concentrating on time, place, and persons, but the scene is
not complete. "While they were talking and discussing," the
Gospel says, "Jesus himself came near and went with them"
(v. 15, RSV). We do not find this particularly unusual, for
Jesus often traveled with His disciples (compare 9:51-56).
Jesus on a journey was Luke's way of reminding readers about
the past. The journey motif is used as a rhetorical device
throughout much of the Gospel.[7]

To this point, nothing out of the ordinary had occurred.
Then, Luke made a critical interpretive comment: "But their
eyes were kept from recognizing him" (v. 16, NRSV). Verse 16
is of crucial importance for two reasons. First, it gives us some
insight about Luke's point of view. Until now, Luke had only
described the situation. In verse 16, however, he presented a

degree of perceptibility beyond mere description. Luke's words reveal to us that the two travelers did not recognize Jesus, and that their blindness was caused. I. H. Marshall notes that the story depends on this important element of "dramatic concealment," which he calls "spiritual blindness."[8] Luke did not tell us what caused the blindness, leaving us free to draw our own conclusions. Secondly, verse 16 is the point where Luke's narrative develops a tension that will not be resolved until the climax of the story. Here, in Burke's terms, is an example of the drama of human relations.

Jesus started a conversation with the two by asking a question. Remember, they did not recognize Him. Jesus asked them about the conversation they were having. Luke broke the dialogue by saying, "They stood still, looking sad" (v. 17, NRSV). At first glance, this statement appears innocent, yet Luke provided important insight into the emotional condition of the two travelers; again, a key rhetorical strategy surfaces. The travelers had lost all hope because of their misinterpretation of recent events. Their journey from Jerusalem was an indication of their hopelessness. They felt they had no reason to stay in Jerusalem now that Jesus was dead. He was their hope, but He was gone. Stillness and sadness are not only outward characteristics of the travelers; stillness and sadness describe the psychological and theological condition of the disciples in their hopeless state. *Stillness* and *sadness* are terms used by Luke to create identification with the feelings his readers were experiencing. This may be a key to understanding the rhetorical significance of this passage.

After making this comment, Luke continued to unfold the events. In verse 18, one of the disciples, named Cleopas, answered Jesus' question with a question: "Are you the only stranger in Jerusalem who does not know the things that have taken place there in these days?" (NRSV). Notice the irony in the question; *irony* is an important rhetorical device because it grabs the reader's attention and dramatically involves the reader in the story. We may be passively strolling through the narrative when the irony of Cleopas' question shocks us by its obvious incongruity. We know that Jesus was the only one in

Jerusalem who *did* know the things that had happened. Our curiosity is teased, wondering what will happen next. We are moved from passive observer to active participant. We want to shout to Cleopas, "Don't you know who you're talking to!"

Jesus responded to Cleopas' question with still another question: "What things?" (v. 19, NRSV). And the tension builds. Picture the moment! Totally baffled by the stranger's ignorance about the events which for them were crucial and life changing, both disciples answered at once. Listen to them, almost yelling the words: first one spoke, then the other, then in unison, then one again. They talked over each other like frantic parents telling a mall security guard that their child is lost. Trying their best, Cleopas and his companion told this traveler things everyone knew:

> The things about Jesus of Nazareth, who was a prophet mighty in deed and word before God and all the people, and how our chief priests and leaders handed him over to be condemned to death and crucified him. But we had hoped that he was the one to redeem Israel. Yes, and besides all this, it is now the third day since these things took place. Moreover, some women of our group astounded us. They were at the tomb early this morning, and when they did not find his body there, they came back and told us that they had indeed seen a vision of angels who said that he was alive. Some of those who were with us went to the tomb and found it just as the women had said; but they did not see him (vv. 19-24, NRSV).

The disciples' response was again a review of recent events. The two related things concerning Jesus of which we, as readers, are already aware: Jesus was a prophet (7:16; 13:33); He was delivered up to be condemned to death (23:22-23); He was crucified (23:26-56); He was the one to redeem Israel (1:68; 2:38). Notice that although the two knew all the facts, they did not understand their meaning.[9] They retold the story of Jesus from their point of view; that is, their immediate and preconceived understanding of the events.[10] Their political, religious, and nationalistic biases generated a mistaken interpretation of the events. They were taught that the Messiah would be a nationalistic figure who would free Israel from the shackles of its political rivals and oppressors. Their religious training instructed them to expect a Messiah who would reestablish Israel to a kingdom of Davidic proportions. The two knew the core teachings of the faith but had not comprehended their true meaning. Like tinted glasses, their biases colored their understanding of what they saw.

Jesus reacted to the travelers' interpretation of the recent events. He chided them for not understanding the Scriptures and how the prophets had predicted that it would be necessary for the Christ to suffer and die (vv. 26-27). Again, Luke used review to evoke previous episodes in the Gospel (9:22; 17:25). Without taking time to provide all the details of Jesus' speech, Luke summarily stated that "beginning with Moses and all the prophets, he interpreted to them the things about himself in all the scriptures" (v. 27, NRSV). Jesus' role shifted at this point from stranger to teacher.

Luke continued the story: "As they came near the village to which they were going, he walked ahead as if he were going on" (v. 28, NRSV). Luke then said that the two constrained Him by asking Him to stay with them because it was almost evening (v. 29). The stage was set for the climactic scene.

Jesus sat with the two travelers, apparently at *their* table having a meal with them, when "he took bread, blessed and broke it, and gave it to them" (v. 30, NRSV). Here is the climactic moment in the story. Jesus has again changed roles: from guest to host. Luke wanted us, the readers, to catch these role shifts. Luke also made an intentional point of contact between the Emmaus meal and the feeding of the five thousand earlier in the Gospel (9:10-17).[11] It is also no accident that Luke explicitly stated that Jesus was "at the table" (v. 30, NRSV) with them. Luke created an image here of the church gathering around the Eucharistic table for the Lord's Supper. With the words "at the table," Luke established identification between the two disciples and the readers of the Gospel.

Luke quickly described what happened next: "Then their eyes were opened, and they recognized him" (v. 31, NRSV).

This is the climax of the encounter. From the beginning of the passage, Luke had been moving the story, ever so intentionally, to this point. The moment of recognition finally relieved the tension between Jesus and the two. The travelers retrospectively asked themselves: "Were not our hearts burning within us while he was talking to us on the road, while he was opening the scriptures to us?" (v. 32, NRSV). The two quickly rose and returned to Jerusalem. When they arrived, they found that the eleven and the others with them had already received their confirmation that the resurrection was indeed a reality because Jesus had already appeared to Simon. Luke closed the section with a crucial statement: the two "told what had happened on the road, and how he [Jesus] had been made known to them in the breaking of the bread" (v. 35, NRSV).

What does this story mean, and what was Luke's purpose in relating it? What can be said about the scene, the historical world, in which Luke wrote? What is the rhetorical significance of this passage? that is, what does this passage *do*? What questions being posed by the situation is this passage intended to answer? These are important hermeneutical questions; when answered, they will help us have a better understanding of this text.

An important issue that aids in comprehending the scene, the immediate context in which Luke wrote, is the obvious misunderstanding the disciples had concerning the meaning of the events both before and after the resurrection. Luke implied that misunderstanding was a major factor, perhaps the single most influential factor, that motivated him to tell this story. The misunderstanding is hinted at in verse 16: "But their eyes were kept from recognizing him" (NRSV). Does this statement give us an answer to the questions being posed by the scene for which this text is a clue? Is it possible that Luke's immediate audience also had problems perceiving the presence of Christ in their situation? Were their eyes kept from recognizing Him? Burke would push this statement to its limit of meaning and suggest that blindness is characteristic of more than just these two disciples.

Another important clue is Jesus asking the two to explain

the conversation they were having. Luke noted that the two "stood still, looking sad" (24:17, NRSV). This editorial comment made by Luke—*editorial* in that it calls upon the narrator to draw a subjective conclusion—is another use of logology language. *Standing still, looking sad* may also characterize those in the church who are the target audience of Luke's Gospel. Luke produced identification between his immediate readers and the two traveling disciples. The inability of the travelers to recognize Jesus and their sullen and sad state have been reported to us by Luke. Because of their misunderstanding of recent events, the two travelers had lost all hope; because of events in the lives of Luke's readers, perhaps they too had lost hope. Luke intentionally attempted to create identification between his readers and the two disciples. The readers not only identify with the two's state of hopelessness but also with their later recognition that Jesus is the promised Christ and is, indeed, present now.

Hence, the rhetorical significance of this passage is to elicit hope and a sense of joy in those who are moved by the story because it also becomes their story. Those in Luke's audience who have misunderstood the presence of Christ in the sharing of Scripture and the symbolic sharing of the Eucharistic meal also have their hopes restored. The point where the tension of the story is relieved is the disciples' recognition of Jesus in the breaking of bread. The breaking of bread in verse 30 with the obvious liturgical formula so important to Luke—"He took bread, blessed and broke it, and gave it to them" (NRSV)—is a reminder to Luke's readers that Christ's presence can be made real to them in the sharing of Scriptures, in the sharing of bread, and in the sharing of fellowship experienced through the Lord's Supper.

Luke 24:13-35 describes the misunderstanding and the subsequent understanding of the two disciples because of their encounter with Jesus—in His explanation of the Scriptures and in the breaking of bread. If Luke's immediate scene was marked with misunderstanding, which is what we suppose, then Luke's act of presenting two travelers, who misunderstood the events surrounding Christ's death and later received the revelation of Christ, is in line with Luke's scene. Luke's obvious use of identification and symbols, images, and metaphors that describe the original scene and speak to issues in the scene of his readers was a well-designed and effective rhetorical strategy.

Language as Symbolic Action

Burke assumes that the basic function of rhetoric is "the use of words by human agents to form attitudes or to induce actions in other human agents."[12] Luke's retelling of the Emmaus Road account is an intentional act to change the attitudes and behavior of his readers. We assume that a rhetorical motive presumes an intentional act; Luke 24:13-35 is that act. Humans primarily act verbally, using language as a medium. Human beings express themselves symbolically with language. For Burke, all literature is symbolic action: symbolic in that it represents something beyond itself; action because it is designed to *do* something. His concern is with the *functional* elements of a literary work; that is, What is the work designed to accomplish?

Literature is the representation of the action or drama of human relations; hence, the term *dramatism* describes his critical system. *Dramatism* sees language as a means of action rather than merely the static description of events or the communication of information.[13] The guiding thesis for Burke's critical approach is that all human relations, and the symbolic representation of those relations in literature, is best described in dramatic terms.

Instead of presenting theology propositionally, Luke communicated theological truth through the drama of the encounter of the two disciples with the unrecognized Jesus. The drama is not only a recounting of past events but becomes an immediate drama, an act in which the readers become active participants. Buttrick argues for the importance of the text addressing the consciousness of the immediate community in which "we are brought before the cross of Christ by means of a remembered gospel message."[14] Luke's readers and our congregations are invited, not merely to recall past events, but to encounter the risen Christ *now* in the remembering of the events. Luke 24:13-35 is not the static description of events that took place on the Emmaus Road; it is itself a dramatic act, purposefully designed to create an immediate encounter with the Christ. Changing attitudes and creating moments evoked by literature is the function of Burke's dramatism.

Literature as Strategic Discourse

Burke understands a work of literature as a strategy for solving a problem. Writers create literary works to change existing attitudes or to move other humans to action: hence, a rhetorical motive. Burke presupposes that literature is designed to do something; there is some purpose at which literature is aimed. Critical and imaginative works of literature are actually "answers to questions posed by the situation in which they arose."[15] Symbolic strategies can be used rhetorically to accept a situation, to correct a situation, or to reject a situation. Dramatistically, a work of literature is the answer of the author who stylistically fits the work to the needs of the situation and the readers of the work. Every situation that motivates a writer is affected by the scene, the predispositions of the author, the modes and methods of the author, and the author's purpose. A literary work is a purposeful answer to the questions posed by the situation out of which it emerged. In the approach taken in this essay, Luke 24:13-35 is understood as an answer to questions posed by its situation. Here, the assumption is that the text was not merely written for conveying information or knowledge, but as an inducement to a change of attitude or behavior. The following are possible questions being posed by Luke's immediate situation: How can we experience Christ now that He is no longer physically present? What is the proper role of Scripture and the Lord's Supper within the emerging body of believers? How is it possible to have a true understanding about who Christ is? A way to understand Luke 24:13-35 is to view it as the answer to these questions. This approach objectively grounds the interpretive method.

On the other hand, Buttrick did not find grounding interpretation in the actual setting of the text necessary. His concern was with the text's ability to create meaning in the modern setting, that is, the communal consciousness of a contemporary congregation. For Burke, understanding the meaning and the function of a text emerged from knowledge about the text's scene, with all its various imposing elements. Burke's approach is to look for the interrelatedness between Luke, his readers, and their immediate life situations. David Buttrick does not think that reconstructing the situation of a text nor understanding the psychological state of the writer has much value for interpreting a text.[16] Burke argues to the contrary, believing that the original meaning and purpose of a work of literature should be the beginning point for interpretation. Buttrick vehemently disagrees:

> The texts we study are not locked up tight in a vault labeled "Original Meaning," but articulate differently as the situation of the being-saved community is reshaped. The world assembled before the cross is ever different, and patterns of being-saved-in-the-world are thus ever-changing.[17]

He contends that we do not preach original meaning because it does not speak to our context. However, Buttrick tempers his argument when he suggests that "there must be some relation between original meaning and the shape of our preaching *now*."[18] He continues: "We must seek a model that will relate contemporary interpretation to both original meaning and, somehow, original *intending*."[19] If they were in conversation, Burke might nod his head, reluctantly, and say: "David Buttrick was not far from the truth."

Burke's Pentad

According to Burke, a work of literature contains a rhetorical motive because of its purposeful design. Where motion can be nonintentional, action is always intentional, presupposing a design and a designer. Rhetorical criticism assumes "the critical interpretation of the significance and purpose" of literary works.[20] A work of literature is an act in symbols. About the act, the interpreter generally asks five questions: (1) Who performed the act? (2) Where, when, and under what circumstances was the act performed? (3) What is the act itself and what does it mean? (4) With what was the act performed? (5) Why was the act performed? Burke reformulates these five questions using his dramatistic *pentad*: (1) What *agent* performed the *act*? (2) What is the *scene* of the *act*? (3) What is the nature and meaning of the *act*? (4) With what *agency* did the *agent* perform the *act*? (5) What was the *purpose* of the *act*? Burke maintains that all statements containing motives develop out of and terminate with this pentad.

In the above analysis of Luke 24:13-35, Luke was the *agent*. The *scene* was the immediate setting of misunderstanding that Luke's readers were experiencing. The *act* to move them beyond their misunderstanding was their encounter with the risen Christ as related in the Emmaus Road story. The *agency* Luke used included the narrative itself, irony, remembrance, and the use of logologic terms. The *purpose* was to move his immediate readers beyond their state of misunderstanding to a new sense of understanding: the risen Christ can be perceived, though He is not physically present. This takes place through a proper understanding of Scripture. Buttrick commented that "Scripture is a good *gift* to the church, a gift of grace. We turn to scripture, search scripture's message, feed on scripture's words, live with scripture, and through scripture remember the message of Jesus Christ crucified."[21] Luke wanted his readers to remember what Scripture reveals about Christ. The risen Christ is also present in the fellowship around the table. He was revealed to the two in the breaking of bread.

The key to the pentad's genius is the interrelatedness of the five elements. The act is charged, controlled, and limited by the scene, agent, agency, and purpose. The scene is a container for the act and the agent. The scene can be the actual historical moment in time when the author wrote. However, the scene is also charged with other background issues and circumstances that motivated and influenced the rhetorical act. Prevailing ideas, prejudices, moral values, the ethical environment, and theological frameworks are scenic factors as crucial as the description of an actual historical setting. The two disciples' misunderstanding was a result of preconceived notions related to religious, political, and nationalistic biases. Often these scenic factors are implied and can be detected in the text of the work of literature. The two disciples said that they had hoped Jesus was the one to redeem Israel, but their preconceived notions about the nature of the Messiah were scenic factors that kept them from recognizing Him when He stood in their midst.

The nature of the agent, the purpose of the act, the agency used, and the act itself must be consistent with the nature of the scene.[22] To show this interrelatedness, Burke describes ten relationships.[23] The purpose of these relationships is to establish that no act takes place in a vacuum. Every rhetorical work—a song, a poem, a play, a novel, a newspaper editorial, and a sermon—is somehow a product of the external forces that came together as part of the motivation for composition. The ten relationships attempt to explain the motivational impact of those various forces.

The primary relationships are the scene-act and scene-agent, along with the act-agent. The relationships describe a causal effect between the two parts. What is the effect of the prevailing theological climate on Luke 24:13-35 (the scene-act relationship)? Perhaps Luke's audience was having difficulty understanding Christ's presence in His physical absence. The scene of theological misunderstanding caused Luke to act to resolve the confusion. Luke's act, the Emmaus Road story, is in keeping with the scene in which it was written. In Burke's terms, the scene-act relationship was maintained. Rueckert notes, "The scene not only controls the act to a certain extent, but often generates the problem for which the [work of literature] is a solution, and often provides the values that the [work] affirms."[24]

How does the scene affect the creator of the act, in this case Luke (the scene-agent relationship)? The scene-agent relationship, perhaps the most obvious, describes the connection between a person (agent) and a setting (scene). Again, Luke acted in light of the scene. The scene is characterized by misunderstanding and confusion; and Luke, perhaps the spiritual mentor of his audience, responded to overcome these obstacles to faith, maintaining the scene-agent relationship. The scene has some control over the nature and actions of the agent. Luke's scene dictated the kind of act he presented.

As seen in the above analysis of Luke 24:13-35, a practical application of Burke's method begins with the following questions: What is the nature of the work of literature itself (act)? What was the specific situation (historically, sociologically, culturally, economically, politically, and religiously, etc.) in which the act took place (scene)? Who performed the act (agent)? What rhetorical devices (metaphor, verse, repetition, review, explanation, and irony, etc.) did the agent use (agency)? What was the agent trying to accomplish through the act (purpose)? Dramatism demands that the answer to any one of these questions be considered in the light of the answers to the other questions; the genius of the pentad lies in the function of the relationships. The key to the pentad's rhetorical significance is to notice that the agent is influenced by the scene, and that the scene controls the choice of agency and the purpose of the act itself, and that there is a a reciprocal influence of these elements. For Burke, ideal criticism was more than historical, biographical, sociological, or psychological criticism.[25]

Identification

The central rhetorical characteristic for Burke, always implied in his writing, is identification. Identification is the key to Burke's theory.[26] Identification becomes the rhetorical motive for the changing of attitudes and the inducement to action. It seeks to minimize differences between persons and to highlight common needs, desires, and concerns. The interpreter will look for hints within the literary work where the agent, both intentionally and unintentionally, attempted to create identification. The rhetorical significance of identification is to motivate the readers to experience and adopt the same attitudes being espoused by the agent. Throughout Luke 24:13-35, Luke implicitly creates identification between himself and his readers, and between his readers and the characters in the passage. These points of identification were mentioned in the analysis.

Identification is created, using Burke's term, *logologically*. Logology is Burke's understanding of the way language is used to express the essence of a rhetorical strategy. Language, by its nature, is the expression of ideas and concepts. Burke suggests that the interpreter must look for word clusters, key words and phrases, and the way these words and phrases transcend material expression to deal with ultimate issues. Burke uses *theology* as the paradigm to show how language functions when it is intended to express ultimate ideas; that is, ideas about God. Since theology expresses ideas about ultimate subjects, an understanding of how theological language works informs how all language performs; hence, logology, the study of words about words.[27] The heuristic device for logology is god-terms, a charged vocabulary designed to create identification. God-terms are part of a unifying vocabulary for creating and maintaining a social order. A vocabulary selected at random lacks perspective; a stylized vocabulary is charged with words, god-terms, that identify with the readers. Some god-terms present in Luke 24:13-35 (NRSV) are: "that same day"; "stood still," "looking sad"; "prophet"; "hoped," "redeem Israel"; "third day"; "Moses and all the prophets"; "scriptures"; "at table with them"; "took bread"; "blessed and broke it"; and, "in the breaking of the bread." When these terms are read or heard, they immediately create vivid pictures in the consciousness of the readers or hearers. This consciousness is the communal consciousness to which Buttrick referred.

The interpreter must be aware that there are many strategies an agent may use in responding to a particular situation. The use of dramatism, including identification and logology, is helpful in directing the interpreter to all the factors and composite strategies that may be present in any particular literary work. An advantage of dramatism is that it considers a work of literature functionally. The dramatistic approach to literary criticism places stress upon symbolic action, which forces the interpreter to view all the elements in the work as they interact to form a complete dramatic and rhetorical strategy.

Evaluation of Burke's Method for Biblical Hermeneutics

Is Burke's method valid in light of the hermeneutical proposals suggested by David Buttrick? His first proposal is that biblical texts were addressed to communal and not merely individual consciousness. Scripture was written to a faith community and, therefore, deals with shared meaning. The interpretation of texts requires that they be understood in this communal consciousness. Burke's serious concern for the scene and its effect on the literature produced in that scene suggests a sensitivity to communal consciousness. Since literature is the response to questions posed by the writing situation, and since the writing situation supposes a faith community, Burke's methodology invites Buttrick's question, "What is the text saying to *our* faith-consciousness?"[28] Also, logology looks for language clusters, phrases, and terms endemic to a particular social group. Burke's whole theory of dramatism is grounded in the idea that language is a product of communal consciousness.

Buttrick's second proposal is a bit more tricky. He contended that "the consciousness which texts address is the 'double' consciousness of being-saved in the world."[29] The double consciousness is that of "being-saved" and viewing the world, and a worldly consciousness startled by being saved. I see this proposal as an attempt to maintain the true nature of the Scriptures. The Bible is divine and human in its essence in that it reveals the eternal God's interaction with humans in worldly situations. When we read a text, we do not understand it apart from who we are as believers, nor do we forget that we are believers living in the world. This hermeneutical proposal guards against Docetism on the one side—failing to admit to the text's worldly setting—and humanism on the other side, failing to admit to the text's divine revelation. Buttrick added that "all biblical texts, though aimed at either worldly ways or the reality of being saved, imply both."[30] The text is both written and read by a double consciousness. Buttrick's proposal is grounded in his theological understanding of the nature of Scripture. While Burke's hermeneutical method offers no theological perspective per se, it allows the text to maintain its address to double consciousness. A hallmark of Burke's method is "to use all that is there to use."[31] Since, according to Buttrick, the double consciousness is inherently present in the interpretive process, taking this into consideration is *using all that is there to use*. A Burkean approach supports Buttrick's proposal.

Buttrick's third hermeneutical proposal is that "the Bible must be interpreted within an interaction of symbol and story."[32] He said that the Christ, the ultimate revealed symbol of God, cannot be understood apart from the story of God-with-us. In Scripture, "story grasps symbol and symbol opens story."[33] This proposal is ready-made for Burke's presupposition that all language is symbolic action. In Burkean criticism, one looks for the way that language, the characteristic symbols of communication, evokes action. Action for Burke is the *story* of human relations. Things move, says Burke, but humans act, and when they act, they act symbolically. Buttrick and Burke are both concerned with the interaction of symbol and story and how the reality of the text is made known through the interpretation of that interaction.

In summary, Luke, as the agent, acting in a scene of misunderstanding, presented the Emmaus Road incident as a symbolic act designed to do something. Luke's strategy was to change the attitudes of his readers. The act was a dialogue between Jesus and the travelers, a dialogue that developed and maintained tension, the same kind of tension that probably existed in the lives of Luke's hearers. Luke used several rhetorical devices (agencies) to highlight the tension: irony, review, logologic remembrance of terms, and the changing role of Jesus. Each of these devices helped maintain the scene-agency relationship of misunderstanding. When Jesus broke the bread at the table with the disciples, their eyes were opened, they perceived who Jesus was, and resolution of the tension took place. Once resolution occurred, Jesus' actual presence was no longer required for His presence to be felt. In Burkean terms, the agent (Luke), the scene (Luke's immediate writing circumstances dealing with misunderstanding within the church), the act (the telling of the Emmaus Road encounter), and the agencies (the rhetorical devices Luke used in creating the symbolic act) all worked together and came together at that crucial moment when the misunderstanding was finally resolved. Herein lies the purpose of the act: to demonstrate that in the experience of Scripture and in the breaking of bread, Christ is perceived and present.

Burke's hermeneutical method allows the symbolic meaning of the text to emerge by evaluating its internal dramatic qualities. His ideas that literature answers questions posed by its situation, and that written works are designed to do something, yield valuable insights as a rhetorical model for interpretation.

The Sermon

It Was One of *Those* Days!

Text: Luke 24:13-35

Have you ever had one of *those* days? Do you know what I mean? One of those miserable, unpredictable days? You're sure you set the alarm clock. You always set the alarm clock. But this morning, the morning you can't be late, the morning that you're supposed to make the presentation, the alarm clock decides (how else could it have happened?) to sleep in! You're supposed to leave the house at 7:30 sharp and it's already 7:35. You shout to anyone who will listen: "It's going to be one of *those* days!"

You jump out of bed directly into the shower and discover that every one else has had their showers. There's no, I mean, NO, hot water for you. You try to make the best of it. "A cold shower is invigorating," you lie to yourself. Out of the shower to the closet you go.

The suit you were going to wear is missing. A frightening thought strikes like a bolt of summer lightning; a chill races up your spine. You remember the errand you were supposed to run last night—stop by the dry cleaners and pick up the suit. You think to yourself, "It's going to be one of *those* days!"

Making the best of existing wardrobe, you dress and race to the kitchen for a quick bite. "Where is all the adult cereal?" you ask as you rifle through the cupboard. Squandering your daily fat-gram quota in one fell swoop, you down a bowl of Cocoa Puffs. Like the refrain of a Beethoven symphony, that haunting thought strikes again: "It's going to be one of *those* days!"

Have you ever had one of *those* days? For the two disciples on the road to Emmaus, it was one of *those* days! The Passover had ended. It should have been a time of celebration. They felt hopeless—dreams gone sour, hopes dashed against the rocks of reality. They went home from church that day totally disillusioned.

Has church ever done that to you? Have you ever gone home from church feeling confused—even empty—and disappointed with the apathy of your Sunday School class? Dissatisfied because the music is never the style you like; mad because the sermon didn't say the things that you believe; frustrated because what happens in church doesn't seem to impact your real life situation? The church world of Sunday seems light years away from the real world of Monday. Have you ever gone home from church feeling let down by God?

As the two disciples headed home, they talked about the things that had happened in recent days: "Just last week, 'Hosanna, blessed is the King who comes in the name of the Lord!' Then it all came apart: untrue accusations, a makeshift trial, and they crucified Him. To make matters worse, the women at the tomb this morning didn't find His body. They said they saw angels who said Jesus was alive. Just wishful thinking if you ask me. It couldn't be any worse than this! We all hoped He was the one to redeem Israel. Just last week He was laughing among us. Now Jesus is dead!" It was one of *those* days, one of those miserable, unpredictable days!

While they are talking, a stranger came and walked with them: "Good evening fellows. Beautiful day. What's new?" They stopped in their tracks; dismay was written all over their faces. The stranger asked, "Why are you so down in the mouth?" To which Cleopas responded, "Are you the only one in Jerusalem who doesn't know what's happened in these days?"

What a strange and ironic question! Pilate was still washing the guilt from his hands. He didn't know what had happened. The members of the Sanhedrin were throwing a party, thinking their problems were over. They didn't know what had happened. The women went to the tomb to anoint their dead friend. They didn't know what had happened. The apostles were hiding out, wondering what they were going to do now. They didn't know what had happened. Peter cowered as each new dawn brought the sound of a rooster crowing. He didn't know what had happened. These two were heading back to Emmaus because their hopes had been spoiled. They didn't know what had happened, and Cleopas asked this unknown traveling companion, "Are you the only one who doesn't know what's going on?" Cleopas, that's Jesus! He's the only one who had any idea about what was going on.

Then Jesus asked, "What things?"

Now, *I* want to know what's going on! Didn't they know this was Jesus? Was this some kind of cruel joke? These two dejected disciples were trying to make sense out of what had happened. Was this a heavenly hoax? Was Jesus playing a game with them? Was this some sort of divine "knock knock" joke? What was happening?

Earlier in Luke's gospel, Jesus had said to the twelve, "We are going up to Jerusalem, and everything that is written about the Son of Man by the prophets will be accomplished. For he will be handed over to the Gentiles; and he will be mocked and insulted and spat upon. After they have flogged him, they will kill him, and on the third day he will rise again" (18:31-33, NRSV). Luke said that they understood none of "these things." *Now* the Gospel of Luke tells us, "Their eyes were kept from recognizing him" (v. 16, NRSV).

Why didn't they understand? Why didn't they recognize Jesus? Was it possible that they didn't recognize Jesus because they were not expecting to see Him? Or is it more likely

that they didn't recognize Jesus because He was not the Christ
of their expectations?

Like many disciples, these two expected the redemption of
Israel, the redemption of Jerusalem. They had hoped for a
kingdom of Davidic proportions. They had hoped for a messiah
riding on a white horse, freeing Israel from all of its oppressors. In their minds, in their theological understanding, there
was no place for a crucified Messiah. To them, Jesus' ministry
was a failure; He had let them down. When they saw Him, He
didn't look like the messiah they had created in their minds.
No wonder they didn't recognize Him.

A local artist was commissioned by a church in Louisville to
do a sculpture of the holy family: Jesus, Mary, and Joseph.
The finished work was to be displayed in the downtown sanc-
tuary when its renovations were complete.

When the work was finished, the artist went by to see the
sculpture in its setting in the church. He looked all over the
building and could not find his work anywhere. He spotted the
pastor whom he knew and asked him about the statue.
Reluctantly, the pastor said it had been moved to the basement.

"Why?" asked the artist, "Is there something wrong with it?
I thought you were pleased with it."

"Well," the pastor said, "nothing is really wrong with it."

"What is it then? Tell me."

"All right," he said, "Some of the people complained about the
sculpture. They said Jesus, Mary, and Joseph looked too Jewish."

That's the problem these two disciples seemed to have: Jesus
didn't fit their image. Jesus didn't look like their picture of the
messiah. Eduard Schweizer said that what stood in the way of
their faith was their belief in an image of Christ that did not
describe Jesus.[34]

What image stands in the way of our faith, keeping us from
experiencing Christ?

J. B. Phillips in his book *Your God Is Too Small* exposes the
trouble with many people today: they have not found a God
big enough for modern needs.[35] There are people who still
carry the understanding of God they had as a young child. I
have talked with students who were struggling with their

spiritual lives. Many have a childish image of God which is inadequate to meet the challenges they now face in life. "Now I lay me down to sleep/ I pray the Lord my soul to keep/ If I should die before I wake/ I pray the Lord my soul to take," is a beautiful affirmation of faith for a child. But such a prayer does not touch the depths of pain we face in the Gethsemane moments of life—moments when no words can express our longing for God who is big enough and real enough to know our suffering.

Phillips describes some of the images people have of God. One is God as "Grand Old Man." Children in a Sunday School class were asked to write down their ideas about what God was like. Their answers went something like this: "God is a very old man living in Heaven." To a child, people in charge are always older. Since God is in charge of everything, God must be the oldest of all.

The problem with this image is that God is not only seen as "old" but as "old fashioned." Here is a God who created heaven and earth, parted the Red Sea, led the Israelites into the Promised Land, and after Jesus' resurrection, has been too tired to do much of anything else.

A group of young teenagers was asked: "Do you think God understands radar? Their first response was no, until they thought about their answer. Yet, in the back of their minds, they were holding onto an idea of God as inadequate for today.

Another "small god" is God as the "projected image" of our own personal morality. We don't drink, so, not surprisingly, this god is against the use of alcohol. We don't smoke. Guess what, this god is also against the use of tobacco. We eat too much. Guess what? This god doesn't mind that. We fudge a bit on our income taxes. This god feels like we do, of course: "Everybody fudges a little bit." Phillips rightly states that unless our image of God is something higher than a magnification of our own moral concerns, our worship will be nothing more than the worship of ourselves.

Another inadequate god is "the God-in-a-box." Some worship a god that they have "captured and tamed and trained" to serve their every whim, to do their bidding for them. Some churches give the impression that God can only move and work within the frameworks they have established.

I was born and reared in Philadelphia, Pennsylvania. My family was religious in their own way, so my ideas about God were not grounded in particularly sound theology. For example, everything that went wrong was blamed on God being mad about something. When things went right, God was not usually mentioned. I understood God as a God of rules and regulations: *Do* this! *Don't do* that! My friends told me, "You'd just better not make God mad."

I had trouble understanding why there were so many denominations, all claiming that they were the "true faith." I felt that the God I learned about was more a God of convenience, a God controlled by whoever was talking about Him.

To fill out the picture, I was raised in a Philadelphia *Italian* family. To my family, God was like Don Vito Corleone, always making deals one couldn't refuse. Even though we were Italian, my family was proud to be in America. When they talked about blessings from above, it was difficult to figure out whether they were describing God or Uncle Sam.

I was twenty-seven years old when I discovered some wonderful things about God: God was not from Philadelphia, God was not Italian or American, and God was not controlled by whoever was talking about Him.

In 1977, my wife and I made professions of faith at First Baptist Church in Sunrise, Florida. We were hungry to find out everything we could about our faith and our new denomination. We heard so much about great Southern Baptists like Lottie Moon—I couldn't wait to meet her—and Annie Armstrong. We learned about our Baptist forebearers, Baptist distinctives, home missions, and foreign missions. Thank God for a wise pastor, who helped us have a healthy loyalty to our new denomination. Under his care and nurture, I made another freeing discovery: God is not from the South! And...God is not a Southern Baptist, nor is God a Roman Catholic or an Episcopalian or a Methodist or a Presbyterian. God is...God!

J. B. Phillips is right: "No denomination has a monopoly of God's grace."[36] If we learn anything from Christ about the nature of God, we know that "the wind [spirit] blows where it wills" (John 3:8, RSV) and is not subject to our restrictions.

Some of you experience God as *angry parent*: always saying no, always disappointed in you: "Can't you do anything right?" Some of you imagine God as a *magic genie*, the granter of wishes, if one will only say the right words. Some of you understand God as the *heavenly rescue squad*: just dial 911 whenever you get into trouble. Some of you understand God as the one who demands success: "You had better be successful if you ever want to get that really big church." All these are inadequate gods, small gods of our own making. God will not conform to our "projected images." God cannot be confined to any of our "boxes," whether national, racial, theological, or denominational.

No wonder they didn't recognize Jesus. They misunderstood what God was like, so they missed the very presence of God in their midst, and Cleopas asked, "Are you the only one in Jerusalem who doesn't know what's happened in these days?"

To help them out of their dilemma, Jesus interpreted the Bible to them. That's just like Jesus, isn't it? When things were confusing, when life didn't make sense, He went to the Scriptures. The devil tempted Him to turn stones into bread; Jesus quoted Deuteronomy 8:3: "One does not live by bread alone, but by every word that comes from the mouth of God" (NRSV). For His first sermon in Nazareth, He read from the scroll of Isaiah: "The Spirit of the Lord is upon me/because he has anointed me to bring good news to the poor" (Luke 4:18a, NRSV). The Pharisees questioned Him about His disciples plucking grain on the Sabbath; He said to them: "Have you not read what David did when he and his companions were hungry? He entered the house of God and took and ate the bread of the Presence" (Luke 6:3-4, NRSV). Even at the moment of His death, He had the Scriptures on His lips: "My God, my God, why have you forsaken me?" (Matt. 28:46, NRSV).

Jesus interpreting Scripture to the two is important because, for Luke, the Scriptures were enough to produce faith. Luke implied that their misunderstanding—the reason they didn't recognize Jesus—was because they did not understand the Scriptures and the Christ they presented.

Jesus is not a conjured-up messiah, one prone to our whims, controlled by our wishes, confined in our boxes. We know Christ, experience Christ, and understand Christ as the One made known to us through the pages of this Book; and out of these pages we move to proclaim Him as Savior and worship Him as Lord.

So why did it take a meal for their eyes to be opened? Perhaps to show the mystery available at the Lord's Supper. Perhaps to show that the Christ of Scripture is present in the ordinary moments of life. Perhaps it was the grace given there; a meal is a wonderful opportunity for grace. Perhaps it was the understanding offered there; a meal is a wonderful opportunity for understanding.

In *Driving Miss Daisy*, Hoke was Miss Daisy's driver. He was the driver her son hired for her, the driver she didn't want. She was a rich Jewish widow used to having things her way; he was a black chauffeur who needed work.

They lived in different worlds. When Idella the maid died, Miss Daisy grieved by eating her meal alone in the dining room; Hoke ate his alone in the kitchen. When Martin Luther King spoke at a banquet, Miss Daisy heard him live from a seat in the hall where he spoke; Hoke heard him on the radio in the car. They lived in different worlds.

In the closing scene, Miss Daisy, nearly helpless, lives in a nursing home. Hoke, who long has been unable to drive, is brought by to visit her. It is Thanksgiving Day. The two are seated at a table. "How are you?" asks Miss Daisy. Hoke says, "You haven't touched your Thanksgiving pie." The film closes with Hoke feeding Miss Daisy the Thanksgiving pie. Here are two people. Barriers are gone. Grace is profoundly given and received.

Jesus explained the Scriptures to the travelers and shared in a time of grace, and their eyes were opened. When they realized what had happened, they went back to Jerusalem to tell all about it. If you listen carefully, you can almost hear Cleopas say, "It wasn't one of *those* days after all."

Well, it's time for us to go to Emmaus. Who do you think you'll see?

Reflection

How did Burke's rhetorical insights help me in preparing the sermon? I was asked to preach in the regular chapel worship service at The Southern Baptist Theological Seminary, Louisville, Kentucky the week after Easter. I looked through several of the lectionary readings for worship after Easter, and the Emmaus Road passage was one. The poignant beauty of the story attracted me; I decided to use it as my text for the chapel sermon.

Following the standard canons of biblical exegesis, I began to work with the text, attempting to have a personal encounter with it. The Burkean concept of literature being the answer to questions posed by the situation in which it was written was the beginning point for me. As mentioned in the above analysis of the text, I looked for the kinds of questions that might have been posed in Luke's situation as he wrote of the Emmaus encounter. The key question that emerged was: How can we experience Christ's presence when He is no longer physically with us? I then looked for analogous questions posed by the contemporary church to see if there were similar modern concerns. I found that the church is seeking to understand the nature of the relationship of the risen Christ and His presence and acting in the contemporary life situations of the church. So often, our preconceived notions about the nature of God and the way Christ acts within and outside the church keep us from experiencing the true Christ. I found this analogous to the dilemma faced by the two disciples on the Emmaus Road. I also discovered that we often misunderstand Christ because we are blind to the truths in Scripture about who Christ is and how Christ acts. This was also a crucial misunderstanding of the disciples. My goal for the sermon was to enable the hearers to feel some of the same tensions felt by the two disciples, tensions I felt as I struggled with the text. Then I hoped the hearers would come to the realization, like the two disciples, that Christ *is* present in the sharing of the Scriptures and the fellowship meal of the church.

I began the sermon by relating a harried, unpredictable day for two reasons. I wanted to create identification between my hearers and the two characters in the story. The two disciples left Jerusalem because it was a day full of bad news. The introduction humorously pointed to the kinds of days each of us has had. If that day was troubling, how much more so the day when we discover that our hopes for life are dashed. I also wanted to create personal identification with the hearers. Humor, carefully used, lowers anxiety on the part of the preacher and his or her hearers. The introduction showed my hearers that I could identify with them because we have all had "one of *those* days!"

My overall sermon strategy was to walk through the text, raising questions about the motivations of the disciples' behavior, of Christ's response, and of why Luke emphasized certain features of the story. This dialectic approach is typical of Burkean rhetoric because it maintains identification by involving the hearers in the process of discovering the truths in the text rather than receiving the truth from the preacher.

Using Burke reminded me that I must continually identify with the needs and interests of my hearers rather than merely my personal concerns. I constantly thought about the language of the sermon and the symbols: how I spoke was as important as what I said. I attempted to create a drama in which the hearers were not passive recipients of a sermon but were intellectually and emotionally involved in the exposition of the Emmaus story. My goal was that Luke's purpose in relating the Emmaus story was accomplished in my sermon.

A rhetorical model of interpretation attempts to discern the meaning and purpose of a passage of Scripture so that the preaching of the passage engages modern hearers, enabling them to have an encounter with God. This model is not only concerned with what the text means but with what the text does. Because of the mystery present in Scripture, it is sometimes impossible to say, "I know what this text means." But one can say, "I know what this text does because, as a reader of the text, it does something with me." The goal of a rhetorical model of interpretation is to allow God's meaning and purpose of a biblical passage to be gladly heard and received.

Notes

1. See *rhetoric* in Webster's *Ninth New Collegiate Dictionary* (Springfield, Mass.: Merriam-Webster, 1987), 1011.

2. David Buttrick, *Homiletic: Moves and Structures* (Philadelphia: Fortress Press, 1987), 241.

3. Ibid., 264.

4. Ibid., 276-279.

5. Richard J. Dillon, *From Eye-Witnesses to Ministers of the Word: Tradition and Composition in Luke 24* (Rome: Biblical Institute Press, 1978), 82.

6. Robert C. Tannehill noted that Luke 24 and Acts 1 rely on review and preview as devices to build a bridge between the two stories and therefore maintain narrative unity. See *The Narrative Unity of Luke-Acts: A Literary Interpretation* (Philadelphia: Fortress Press, 1986), 277.

7. Luke 9:51—19:27 describes events and teaching on the journey to Jerusalem. B. P. Robinson described *journey* as one of the four major Lukan motifs that come together in the Emmaus story. See "The Place of the Emmaus Story in Luke-Acts," *New Testament Studies* 30 (1984):481.

8. I. H. Marshall, *The Gospel of Luke: A Commentary on the Greek Text* (Exeter: The Paternoster Press, 1978), 893.

9. Hans Dieter Betz, "The Origin and Nature of Christian Faith According to the Emmaus Legend," *Interpretation* 23 (1969):36.

10. Tannehill, *The Narrative Unity of Luke-Acts,* 279.

11. Ibid., 290.

12. Kenneth Burke, *A Rhetoric of Motives* (1950; reprint ed., Berkeley: University of California Press, 1969), xiv-xv.

13. For a complete discussion of dramatism, see Kenneth Burke, *A Grammar of Motives* (1945; reprint ed., Berkeley: University of California Press, 1969), xv-20.

14. Buttrick, *Homiletic,* 247.

15. Kenneth Burke, *The Philosophy of Literary Form: Studies in Symbolic Action,* 2d ed. (Baton Rouge: Louisiana State University Press, 1967), 1.

16. Buttrick, *Homiletic,* 275.

17. Ibid., 259.

18. Ibid., 273.

19. Ibid., 274.

20. Alfred G. Smith, "Entropy and Synopsis," in *Communication: Concepts and Perspectives,* ed. Lee Thayer (Washington, D.C.: Spartan Books, 1967), 427.

21. Buttrick, *Homiletic,* 248.

22. Burke, *A Grammar of Motives*, xv.

23. The ten relationships are: scene-act, scene-agent, scene-agency, scene-purpose, act-purpose, act-agent, act-agency, agent-purpose, agent-agency, and agency-purpose. See Burke, *A Grammar of Motives*, 15.

24. William H. Rueckert, "The Analysis of Poetry as Symbolic Action," *Kenneth Burke and the Drama of Human Relations*, 2d ed. (Berkeley: University of California Press, 1982), 75.

25. L. Virginia Holland, "Kenneth Burke's Dramatistic Approach in Speech Criticism," in *Critical Responses to Kenneth Burke, 1924-1966*, ed. William H. Rueckert (Minneapolis: University of Minnesota Press, 1969), 301.

26. Kenneth Burke, "Rhetoric—Old and New," *The Journal of General Education* 5 (1951):203.

27. See Kenneth Burke, *The Rhetoric of Religion: Studies in Logology* (1961; reprint ed., Berkeley: University of California Press, 1970).

28. Buttrick, *Homiletic*, 277.

29. Ibid.

30. Ibid., 278.

31. Kenneth Burke, *The Philosophy of Literary Form: Studies in Symbolic Action,* 3d ed. (Berkeley: University of California Press, 1973), 23.

32. Buttrick, *Homiletic*, 278.

33. Ibid., 279.

34. Eduard Schweizer, *The Good News According to Luke*, trans. David E. Green (Atlanta: John Knox Press, 1984), 372-373.

35. J. B. Phillips, *Your God Is Too Small* (New York: Macmillan Publishing Company, 1961), 20. The following descriptions are found under the topic "Unreal Gods," 9-64.

36. Ibid., 40.

5

AN AFRICAN-AMERICAN MODEL

James Earl Massey

Preachers who take their calling and task seriously know that hermeneutical work is an almost daily necessity and that this regular exercise in faith and study is imperative to grant the substance, sustenance, and proper focus needed for effective pulpit work. Since the art of preaching has to do with applying the insights of Scripture to meet human needs, it is incumbent upon the preacher to know and follow the principles for interpreting Scripture rightly, fully dependent upon the sacred writings as a primary source of witness about God's way with humankind. Hermeneutical work is germane to this task, granting understandings that are basic for dealing with the nature and range of the biblical materials, and with the import and application of the biblical witness for changing generations and for life in new settings.

The term *hermeneutic* is a many-sided word: it reminds us, on the one hand, that human language is intended to express meaning and that understanding of meanings should be available in the words that are used; on the other hand, it implies a process by which the meaning intended can be sought and gained. In the background, however, lurks the awareness that words can be problematic, so care must be given as to how meanings are best represented and conveyed in relation to a commonly shared view of reality. Robert W. Funk has explained: "The hermeneut—the one who practices hermeneutics—is he who, having been addressed by the Word of God and having heard, is enabled to speak, interpret, or translate what he has heard into the human vernacular so that its power is transmitted through speech. If the minister is not a hermeneut, he has missed his vocation."[1]

This chapter treats the hermeneutical perspectives which traditionally have governed the African-American approach to the preaching task. Three basic hermeneutical perspectives will be set forth as distinctives in sharing the Word within the African-American community. The first of the three perspectives will show the extent to which African-American hermeneuts honor general hermeneutical principles shared by all who seek rightly to understand and interpret Scripture. The other two will isolate principles which are distinctive for pulpit work in the African-American church setting, a sociocultural environment within which a shared set of experiences has occasioned some distinctive social understandings, assumptions about the world, expectations from religious faith, and unique leadership demands.

Perspective One:
The Adequacy and Immediacy
of the Biblical Witness

It is axiomatic in the African-American church that the Bible must be honored as the basis for pulpit work. The black hermeneut, like all others, must deal with the manifold forms and genres found in the Bible. He must interrogate them for their intended meaning, using any and all skills and tools available through training and experience, but attention is centered mainly on "the life meanings of the Bible, for which it was handed down orally in the first place."[2] The Black hermeneut seeks to escape the limitations of a skewing literalism in his or her study of the Scriptures and to avoid getting entangled in the analytical technicalities of modern critical approaches which can deaden lively imaginativeness and vital utterance. The concern is ever toward meanings for living. As Mitchell has rightly explained it: "Few if any of the controversies over Scripture itself or any of the doctrines would have lasted very long if focused on the kinds of issues people face in real life."[3]

In the African-American church setting, the preaching emphasis is seldom, if ever, upon analytical absoluteness as to concepts about the nature and scope of Scripture. Rather, the preaching focuses upon an openness to the basic message and purpose for which the Word was given and preserved. The cultural roots of the black approach to Scripture honors the folk appeal reflected throughout the biblical record. This cultural difference in the way Scripture is approached by African Americans has been responsible, in part, for keeping black preaching free from divisive theological controversies and from deadening abstractions. In black preaching, and in the hermeneutic by which it happens, the focus is not on concepts to be voiced and treated intellectually but upon an experience to be expected and enjoyed through an openness to the biblical witness. The Black preacher studies Scripture for preaching with a view to discern the experience toward which the text points, and to plan the best means by which a vision of that experience can be shared in the pulpit.

In a written treatment about how sermons "come" to the preacher, Gardner C. Taylor admitted that sermons come in many ways but most particularly through a study of the Bible. "Anyone who will open himself or herself to the revelation of God contained in the Bible will find endless preaching, better still, will be found by it, which demands to be delivered of the preacher by pulpit presentation."[4] Taylor went on to stress the importance of opening the whole self to the biblical witness, to "catch the sounds and sights and smells of the accounts recorded in the Bible. Enter as much as you can into the climate of each scene. Let the imagination and the mind work at the same time"[5] but always with the central message informing the self, namely, "God reaching out in this way and that for a people whom He loves,"[6] and with His hand seen supremely stretched out toward everyone in the person of Jesus Christ on Calvary.

The ruling principle by which the Black hermeneut operates in reading Scripture is to see all things in light of the deliverance theme highlighted there. The basic methodological perspective by which the entire revelatory canon is finally viewed is the biblical theme of God acting to deliver humans from their plights. This perspectival theme of freedom is a constant in Scripture, whether one is reading the narratives of the earliest patriarchs, the stringent remonstrances in the prophetic books, or exploring the diverse and impressive imagery Paul used in the New Testament Letters to describe the human condition under benefit of divine grace. In fact, the majority of that apostle's images about salvation spill over with grand implications about the meaning of deliverance.[7] Paul's shared understanding of what God has accomplished in the human interest through Jesus Christ is best summed up in the word *freedom,* since he used it in so many connections: freedom from sin, release from subjection to the powers of the evil age, escape from bondage to the elemental spirits of the universe, freedom from confinement to legalisms, and even ultimate release from a limiting mortality by means of a coming resurrection from death.

Two related concerns merge in the African-American pulpit: liberation and community.[8] Black preaching at its best is never far from these two concerns, and the Black hermeneut has high warrant for emphasizing them because the whole of Scripture does so.

The concern to understand Scripture in light of its leading theme of God as deliverer should not be misunderstood as but a reading of the biblical record through the lens of a modern social or political concern. Far from it, this way of reading Scripture keeps the basic facts of the human experience in clear view and the divine concern about the human condition in fresh focus. The concern for freedom, justice, love, and hope is reflected on nearly every page of Scripture; not to see this when the Bible is read is to miss what is most germane for life as God intended it. Such an approach to understanding the biblical record honors the historicity of the Scriptures, forbidding a purely academic handling of its witness.

This approach to Scripture does not answer all of the questions which rightfully arise through confronting its pages; neither does the covenant-theme approach, nor the promise and fulfillment approach, nor the revelation as history framework, nor the sacrifice motif. Like every other hermeneut, the

black hermeneut needs to use more than one conceptual framework in order to view the materials in the two Testaments
with increased understanding. It is a fact that not everything
in the Bible can be made to fit neatly into any one scheme.
However, it is an observable fact that the theme of freedom,
with God as Deliverer, is one of the leading thematic continui-
ties by which the two Testaments cohere. It is certainly one of
the strongest themes for addressing persons with a history of
oppression and social trauma. It is a theme that does not allow
for abstractions in preaching nor for fruitless intellectualizing.
To quote Mitchell again: "The Black devotion to the Bible is not
anti-intellectual; it simply and wisely avoids intellectual*isms*."[9]

Perspective Two:
The Importance of the Hearer's
Situation in Planning the Sermon

A sermon can rise from a text that generates it or from
musing about some human need or concern. Whatever the
original occasion that shapes it, the final focus of the sermon
must apply its message to the hearer's life; the truth it contains must match an end to which it is projected. This hermeneutic principle demands that the hearers be taken seriously
and their life situation be given due regard. This perspective
highlights the need to keep the fundamentals of the text
properly wedded to the function of the sermon as a medium of
intended help.

The traditional emphasis in Black preaching on the importance of storytelling grows out of this concern. It is for this
reason that *story* is the chief mode used by African Americans
in preaching.

Thirty years ago the scholarly religious world was in disar-
ray, puzzled about the problems associated with speaking about
God; the need was being voiced to rediscover ways and means
to communicate religious meanings effectively. Many modes of
utterance were being vigorously explored as the question continued to be asked about how to speak meaningfully about
God in a secular and nihilistic age. During that questioning
time, Amos N. Wilder published those seminal studies, *The*

Language of the Gospel, and called attention to the modes, genres, and immediacy of the early Christian rhetoric reflected in New Testament literature. One of the genres Wilder treated in some detail was that of story, and he highlighted narrative form as an engaging, illuminating, revealing language mode.[10] Considerable scholarly interest was shown in Wilder's study because he directed attention back to the qualities of the language modes by which the early Christians captured the attention and, later, the recognition of a world hungry for meaning.

The strategic use of story is proverbial in the Black preaching tradition. The story mode touches every one, leaving no hearer disengaged. Whereas critical treatment of some texts can show many what the preacher has discovered and brought to view—sometimes leaving them with little more than interesting ideas about the text—story can engage the hearer immediately, granting access to the very living current of life within the text. This popular mode for preaching addresses the hearer at the deepest level of need because it not only interests but invites; it challenges and engages; it opens the self to new possibilities. A specimen of such story preaching will soon be shared as part of this chapter. The choice of story will be explained, and a preliminary hermeneutical treatment offered to set the stage for understanding the focus by which the sermon took its shape and direction.

By necessity, the Black hermeneutic has as its concern the matching of some textual help with someone's soul struggles; it fulfills itself in relating to that range of human issues that Martin Luther once described as *anfechtung,* a word without any real equivalent in English but one that should be understood to include "all the doubt, turmoil, pang, tremor, panic, despair, desolation, and desperation which invades the spirit of man.[11] Black life in America has been the context for struggle, combat, continual pressures due to unfair treatment and unmitigated woes, always under attack, and the African American's need for spiritual resources has been acute. The Black pulpit has had to address such situations, calling attention to the properties and power of faith and hope for facing and handling it all. The Black hermeneut understands the struggle and preaches with insight because of having had a common share in it. This is why African American preaching has appealed so often and so effectively to the biographies of struggle found in Scripture, highlighting how those who suffered in that earlier day overcame or endured by the help of God. The character of such preaching is thus more interpretative than descriptive, more pastoral and therapeutic than didactic and propositional. It does not grow out of a system but out of the soul, a soul that reads the Bible in the light of its own experiences, and whose preaching reflects the sustenance that an open and intense reading has granted. This is a point of vital necessity for preaching to those who live with their backs against the wall. So the importance of the hearer's situation in planning the sermon is imperative for the particularism so native to African-American pulpit work.

The Black preacher knows that where the hearer stands in life will make all the difference for being understood and relevant. It is only out of such an awareness of the hearer's situated place in life that the sermon approach can be planned well, the sermon aim determined with aptness, and the sermon application effectively made. The Black hermeneutic keeps this in view. The grammatico-historical approach to the text can be ever so valid, but it is never vital until what it makes clear is matched against the faces and needs of those to whom its insights will be shared through preaching. From the earliest period of Black life in America until now, the preaching needed by those who are part and parcel of the African-American community must be geared to deal with "the sufferings and needs of their days."[12]

Perspective Three:
The Centrality of Preaching as an Agency for Hearing and Faith

Deeply rooted in the African-American preaching tradition is the view and belief that preaching is an agency both for mediated meaning and a sense of divine presence. The person of the preacher is crucial because he or she is the visible and vocal agent of the God who sends and shares His word:

1. The preacher is traditionally and expectantly *identified with the divine Word*. He or she is both an authorized handler of the sacred text and the one who applies its message to the situated lives and needs of the hearers. Expected to be filled with the word God intends to be uttered, the preacher is understood traditionally as the bearer of an answer and the sharer of a solution. This was part of the rich understanding out of which the late Bishop Joseph A. Johnson, Jr., wrote when he commented: "The Black preacher does not merely use the Bible, but rather he permits the Bible to use him."[13] This being used by the Bible has to do with being an agent of the biblical witness and gospel message, and this begins with and is sustained by an open hearing from God through acquaintance with the Scriptures and their import.

The preacher is expected to be a hearer in preparation for being a speaker. In any discussion of the preacher as a hearer, one must recall the ancient biblical tradition in which the Hebrews were again and again addressed by God—always with an invitational imperative to listen. This is clear from the hallowed call in the Shema (Deut. 6:4) and all the other instances when God issued an attention-claiming summons, as recorded throughout the prophetic literature (see Isa. 1:10; 7:13; Jer. 2:4; 7:2; 10:1, etc.). In His teaching and preaching, Jesus knew that the people understood His call to "hear" what He was saying as invitational, as promising something of importance, as an indication that what He sought to share should be received with openness, regard, and concern about its implications. Thus His admonitions: "Everyone then who hears these words of mine and acts on them will be like a wise man who built his house on rock" (Matt. 7:24, NRSV); "Let anyone with ears listen!" (Matt. 11:15; 13:9,43, NRSV); and "Pay attention to what you hear" (Mark 4:24, NRSV). The preacher is rightly expected by the people to assume the stance of an eager hearer in order to know what is to be preached, since hearing is preparatory to knowing what God wants said. The African-American church tradition honors the preacher as a person who has been called by God to hear first, and who is then sent to speak for God. This view has a biblical warrant in that awesomely promising word from Jesus about those sent to represent and speak for Him: "Whoever listens to you listens to me" (Luke 10:16, NRSV).

2. In the African-American church setting, the preacher is understood as *related by service to the highest frame of reference* as a man of God or woman of God. This view of the preacher makes a world of difference in how the preaching can be encouraged or projected. It is instructive to notice the strength and stamina the African-American preacher tends to show in handling the pulpit task as compared to the hesitancy and unease some preachers from other cultural settings have confessed about facing their pulpit work. Adolphus Julius F. Behrends, in giving the Beecher Lectures at Yale in 1890, took time in his course to warn white seminarians about a struggle which could disarm their spirits as preachers. "There are men who will treat you with haughty indifference, or with condescending civility," he cautioned, "simply because you are a clergyman. They do not believe in the manliness of your vocation."[14] He advised them that they could persist and endure in such circumstances only if convinced of the eternal worth of what they were called and sent by God to do. The African-American church setting has a mind-set that conditions the freedom of the black preacher for his or her work, associating that work with the highest frame of reference— the God who speaks.

3. In addition to the expectation that he or she is divinely called and gifted for what is to be done, *the black preacher is honored as someone intimately related to the need and future of the church*. This also makes the preaching task an honored and desired one. There is the perennial need to build bridges between the meanings in the Word and the daily concerns of the people. There is the need to represent in character and work the incarnation of universal truths and the particularized application of them in personal experience—in a word, modeling the message.

Given all of these levels of expectation and regard, the

preachers in the African-American church setting who honestly meet such expectations and show evidence of being truly charismatic leaders are usually granted the freedoms necessary to fulfill their course with joy as well as widespread communal support. All of this follows from the traditional view and belief that preaching is still a central agency for hearing from God and for gaining and sustaining faith in His deep and sometimes "mysterious ways."

Such faith in the preacher, and such ties between the preacher and the people, will also explain in part why black preaching is so often subjective rather than objective in tone. There is little need on the preacher's part to fear making personal references to his or her experiences, or even saying "I." The African-American church knows that the best preaching involves personality—and demands it. Little is ever lost, but much is usually gained when the preaching person has identified intimately with the people in their journey and struggles, for if that is the case, then the saying of "I" will make the hearing all the more revealing and relevant. As James H. Robinson, echoing Phillips Brooks, once put it: "Preaching may be defined as truth through personality, but a personality which touches life at every point." He added, "If our preaching is to be a revealing ministry, it must grow out of involvement with people in their search for God's will in their lives. Otherwise, it becomes highly irrelevant."[15]

The perspective being traced here involves both religious and social elements, since the Black preacher, as the spiritual leader of a church, is one whose ministry is needed by all and whose identity is shared with all. The group that relates to him or her does so for its life, orientation, guidance, and future. The preacher's influence is extended ever deeper because it is associated with God; this makes the preacher a figure of incarnate meanings and a symbol of hope. This is why the late Kelly Miller Smith commented that "communication actually begins not when the text and the sermon title are announced, but when the minister functions in the community in relation to critical social circumstances and shows social sensitivity prior to proclamation."[16] This understanding also appears in James H. W. Howard's treatment of Preacher Belton in his novel *Bond and Free* (1886) when the reactions of the people to him are described: "In him [they] confided; him they honored; in him they saw the messenger of the Lord bearing the only consolation which was like balm to their deepest sufferings."[17]

Overview of Other Treatments of the Black Hermeneutical Tradition by African-American Scholars

I have treated three hermeneutical perspectives which I have found reflected in the African-American preaching tradition: (1) the adequacy and immediacy of the Word of God as found in the Holy Scriptures of the Christian church; (2) the importance of the hearer's situation in planning the sermon; and (3) the centrality of preaching as an agency for hearing God's Word and gaining an informed faith. It is necessary at this point, however, to offer a brief overview of assessments other African-American scholars have made after studying this preaching tradition. The reader will therefore discern some essential agreements between the hermeneutical perspectives set forth more recently in published works, and the overview may prove helpful in isolating aspects which call for even greater exploration, research, and discussion.

The most recent and extensive critical study of the African-American hermeneutic (both for preaching as a practice and for biblical interpretation as a science to which African Americans are contributing) today is Felder's *Stony the Road We Trod: African American Biblical Interpretation*.[18] The chapters by Thomas Hoyt, Jr.,[19] William H. Myers,[20] and David T. Shannon[21] have opened lanes of interest along which serious preachers will readily travel in rehearsing Black preaching history and projecting their part in its future. Felder's edited volume is the most recent treatment, but the first study dealing with the Black hermeneutic from critical research was Henry H. Mitchell's *Black Preaching*, first published in 1970, and already cited. From his in-depth study of the tradition, Mitchell isolated and expanded upon two major hermeneutical principles honored by the "Black Fathers": (1) the necessity to declare the gospel in the language and culture of the people, using the vernacular; and (2) the necessity, when preaching, to deal directly with human needs.[22] Mitchell's book became the basic text by which others—black, white, and others—were guided in examining the Black preaching rationale and its heritage.

Joseph A. Johnson, Jr. acknowledged his indebtedness to Henry Mitchell in his rather full study, *Proclamation Theology*, also already cited. From his assessment of the tradition, Johnson isolated four hermeneutical principles: (1) The necessity to proclaim the gospel in the vernacular of Black people, with commentary on the Scriptures being drawn from the Black experience; (2) the understanding that God is actively engaged in the work of liberation; (3) the understanding that Jesus Christ is God's revelation in the world, and He is actively engaged in healing, liberating, and reconciling; and (4) the understanding that by His life, ministry, death, and resurrection, Jesus has radically transformed the human condition and has made possible triumphant Christian living.[23]

Warren H. Stewart, Jr., who studied under Mitchell, was the first to write a book devoted exclusively to a documentation of illustrated instances of Black pulpit hermeneutics. Titled *Interpreting God's Word in Black Preaching*, Stewart's study identified five basic hermeneutical principles honored by the African-American preachers with whom he had worked or whose work he had examined in detail. The principles can be summarized as: (1) faith in God's concern; (2) identification of the preacher with the hearers; (3) internalization of the biblical Word by the preacher; (4) translation of the Word into the common tongue of the hearers; and (5) dialogue with the hearers.[24] Stewart's study was brief, but insightful, with valuable references to then-living pulpit figures whose work and witness went beyond denominational walls.

Apart from a few articles on the subject as published in scholarly journals,[25] the most notable studies related to this issue are appearing in anthologies edited by African-American scholars. One previously noted is *Stony the Road We Trod*, edited by Cain Hope Felder; another is *African American Religious Studies: An Interdisciplinary Anthology,* edited by Gayraud S. Wilmore.[26]

In addition to the volumes cited, attention must be called to an earlier study by Cain Hope Felder: *Troubling Biblical Waters: Race, Class, and Family.* Sections of the book treat hermeneutical issues in the preaching task.[27] Mention must likewise be made of the late Kelly Miller Smith's *Social Crisis Preaching,* his Lyman Beecher Lectures delivered at Yale Divinity School in 1983. Smith's thesis audaciously argued the case based on the hermeneutical principle that "a Christian imperative . . . requires adherents of the Christian faith to initiate action regarding social conditions," and preaching is to motivate people to social action.[28] Still another hermeneutical principle is treated by James A. Forbes in his 1986 Lyman Beecher Lectures on *The Holy Spirit and Preaching:* Holy Spirit-anointed preaching is imperative for revitalizing the church.[29]

It is quite clear from these studies that much more remains to be searched out, assessed, and set forth before any full-scale definitive treatment of the African-American hermeneutic for preaching can be prepared and sent forth. The studies listed above are in general agreement, some quite dependent at points upon the earlier publications. My own treatment has been set down under three major perspectives; and from within the history of the tradition under review, these three are, in my judgment, the most central in scope and influence.

Working with the Text

A sermon prepared for an African-American congregation follows. Based on a biblical account, it has been readied and treated in the narrative mode. This understanding is important in following the brief discussion here about the hermeneutical procedures I honored in working with the chosen text: Genesis 47:7-10.

The Hermeneutical Procedure

The right and effective use of a text must be preceded by a right understanding of it; so in working with the chosen text, I

first sought to discern its boundaries as a sense unit. Although the setting and court scene allowed this to be done
with readiness, the whole report is related to the larger context in which Jacob's arrival in Egypt is explained.

I next sought to discern the mood within the structured
sense unit. This was essential because of Jacob's strange answer to Pharaoh's rather clear-cut question about the patriarch's age at the time. Interestingly, Pharaoh and Joseph
seemed gladdened by the old man's presence, but Jacob's mood
did not match their joy. Actually, Jacob's mood was ill-suited
to the occasion as well as the place. The probing of the text
with concern to discover the reason for Jacob's strange demeanor made me remember what novelist Thomas Mann once
lamented about in print—our inability to know in depth "the
colour of the original happening."[30] It is always something we
are striving to sense. My search to "catch the sounds and
sights and smells of the account," as Gardner C. Taylor has
put it,[31] allowed me imaginatively to "overhear" the inner
churnings within the old patriarch's spirit—the rumbling noise
of fear, the lamented memories of a life now almost over, and
the threat of life coming to its end in a foreign land—all this
in the face of Joseph's depth of joy in having his aged father
and family with him in a land where they were freed from the
famine crisis back in Canaan. Sensing Jacob's fear and
tormented memories helped locate the field of concern and
focus out of which the sermon was projected.

As for a critical accounting of the narrative, the text is from
the Jacob cycle embedded in the larger story of Joseph found
in Genesis 37; 39—50, the section of the historical tradition
showing how Israel (the people) came to be in Egypt. As a
written statement the section can be classified by source analysis as part of the P tradition (47:5-6a,7-11,27b-28), but this
consideration about source is not germane to the use to which
the story line I sensed was put; nor is the debated chronology
of 1360-1350 B.C. germane to the sermon purpose, except that
Joseph's role and rank in Pharaoh's court provides the background against which his father's presence in court became
possible.

No textual problems needed to be solved before proceeding to ponder the mood of the man under study. The patriarch's peculiar answer to Pharaoh's question about his age provided the suggestive angle from which an interpretation of his answer came into focus.

Jacob, the Old Testament character, is often viewed, like Simon Peter in the New Testament, as a tragic but representative figure. The many episodes recounted about him in the Genesis narratives are experientially concrete and highly illustrative of how we humans can flaw ourselves. They show what happens within us when we feel the pressures of sad memories, irreparable mistakes, lost opportunities, and feel that our grounds of hope are severely undermined. Jacob's demeanor in court will become a mirror for those who hear the sermon, and by means of that mirror they will be guided to see their need to deal with thwarted ambitions, fears, emotive states that bind and constrict, and especially attitudes that block faith and forbid the necessary upward look that a happy life requires. The textual story speaks most tellingly about Jacob, but it uncovers as much about the hearer's story as about the patriarch's problematic mood.

The reporter has been more suggestive than exhaustive in what stands detailed about Jacob's visit as a guest in Pharaoh's court that day. So much begs to be discovered by the interpreter. Some understanding seems evident through Jacob's assessment of his life: his years are assessed as "few" and "evil," which triggered my recollections from counseling sessions, on the one hand, and the history of the race, on the other. All of this will form the basis for the conflict element in the sermon, against which the gospel can be projected for a needed resolution. The very leanness of the account heightens its appeal because, as a preacher, I knew I had to probe the scene and ponder its implications and links with modern needs before the narrative could be used with effective focus and applied wisdom.[32]

The Homiletical Approach

As a narrative, the story line must be introduced in such a way that the hearers will be gripped, as I was, by the need to

understand why Jacob answered Pharaoh as he did. Afterward, an ascensive handling of the suggested reasons is
demanded, along with the device of strategically timed rhetorical questions that are prods into the hearer's consciousness. The scene must be so vividly felt that it will generate a
rerun within each hearer's own mind, making clear the need
for a serious faith in God's concern and applied grace. The
application-possibility points in the sermon will be many, as
in any such narrative, but the strongest thrusts are planned
through the use of pictured problems: being a misfit in one's
setting, being victimized by sad memories, etc. This seems
evident about Jacob in court, and it becomes the cue for
offering guidance on how to break free from the power of sad
lamenting. The illustrations chosen to deepen the sense of
being a victim on the one hand, and those used to highlight
the gospel message of hope on the other, are all drawn from
the black heritage, keeping the tone of the sermon in full
touch with the lives of those for whom the sermon was prepared. The fact that Jacob holds a treasured place in the folk
tradition of the African-American church (he is the subject of
many of the Black spirituals) provides an additional factor for
those hearing the sermon to identify with him. Finally, the
hearer's attention is moved away from that aged patriarch's
tragic view of life to consider anew his or her own faith or
sense of fate. The final concern, then, is not with Jacob in
Egypt but the self in its history before the God who sees,
cares, and graciously provides us needed help.

The Sermon

Looking Beyond Our Laments

Text: Jacob said to Pharaoh, "The days of the years of my
sojourning are a hundred and thirty years; few and evil have
been the days of the years of my life, and they have not
attained to the days of the years of the life of my fathers in the
days of their sojourning" (Gen. 47:9, RSV).

I

In the scene before us, Joseph's father, Jacob, has come down from Canaan to live in Egypt. It was a necessary move. Canaan was famine-stricken, and Joseph had arranged for the whole family to join him in Egypt where food was still available. The scene concerns the day on which Pharaoh gave Jacob audience, intent to show favor to Joseph, his wise and trusted grand vizier.

Pharaoh asked Jacob his age: "How many are the days of the years of your life?" (v. 9, RSV). Jacob's reply was rather strange; it told his age, but not in the spirit one would expect after being greeted so warmly as a guest in the land. The reply reeked with lament, its wording full of evident unpleasantness. Jacob's reply had no lift in it; it was moody, as if something other than the benefits now available to him had burdened his spirit. What was it that overshadowed his mind in this place of opportunity, a place where food would no longer be scarce? What so affected Jacob's reason that he spoke as if he had none? Whence this moodiness at a time when rejoicing was in order?

II

1. Jacob's moodiness was occasioned in part by *fear*, fear that he might not live long enough to return to Canaan. He was feeling like a refugee because he was now so far from home. His ancestors were buried back there, and Jacob feared that dying in Egypt would mean that he would not be taken back to lay beside them in the family burial plot. Surely we can understand the importance of this to one who like us was concerned about a proper burial, and in the prescribed place. Jacob was now one hundred thirty years old, and he feared that he did not have much longer to live. He thus lamented to Pharaoh, "*Few* and evil have been the days of the years of my life" (v. 9, RSV, author's italics). Actually, Jacob lived on for seventeen more years, dying at the advanced age of one hundred forty-seven years (Gen. 47:28). He had wanted to live longer than his grandfather Abraham, who died at one hun-

dred seventy-five (Gen. 25:7), and longer than his father Isaac,
who was one hundred eighty when he died (Gen. 35:28). And
why did he want to outdistance their years? Only Jacob knew,
but whatever the reason behind his apparent fear of dying
outside the promised land, his lament was out of place on the
occasion of being greeted by Pharaoh; but it is still true: of all
our many emotions, it is fear that weakens our judgment the
most.

2. Jacob's moodiness was stirred by another problem also:
remembered frustrations. His statement to Pharaoh shows
that his memory bank was overflowing with sad scenes from
across his life: "Few and *evil* have been the days of the years of
my life" (v. 9, RSV, author's italics).

Standing before Pharaoh was a man, an old man, troubled
by a sad emotive state at a time when joy was expected. The
depth of his evident disturbance is clearly in view when he
lamented his life as "evil," that is, a spoiled, ruined, worthless
affair of just living on. And we rightly ask: Was this a right
assessment? Yes, he had lived by his wits; he had been a
cunning fellow, ambitious beyond principles, and his lack of
care for others had led him into some tragic tangles and
produced for him some tragic times. Yes, he had been a man
intent on making things go his way, even if he had to force
matters by outsmarting people—as he did his older brother
Esau in seizing the birthright privileges for himself. Thus, he
was afterward on the run for years, trying desperately to stay
out of his angered brother's reach so as to escape that brother's wrath. If Jacob's life was a ruined one, he ruined it, as we
humans can surely do to ourselves.

As Jacob stood answering Pharaoh, surely he had not forgotten how God had so often blessed his life. How could he
have forgotten those fresh starts God had given to him—those
great times of vision when God showed him anew how life
could be, and had given him the favor of starting over again?
How could Jacob have forgotten the experience of that ladder
dream God gave him (Gen. 28:10-22)? How could he have
forgotten that all-night wrestling match with the angel when
he won by valiant struggle a change of name (Gen. 32:24-32)?

How could he have forgotten that vision time at Bethel (Gen. 35:9-15)? What is there about us that makes sad times stand out larger in our memories than glad times? Is memory something with which we catalog events or forget them? Yes, God had been good and gracious; He had often blessed Jacob, but now the man stood victimized by a mood, imprisoned by sad memories. Thus his lament, even at this time when joy was the expected emotion.

What frustrations make you moody? Watch how you handle them because laments can not only change your countenance, but also they can block your reason and distort your perspective. Laments can make us sorry company. I wonder what Joseph thought as he listened to his aged father darken the scene in the court with his moody words. I wonder what Pharaoh thought as he watched and listened to the old man.

III

The late Martin Luther King, Sr., "Daddy King," as we affectionately called him, told in his autobiography about the bitter days he knew as a boy with his sharecropper father in Stockbridge, Georgia. Their lot on the farm was unreasonably hard: the field-work was plentiful; it was never over, and the pay his father received was never a fair share. Black, broke, and without hope that he would ever own land and work for himself, James Albert King sometimes tried to drown his troubles in strong drink, and he had a lot of weekend binges.

One season when farm work was going badly, James King went to Atlanta where his son had gone to complete grade school. King had been drinking, and this was evident to both the son and the school principal who was standing in the office as the father spoke harshly to the boy. James King was insisting that his son would have to stop school and return with him to the farm, while the boy was pleadfully resisting the notion. Soon it was plain to the principal that he would have to intervene. Knowing that the man's son was now in his twenties and just about to complete grade school after a late start in life, the principal advised: "Don't ask your son to do this, Mr. King. Not when his future is so clearly tied to his getting an education. We can only give him some of that here, maybe not enough, but let us, and let him try."

James King bit his lip hard, paused briefly despite his anger, then lurched toward the office door and left. His eyes had narrowed in defiance as he headed out along the road that would take him back to face things on the farm without his son's help. He walked out loaded with lament, his years unpleasant, unreasonable, unrewarding, and unfair. The son walked back down the hall, reentered the classroom from which he had been summoned, sat down, and tried to be attentive as the teacher talked to the class. "I listened," he wrote, "but I heard very little."[33]

There is much in life that can stir a lament within us. There are indeed conditions which can make life unpleasant and unrewarding, conditions which to any reasonable mind are apparently unreasonable and unfair. You are thinking about some of those conditions as I speak, conditions that you have known. We all know what it is to lament, and we all know why we sometimes indulge in the moodiness out of which laments rise.

Any reasonable mind also knows that moodiness can make us like misfits—like Jacob before Pharaoh, so locked in the prison of his moods that his spirit lacked the openness needed to receive the hospitality being extended to him as a privileged guest in the land. Yes, moods can make us misfits. Lingering laments can affect our work, our family, our friendships, our very souls.

There is a way out of the lament mood. There is a way out of the prison of our feelings. The road of faith is that way: faith that life is not through with us, faith that feelings are not the final facts in any case, faith that God still knows and cares about who and where we are. This is the open secret for the courage of our slave ancestors as they faced the unyielding demands of their hard lot in life. When their frustrations seemed unrelenting, when their troubles seemed unending, when their sorrows continued to multiply beyond all counting, and when their hopes were like raisins shriveling under the hot sun, they caught a glimpse of God that helped them to look beyond their laments. Yes, they did sing "Nobody knows the trouble I see, nobody knows my sorrow," but having looked beyond themselves to catch a vision of the justice and mercy of God, they went on to sing, "Glory, Hallelujah!" Our slave ancestors made it through the dark valley of slavery because they learned to look beyond their laments to see the bright mountain peak of a coming freedom. They looked, and God took care of the *seeing*.

IV

In the economy of God, courage to look in His direction has always been the means for human benefit; across the pages of Scripture it has been the sure way to gain hope and find needed help. Childless Abraham learned this as he obeyed the Lord who told him to "Look toward heaven, and number the stars, ... So shall your descendants be" (Gen. 15:5-6, RSV). And in God's time, it happened! Ancient Israel, Abraham's descendants, had to be rebuked again and again by the prophets for looking down rather than up, looking to human alliances with foreign nations for safety instead of trusting fully in their faithful God. The words of Isaiah had a sting in them for all whose eyes were not turned in the right direction:

> Woe to those who go down to Egypt for help
> and rely on horses,
> who trust in chariots because they are many
> and in horsemen because they are very strong,
> but do not look to the Holy One of Israel
> or consult the Lord! (Isa. 31:1, RSV).

Yes, the plea had to be voiced again and again to remind the erring nation about the means for true help:

> "Turn to me and be saved,
> all the ends of the earth!
> For I am God, and there is no other" (Isa. 45:22, RSV).

Have the conditions of your life so narrowed that you are lamenting? Have you lost perspective during your journey, soured because you fear that something important has eluded your grasp? That explains Jacob's demeanor: he was in an emotional rut, and this late in his life. He was so imprisoned in his feelings, so locked into lamenting he did not see that his best years were just ahead of him. The Genesis record tells us that Jacob finally lifted his eyes and looked beyond himself, and as he did, God gave the old patriarch some prophetic insights for the family members gathered about his bed as he faced death. Look beyond your laments! Unless we learn to *look* beyond them we will never be able to *live* beyond them!

Look beyond your laments! Look up, and catch a fresh vision of the glory and grace of God in the face of Jesus Christ. His promise still stands: "Come to me, all who labor and are heavy laden, and I will give you rest" (Matt. 11:28, RSV). This includes rest from strength-sapping, faith-denying, mind-muddling laments! Look beyond your laments! Look around, and catch a fresh awareness of the needs and hurts of others whose lives call out for what your hands and heart can make possible for them in their plight. Look back, and count anew the many blessings you have known from the hand of the Lord! You have seen far too much of His goodness to remain a victim of your own sad moods. Look beyond your laments! Look forward, and see the light shining forth from the future, and those outstretched arms of a Savior ready to welcome your coming in prayer, in trust, and finally, in a death that admits you to the best that can ever be—eternity in His presence!

> I heard the voice of Jesus say,
> "Come unto Me and rest,
> Lay down, thou weary one, lay down
> Thy head upon My breast!"
> I came to Jesus as I was,
> Weary, and worn, and sad;
> I found in Him a resting place,
> And He has made me glad.

I heard the voice of Jesus say,
"I am this dark world's Light,
Look unto Me; thy morn shall rise,
And all thy day be bright!"
I looked to Jesus, and I found
In Him my Star, my Sun;
And in that light of life I'll walk,
Till trav'ling days are done.[34]

Notes

1. See Robert W. Funk, *Language, Hermeneutic, and Word of God: The Problem of Language in the New Testament and Contemporary Theology* (New York: Harper and Row Publishers, 1966), 13-14.

2. Henry H. Mitchell, *The Recovery of Preaching:* The Lyman Beecher Lectures, 1974 (San Francisco: Harper and Row Publishers, 1977), 89.

3. Ibid.

4. Gardner C. Taylor, *How Shall They Preach:* The Lyman Beecher Lectures, 1976 (Elgin, Ill: Progressive Baptist Publishing House, 1977), 59.

5. Ibid., 60.

6. Ibid.

7. See Eldon J. Epp, "Paul's Diverse Imageries of the Human Situation and His Unifying Theme of Freedom," in *Unity and Diversity in New Testament Theology: Essays in Honor of George Eldon Ladd,* ed. Robert A. Guelich (Grand Rapids: Wm. B. Eerdmans Publishing Co., 1978), 100-116.

8. See Olin P. Moyd, *Redemption in Black Theology* (Valley Forge: Judson Press, 1979).

9. Henry H. Mitchell, *Black Preaching: The Recovery of a Powerful Art* (1970; reprint ed., Nashville: Abingdon Press, 1990), 59.

10. See Amos N. Wilder, *The Language of the Gospel: Early Christian Rhetoric* (New York: Harper and Row Publishers, 1964); reissued, Cambridge, Mass: Harvard University Press, 1971, with an extensive introduction by the author, using the title *Early Christian Rhetoric: The Language of the Gospel.*

11. Roland H. Bainton, *Here I Stand: A Life of Martin Luther* (Nashville: Abingdon-Cokesbury Press, 1950), 42.

12. Albert J. Raboteau, *Slave Religion: The "Invisible Institution" in the Antebellum South* (New York: Oxford University Press, 1978), 213.

13. Joseph A. Johnson, Jr., *Proclamation Theology* (Shreveport, La.: Fourth Episcopal District Press, 1977), 45.

14. Adolphus J. F. Behrends, *The Philosophy of Preaching* (London: Richard D. Dickinson, 1890), 5-6.

15. James H. Robinson, *Adventurous Preaching*: The Lyman Beecher Lectures, 1955 (Great Neck, N.Y.: Channel Press, 1955), 36.

16. Kelly Miller Smith, *Social Crisis Preaching*: The Lyman Beecher Lectures, 1983 (Macon, Ga.: Mercer University Press, 1984), 80-81.

17. James H. W. Howard, cited by Bernard W. Bell in *The Afro-American Novel and Its Tradition* (Amherst, Mass.: University of Massachusetts Press, 1987), 31. James Howard's novel was the first Afro-American novel published after the Civil War.

18. Cain Hope Felder, ed., *Stony the Road We Trod: African American Biblical Interpretation* (Minneapolis: Fortress Press, 1991).

19. See Thomas Hoyt Jr., "Interpreting Biblical Scholarship for the Black Church Tradition," Felder, ed., *Stony the Road We Trod,* 17-39.

20. See William H. Myers, "The Hermeneutical Dilemma of the African American Biblical Student," Felder, ed., *Stony the Road We Trod,* 40-56.

21. See the perceptive and illuminating analysis David T. Shannon has given to Paul Laurence Dunbar's specimen of early black preaching, " 'An Antebellum Sermon': A Resource for an African American Hermeneutic," Felder, ed., *Stony the Road We Trod,* 98-123.

22. See Henry H. Mitchell, *Black Preaching: The Recovery of a Powerful Art*; also idem, *Celebration and Experience in Preaching* (Nashville: Abingdon Press, 1990).

23. Johnson, *Proclamation Theology,* 30-51.

24. Warren H. Stewart, Jr., *Interpreting God's Word in Preaching* (Valley Forge: Judson Press, 1984); see pages 13-24; 25-39; 41-51; 53-59; and 61-69.

25. See Robert A. Bennett, Jr., "Biblical Hermeneutics and the Black Preacher," *Journal of the Interdenominational Center* 1, No. 2 (Spring, 1974): 38-53.

26. Gayraud S. Wilmore, ed., *African American Religious Studies: An Interdisciplinary Anthology* (Durham, N.C.: Duke University Press, 1989); see especially the chapter by Robert A. Bennett, "Black Experience and the Bible," 129-139; Vincent L. Wimbish's chapter on "Biblical Historical Study as Liberation: Toward An Afro-Christian Hermeneutic," 140-152; and Henry H. Mitchell's chapter, "Toward a Theology of Black Preaching," 361-371.

27. Cain Hope Felder, *Troubling Biblical Waters: Race, Class and Family* (Maryknoll, N.Y.: Orbis Books, 1989). See especially pp. 79-101 for Felder's most pointed contribution to the question of a hermeneutic for preaching.

28. Smith, *Social Crisis Preaching,* 8. The thesis is treated throughout the book.

29. See James A. Forbes, *The Holy Spirit and Preaching,* The 1986 Lyman Beecher Lectures (Nashville: Abingdon Press, 1989).

30. See Thomas Mann, *Joseph the Provider*, trans., H. T. Lowe-Porter (New York: Alfred A. Knopf, 1944), 370.

31. Taylor, *How Shall They Preach,* 60.

32. For guidelines for doing this, see James Earl Massey, *Designing the Sermon: Order and Movement in Preaching* (Nashville: Abingdon Press, 1980), 35-39. For additional insights on handling a narrative, see Henry H. Mitchell, *Celebration and Experience in Preaching,* 79-107.

33. Martin Luther King, Sr., with Clayton Riley, *Daddy King: An Autobiography* (New York: William Morrow and Co., 1980), 66-67.

34. Horatius Bonar, "The Voice of Jesus," in E. E. Ryden, *The Story of Christian Hymnody* (Rock Island, Ill.: SugarCane Press, 1959), 398.

6
A
PHILOSOPHICAL
MODEL

Dan R. Stiver

Jesus' haunting question to the disciples gathered at Caesarea Philippi—"But who do you say that I am?" (Mark 8:29, RSV)—endures as one of the focal points of the entire Bible. Given its eternal significance, it is the most critical question that we answer in our lives. It is not only a climactic point in each of the Synoptic Gospels (Matt. 16:13-23; Mark 8:27-33; and Luke 9:18-22), but also it is a climactic point in the whole body of Scripture. The Scriptures as a whole are addressed to posing this question and answering it.

Quite apart from the intrinsic significance of the question and of the fact that this event appears as a major turning point in Jesus' ministry, it seizes the reader's attention because of the central incongruity that leaps out even at a cursory first reading. The question is not posed to those whom one might expect. It is not a question to those hearing the gospel for the first time, nor to those who have already heard but are still considering; no, it is addressed to the small circle of the committed. It is addressed to the disciples themselves, who had already been convinced enough of Jesus' significance and identity to leave home and work to follow Him. By this time, one would expect that they would be putting the question to others, not having to face the question themselves. Yet the text reveals that even their answer to the preliminary question—"Who do men say that the Son of man is?" (Matt. 16:13, RSV)—is singularly disappointing. It is not without good reason that Jesus follows up the preliminary question rather curtly with the sharply personal alternative formulation, "But who do you say that I am?" (Matt. 16:15, RSV). Of course, anyone familiar with the Gospels is aware—perhaps too aware in that one is deadened to the original scandal—of the lagging understanding of the disciples. As if anticipating this narcotizing effect, Matthew and Mark followed up one jolt with another. Peter gave the ringing declaration, "You are the Christ, the Son of the living God" (v. 16, RSV), which is no shock by now to our expectations. Nevertheless, following Jesus' equally ringing endorsement of Peter, Peter fell from the pinnacle to the pit by, of all things, Jesus addressing him as Satan! It is this second shock in the passage (in Matthew and Mark) that is not so familiar, not so dead to our sensibilities, and, therefore, retains much of the original offense of the entire passage. It is this second conclusion to the story, this demand to "recognize" Jesus as it were, that is not so often assimilated.

This passage about a question raises more questions. Why is this second stage of the story more difficult? What light does it shed on the first stage, on the questions asked by Jesus? Why is it included in Matthew and Mark and omitted in Luke? These are questions that will be addressed by the exegesis and the sermon. In addition, in a passage highlighting the drama of differing interpretations of Jesus that is just as lively a question today as then, what help can a contemporary philosophy of interpretation provide? In other words, does "philosophical hermeneutics" that focuses on the issue of interpretation have anything to say to those struggling with hermeneutics? Does it help with the broader question opened up by this passage, with the interpretation of Jesus Christ in general, not just the interpretation of this passage in particular?

Analysis of the Text

We begin exegesis of the passage by asking: What is its location in Matthew's Gospel? Without having an exact chronology of Jesus' ministry and without denying that these pericopes could well have been told separately and in different contexts as they were preserved through oral tradition, it is clear that they are structurally located in Matthew's Gospel in the midst of Jesus' ministry and represent a dramatic change of direction. Jesus had enjoyed initial success, culminating with the feeding of the multitudes. However, Jesus appears to withdraw for reorientation, going as far north as He ever traveled, twenty-five miles north of the Sea of Galilee.[1] This removal from the heat of ministry is as much a hinge of the Gospels as the temptations in the desert, and can be seen as a recapitulation of what Jesus learned there: His role was not going to fit public expectations.[2] In fact, what comes to prominence here is not only Jesus' first acceptance of the title Messiah but an identification with suffering. "From that time Jesus began to show his disciples that he must go to Jerusalem and suffer many things" (16:21, RSV). As the passage makes clear, none of these shifts in orientation could be taken as a matter of course.

All of the possibilities mentioned by the disciples would have been an honor to Jesus but would still have left Him with a preparatory and not a decisive role.[3] John the Baptist is clearly seen as precursor, even if somehow still alive after his death in Jesus' ministry! (Matt. 14:1-13).[4] Elijah was a classic apocalyptic figure who was to appear before the coming of the Lord.[5] John the Baptist in fact is identified by Jesus as Elijah in 17:10-13. Jeremiah is mentioned in Matthew alone, and his role is not clear. He may represent a major example of "one of the prophets" (v. 14, RSV) who spoke authoritatively for the Lord; still, he is certainly not a messianic figure himself.[6]

What makes this passage so central is that it is, according to the synoptic writers, Jesus' first acceptance of the title "Messiah," (*christos*, the anointed one). In general, Jesus seemed reluctant to accept the designation, probably because of the misunderstanding such an acceptance would provoke. This assumption is well supported by the Gospels, and particularly by this text. The expectation of a triumphant, powerful, nonsuffering Messiah posed an almost insuperable barrier for the understanding of Jesus, as the disciples' difficulties reveal. What Jesus apparently preferred was to draw on the apocalyptic tradition of the "Son of man" (rooted in Daniel 7:13), tying it by a creative twist to the Suffering Servant of Isaiah. The genuineness of this combination is attested by the fact that neither tradition was emphasized in the early church.[7] The Son of man tradition, which connoted dominion, was in tension with the suffering implicit in the Isaiah passages. The same could be said for the Son of God tradition, tied in with both kingship and with the Messiah in Psalm 2. Jesus' inclination for the Son of man tradition may have been due to the fluid state of its meaning as compared with other available designations, making it more open for Him to fill it with His own interpretation.[8] It may, of course, be likely that Jesus' use of "Son of man" in verse 13 is only, or would have been interpreted as only, a circumlocution for "I"; that is, Jesus could have been heard as asking simply, "Who do people say that I am?" This is the way the question reads in Mark 8:27.[9] Since Matthew added the reference here, it is odd that he omitted the reference to "Son of man" in verse 21 (compare Mark 8:31; Luke 9:22). This, however, does not detract from Jesus' identification with the Son of man tradition, for example, in verses 27 and 28, and certainly would have had significant reverberations for the hearers of this passage in the early church.

Matthew also added the reference to the Son of God in 16:16 to the simple confession of Jesus as the Messiah in Mark; however, this is quite consistent in that Matthew emphasizes a Son of God Christology.[10] Matthew particularly emphasized Jesus as the Son, with the disciples confessing Jesus as the Son of God after His calming of the storm (14:33). Peter's earlier confession, found only in Matthew, takes away some of the innovation in the confession at Caesarea Philippi, but it may be seen as preparatory in a moment of crisis to a deeper, more reflective confession in chapter 16, coupled with the first attribution of Jesus as the Messiah.[11] Even with this further revelation, Jesus continued to be cautious about the use of the title *Messiah*, for He immediately followed Peter's confession with the admonition "to tell no one that he was the Christ" (v. 20, RSV).

What is also significant is that this first acceptance of the title *Messiah* was combined with His first occasion to speak openly about His passion.[12] It is this sharp turn in Jesus' ministry that is underscored by the following fiasco involving Peter. It is precisely the clash of expectations between Jesus as the Messiah and, therefore, the Messiah's suffering that leads to Peter's sharp rebuke of Jesus followed by Jesus' even sharper rebuke of Peter.[13] Structurally, the association of the Messiah with suffering is more climactic than the identification of Jesus as the Messiah.[14] In Matthew, as in the other Synoptic Gospels, the reader is led to increased expectations of Jesus, countered by the challenges of the Pharisees and Sadducees (16:1-12), a tension that is heightened by the disciples' own hesitant response to Jesus' question to them about His identity. The resolution of the tension seems to be reached in Peter's confession, inspired by the Holy Spirit, heightened in Matthew by the fact that Matthew alone recorded the affirmation of Peter as a "rock" and the giving of the keys of the Kingdom (v. 18).[15] However, Peter's great insight is followed immediately by an even greater blindness, inspired by quite another spirit, precipitated by Jesus' own introduction of a new tension between the commonplace expectations of the Messiah and Jesus' own expectations. The importance of Jesus as the suffering Messiah could hardly be emphasized in a more powerful way.

Given the centrality of this story of Peter's failure combined with his earlier achievement, what can we make of the odd fact that it is omitted by Luke? The omission is hardly accidental. Luke certainly included the weaker side of Peter, too, when one looks at Luke-Acts as a whole; and Luke omitted, as does Mark, the positive praise of Peter. There are indications, however, that Luke likely represents a tradition that regarded Peter's leadership more highly than did the traditions behind Matthew and Mark.[16] For our purposes, however, what is significant is that even Matthew and Mark, who included this story of Jesus calling Peter "Satan" (v. 23), had high regard for Peter. In Matthew, the dramatic confession of Jesus as the Christ is included, followed by the giving of the keys of the kingdom, which focuses at least on Peter as a central representative of a disciple's confession. In Matthew and Mark, Peter is seen with James and John as the closest to Jesus among the twelve. Peter is also the most emphasized among the twelve to whom Jesus appeared after the resurrection.

This regard of Peter by all of the Gospel writers makes Jesus' rebuke all the more startling. The sermon concerns not so much the original situation but the text as Scripture, as that which was read by the early church as inspired and later as canonical. Matthew and Mark intentionally included this story, as Luke did not, for these hearers. What was the intended effect? One must try to imagine what must have gone through the minds of those early hearers as they listened to, or perhaps, read this story. If it was read during the church service, most of the hearers then, as today, would have already been believers. They could have identified as believers with Peter's confession of Christ. It likely struck chords of memory of their conversion, their becoming a Christian, when they, too, first clearly recognized and confessed that Jesus was the Christ, the Son of the living God. However, what about Peter's failure that immediately followed?

This episode is clearly *after* Peter's confession. How would they relate to it? This was a place where they would be reminded of their current status as disciples. It would have directed them not at what *had* happened before but to what *can* happen as a disciple, as someone who has confessed Christ. It drives home the point, as only a dramatic story can, that one can be a disciple and yet radically misunderstand Jesus. It accentuates the fact that one can have been inspired by the Spirit and yet need a great deal more insight.[17] At this point, Peter functioned as a bad example, much as he functioned as a positive example as the "rock" on which Jesus founded His church.

This likely was a painful message, as it is today, if we do not deflect it by seeing it just as a personal failure of Peter, having only to do with him and no one else. We may take it to refer only to Peter's unique situation of being a follower of Christ before the fuller revelation of Christ through the resurrection. These strategies, however, defang the text, turning it into only an interesting biographical story with no further relevance. All of the indications are that the Gospel writers did not write and shape their material only to be interesting. They had an instructive purpose in mind. It was history, yes, but history with a message. They desired to change the lives of the readers and hearers of their Gospels. As Frank Stagg pointed out in regard to this passage, the call to suffering "belongs essentially to the Christian calling; it is not optional equipment for 'deluxe model' Christians."[18]

With this larger understanding of the nature of the Gospels in mind, we can return to the question: What is the purpose of this story? Without trying to guess at what Matthew or Mark had in mind, we can ask this in a more objective way: What function does this story have in the Gospel? In other words, what does it do to the reader? Or rather, what does it lead the reader to do? Answering this question indeed requires imagination on the part of the interpreter, but it is not unfettered imagination. It is imagination guided by the text.[19] Put in this way, the message that was indicated above is clear. It is a forcible reminder to believers—as Paul would later remind those observing the Lord's Supper—of an obligation to examine themselves (1 Cor. 11:28).

Drawing further upon Paul, it is a call to theological humility, to realize that "now we see in a mirror dimly" (1 Cor. 13:12, RSV). It is an appeal to be able to say with Paul, "Not that I have already obtained this or am already perfect; but I press on to make it my own, because Christ Jesus has made me his own" (Phil. 3:12, RSV). It is a stern reminder about falling into the situation, as Peter did, of instructing Jesus about what Jesus is really like! It is a caution against knowing better than God what God wants of us. The proper attitude is one also expressed by Paul: "Work out your own salvation with fear and trembling" (Phil. 2:12, RSV).

Given the contrast with the role of the Holy Spirit in Peter's messianic confession, it appeals also, and none too subtly, for humility towards inspired claims to speak for the Holy Spirit. The importance of prophets in the early church indicated throughout the New Testament, who relied on such inspiration, heightens the relevance of this admonition.[20] Peter's experience here is a graphic reminder that one can genuinely be inspired by the Holy Spirit at one moment and by Satan the next! This calls for care and discernment on the part of those who hear, one of Paul's characteristic emphases to the churches under his care (1 Thess. 5:19-21; 1 Cor. 12:3). It is also an appeal to be discerning of oneself, as walking "by the Spirit" is ostensibly to be a part of every Christian's life (Gal. 5:16). One cannot assume that one has properly interpreted God's guidance simply because one is a Christian or even because one has convincingly spoken before "in the Spirit." The passage provides some aid in discernment, namely, no one speaking by the Spirit of God ever denies the call to suffering on the part of the Christian (compare 1 Cor. 12:3). Nevertheless, the difficulties in understanding Jesus underscored by this passage serve as a sober reminder of the complexity inherent in religious judgments. Interpreting the Spirit, while not subjective in a pejorative sense, is marked by ineradicable elements of personal judgment. This fact again calls for cognitive humility on the part of the interpreter.

Such a broad exhortation, however, though salutary, could be paralyzing. It could lead to a state of indecision since we could always doubt that we understand sufficiently, therefore dare not act. It is clear from the text and from the wider context of Scripture that this is certainly not the goal of the text. The fact that Peter was corrected in the same context that his prospects as a reliable disciple for the future are affirmed offers hope. It is not insignificant, too, that the story of the transfiguration which features Peter again as a central character immediately follows (17:1-9). The hearers of this Gospel, the Matthean community, would also be able to confirm in their own experience the high esteem that Peter later attained as a disciple, further providing an implicit background of hope, despite the warning about being mistaken.

As serious as Jesus' charge is, He neither dismissed Peter from the ranks of the disciples nor implied that Peter was irrevocably captivated by Satan. Rather, He challenged Peter, and all other disciples, to further discipleship. The intent is action, not paralyzed indecision, as is clear from the admonition that follows Peter's rebuke, "If any man would come after me, let him deny himself and take up his cross and follow me" (v. 24, RSV). For all those later disciples who have experienced the pattern exemplified by Peter, initial success and confirmation followed by increasing difficulties and perhaps dismal failure, the passage points to an important truth. What is important is to continue on the Way. One day does not a disciple or a season make. Jesus' very reprimand is framed in a context of grace. It was not meant to reject or to abandon Peter; it was meant to rehabilitate and to deepen Peter's discipleship. In this way, too, Peter serves as a model for general patterns in the Christian life.[21]

The message of the passage does not remain, however, on the level of generality. It focuses on a particular stumbling block for Peter: suffering. It is not surprising that this could be a problem. The initial enthusiasm of the disciples for Jesus, that led them to such radical discipleship, probably did not include suffering as a central element. Suffering might occur along the way, but the focus was likely triumph, especially for Jesus. Simply put, the key to the common Gospel theme of the dismal incomprehension of the disciples is the cross, and what was most likely significant for the Gospel writers in retrospect was that it continued to be a stumbling block for those who believed in Jesus Christ after the cross. As the juxtaposition of verses 24-26 with Peter's failure underscores, a suffering Messiah means suffering disciples. Jesus Himself said in John with reference to the suffering of the disciples, "A servant is not greater than his Master" (John 15:20, RSV).

From what is known of the early church and of the context in the later years of the first century when the Evangelists wrote, suffering was a challenge. Even though Matthew was probably written after the persecution of Christians in Rome under Nero in A.D. 64, the heavy persecutions from Rome largely came later. However, there was already strife with the Jewish synagogue, strife within the fledgling church itself, and enough persecution for many of the disciples to become martyrs. We should be able easily to grasp this context, for suffering is still a problem for the church. Again and again, the tempting idea arises that the Christian can somehow be exempt from suffering—despite the clear words of Scripture, like this text, that contradict such an idea.

There are many passages that underline the fact that the Christian faces suffering; this text, however, is shocking in the severity of the rebuke towards misunderstanding on this point. Compare, for example, Jesus' gentleness towards the later request that James and John be allowed to rule at His right hand and His left, also a great misunderstanding of what Jesus' messiahship meant! (20:20-28). Jesus was probably keenly aware of how people would shrink from such a realization. It is apparent that dealing with the reality of the cross was a key to His own realization of what messiahship and sonship meant. In the garden of Gethsemane, Jesus Himself prayed, "My Father, if it be possible, let this cup pass from me" (Matt. 26:39, RSV). The importance of the issue perhaps accounts for the stringency of the response: "Get behind me, Satan!" (v. 23, RSV).

The Art of Interpretation

This text is provocative in that it not only raises questions *of* interpretation but is itself *about* interpretation. Peter was confronted with the challenge of interpreting who Jesus really was. As such, He embodies the kind of perplexity that moderns face as they, too, attempt to understand Jesus. We face conflicting views of Jesus' identity. Our deeply held convictions about Jesus are often confronted—sometimes by those outside the church, sometimes by prophets within the church. We face then the problem of determining the truth of the matter. Given the possibility of the kind of radical misperception that Peter exemplifies, is there any way that our judgments can be validated? Are we reduced to leaps in the dark? Are our judgments simply quixotic inclinations doomed themselves to be called into question without any possibility of adjudication? The way out of this dilemma has often been to latch onto some strict methodology that will provide assured results. These have one after another, however, proved to be partial and inadequate. The movement in contemporary philosophy called "hermeneutical philosophy" attempts to forge a way between the instability on the one hand and the overestimation of methodology on the other. It certainly affords insights into how one approaches the exegetical task, but it also offers a way of looking at Peter's experience as a common, if distressing, experience faced by many Christians, and it suggests a way of coming to grips with it.

Hermeneutical philosophy stems, as one might suppose, from the traditional discipline of hermeneutics, defined as the theory and principles of interpreting ancient texts, above all, the interpretation of sacred Scripture. Indeed, the act of interpreting an ancient text forms the root metaphor or paradigm for hermeneutical philosophy. In turn, the elaboration of this root metaphor on the more general philosophical level has implications that enrich the understanding and practice of biblical hermeneutics. This paradigm is a striking example itself of a key hermeneutical principle, namely, the hermeneutical circle, meaning that the parts and the whole reciprocally affect one another.

In order to see this development more clearly, think of what is involved in interpreting a text. In the case of Scripture, one is confronted with a text from another language and another culture, demanding—and assuming—an ability to cross that historical gap by an act of empathetic imagination, often necessarily combined with technical skills in foreign languages, historiography, and perhaps a myriad of other related disciplines. The experience of controversies in interpreting classic texts underscores the fact that this is neither an easy nor an exact task. On the other hand, it is one that is often met with surprising success. A layperson, relying on an expert's translation and perhaps a lifetime of background tradition concerning the New Testament milieu, can grasp rather well, for example, the gist of Jesus' conflict with legalism, or in our case, the conflict over Jesus' identity in Matthew 16. Such a person in approaching a specific text like this must bring all of his or her background knowledge to the specific text, including some knowledge of the nature of the Messiah in the whole of Matthew's Gospel, the New Testament, and certainly the Old Testament. As an example of the hermeneutical cir-

cle, study of a specific text like this then enriches the understanding of those broader contexts.

Despite the degree of understanding that is possible, even
experts often disagree on finer points of interpretation without any clear and decisive way to resolve the disputes, for
example, the significance of the reference to Jeremiah in
Matthew 16:14 or the meaning of giving Peter the keys of the
kingdom of heaven in 16:19. The difficulty of resolving disputes in a completely impartial, objective way makes hermeneutics more akin to an art than to the application of a
mechanical method.

To turn from the specific instance of interpreting a passage
of Scripture, what relation does such hermeneutics have to
philosophical hermeneutics? Historically, hermeneutical principles were developed, such as that of the hermeneutical circle
or of interpreting obscure passages in light of the clear, in
connection with the interpretation of Scripture, of classic Greek
and Roman texts, and of legal texts.[22] These specific disciplines Paul Ricoeur called "regional hermeneutics."[23] It was
Friedrich Schleiermacher who, above all, emphasized the importance of developing general hermeneutical principles, or
"general hermeneutics," that would be common to any act of
interpreting ancient texts, whether it be Scripture, classical
Greek texts, or legal texts.[24] Although Schleiermacher intimated
a more philosophical approach, Martin Heidegger gave the
impetus to moving on a more general, "ontological" level,
where any hermeneutical act whatsoever was understood to
follow the dynamics of interpreting an ancient text. For
Heidegger, human beings do not just occasionally engage in
hermeneutical acts; all of their understanding is hermeneutically
shaped; in other words, human beings do not just *do* hermeneutics, they *are* hermeneutical.[25] Heidegger's stimulus was
extended and developed above all by his student Hans-Georg
Gadamer in *Truth and Method* and by Paul Ricoeur, who
translated Gadamer's work into French.[26]

Gadamer stressed that in any act of understanding, whether
it be that of conversation with a friend, studying modern
physics, engaging in political debate, watching a movie, or

interpreting a passage of Scripture, one brings one's own "horizon" to another horizon. *Horizon* means one's total perspective on the world. This is especially clear in grasping a text from another culture, but it is also true, if only on a lesser scale, in communication with those with whom one is most familiar. Understanding, then, for Gadamer was a "fusion of horizons," in extreme cases a creative transfiguration of one's view of the world.[27]

Gadamer emphasized several points. One was that understanding is a creative act irreducible to a precise method. This is of great significance in biblical studies. Methods may be helpful, but they are not ends in themselves, despite the endemic tendency to make them so. Methods cannot take the place of the individual, personal judgment of the interpreter. Ricoeur made this point through emphasizing the role of the "productive imagination."[28]

It is easy to miss the significance of this reversal of the priority of personal (or one might say, "hermeneutical") judgment over objective methodology. The history of Western thought, particularly modern philosophy since Descartes and the Enlightenment, has emphasized the priority, even the necessity, of method as a safeguard against the inexactitude and possible prejudice of such personal judgment. What hermeneutical philosophers emphasize is what Gadamer provocatively termed the Enlightenment—"prejudice against prejudice."[29] What this means is that there is no way to escape human judgment by a retreat into an impersonal methodology; in other words, one cannot escape the human condition. In religious terms, it means that one cannot have a "God's-eye" perspective. The tradition has tended to relegate the so-called hermeneutical disciplines that explicitly rely on such judgment such as history, literature, aesthetics, and religion to a secondary status in comparison to the "hard" sciences whose methodology supposedly brackets out the distortions of the human element. The striking inversion for which Gadamer, and an increasing chorus of other thinkers, appeals is to see that the hard sciences themselves are based on hermeneutical judgments, meaning that, if anything, the priority lies with hermeneutical reasoning. The traditional dream of a certain, completely objective, completely secure, impersonal knowledge has been seen to be a will-o'-the-wisp that detracts from the value of what is actually possible to do and to know.

There is no compelling philosophical reason, as is commonly supposed, to view the interpretation of Scripture as somehow less scientific, less rational, or more flawed due to its subjectivity than other disciplines. This fact has important implications for the attitude in which one engages in exegesis. This truth should inhibit the tendency to evade the work—and risk—of interpretation by preoccupation with more "objective," yet limited methods.

A second point that Gadamer emphasized was the role of tradition in the fusion of horizons. One cannot always assume a sharp distinction between the past horizon and one's present horizon. In most cases, especially in the case of Scripture, the past has had some formative influence on the nature of the present horizon.[30] Horizons do not just spring up fully formed! There is, therefore, a process of historical mediation already at work that gives us a foothold from which we can encounter a text. Lessing's so-called ditch, the gap between present and past, is not necessarily an unbridgeable chasm! This relates to Gadamer's previous point about prejudice. He is aware of, and critical of, the negative dimension of prejudice. Nevertheless, he is concerned to make us aware that without some preunderstanding, we would not be able to make contact with the text at all. The fact that our current horizons are already formed in part by the way ancient traditions and ancient texts have been historically mediated to us means that we often have some predisposition to understand a text. Clearly, in the text at hand, our Christian heritage—and our experience of failure—gives us an entree to the text that might be very different for someone raised in a Buddhist culture with very little contact with the Judeo-Christian heritage of the West. Even in such extreme cases of a wide gap, universal human experience, such as the problem of suffering that is so crucial to understanding our text, can provide a bridge of preunderstanding to just such a tradition. Our prejudices, therefore, can be helpful as well as harmful; what is clear is that we cannot escape history into some presuppositionless realm. As Anthony Thiselton expressed it, we live in tradition as fish live in the water.[31] The key is to work with our preunderstandings in the encounter with other horizons in such a way that we become aware of them and mitigate the destructive power of prejudice.[32] The goal might be expressed as preventing preunderstandings from becoming prejudices.

A third emphasis of Gadamer is that one should not elevate either horizon over the other. One cannot understand the past horizon apart from the aid of the present horizon. Contrary to some interpretations of Gadamer, however, it is also untrue that the present horizon is somehow imposed upon and completely dominates the other horizon. Relativism is precisely what Gadamer was attempting to avoid. In fact, he stressed the salutary potential of ancient texts to challenge and confront current horizons. The past can, therefore, exercise a critical function. In our text, the recognition that the way of the Messiah is the way of suffering can be a sobering challenge, even a shattering of a self-satisfied, indulgent Christianity of comfort. Therefore, the fusion of horizons can be seen with respect to one's current horizon as confirmation, mild modification, significant expansion, or radical challenge and transformation.

Gadamer's arresting analogy for this dynamic relationship between the past horizon and the present, between text and interpreter, is that of a game.[33] In a game, the players (more than one) are important. The viewpoint of the modern paradigm is often that of a sovereign subject scrutinizing passive objects. Yet a game is not truly played unless the players lose themselves in the game. One is not entirely in control of a game. There is a sense in which one is "played" by the game itself rather than that one "plays" the game. By this point, Gadamer stressed the way texts grasp our attention, the way we are seized by texts such as Scriptural texts, that is foreign to the ideal of a dispassionate spectator. This model of a game sheds light as well on Gadamer's other favorite model, that of the dialogue.[34] A dialogue, too, consists of an interchange in

which often a new outlook emerges beyond the initial understanding of either partner. He also wanted to underscore the
fact that a game must be played to exist at all. Without
making the meaning of the text subjective, momentary, or
capricious—which should be clear by now in light of the wider
context of Gadamer's concerns—he pointed to the way the
meaning of a text is realized ever anew, and that is only
through giving oneself to the text. Meaning is not temporary,
but it is realized only through new acts of reading, meditat-
ing, or praying.

The events at Caesarea Philippi illustrate internally the
way one's preunderstanding or previous horizon can be caught
up in this to-and-fro movement. Peter would probably never
have been interested in Jesus apart from broader traditions
such as those about a Messiah or Son of God. These drew him
into the game, so to speak. At Caesarea Philippi, however,
Peter found that he was not in control of the game. His
horizon of understanding was confronted, and he found himself suddenly in a "new ball game," one that was disorienting.
Jesus' hope was that through the transformation of Peter's
understanding of the Messiah, Peter would be reoriented. In
fact, Peter was to emerge with quite a new horizon.

A final implication for biblical understanding is that the
traditional sharp differentiation—between exegesis as determining "what the text meant" and then of hermeneutics as
the determination of "what it means" today—is untenable.[35]
Of course, Gadamer recognized the need to distinguish between the present and the past horizon—fusion is not confusion—
but this is only a relative, not an absolute, distinction. A valid
practical contrast can be made, as the above exegesis shows,
but the past and present interpenetrate more than the typical
approach allows. Gadamer asserted that the grasping of what
the text meant is already shaped by the current horizon and
even by some sense of what the application of the text means
for today. Consequently, he also criticized the rigid distinction
between the interpretation of the text and the application of a
text, as if one can first establish the meaning of a text before
raising at all the question of application. It is difficult to miss

the fact that the differing current appropriations of the granting of the keys to Peter has an effect on the way people "objectively" establish what the text meant then! The important thing again is to become aware of these preunderstandings; complete escape is not an option.

Gadamer challenged the hegemony of method but did not elaborate what legitimate place it might have, a task taken up by Paul Ricoeur. Ricoeur emphasized that methods are often crucial in eliminating the negative influence of prejudices, even though they do not replace the importance of hermeneutical judgment. He therefore suggested a hermeneutical arc, or perhaps better, a hermeneutical spiral, in which one approaches the text with an initial understanding, tests that through the use of critical methodologies, leading to a third, postcritical, act of understanding and application.[36]

A critical moment is necessary, although not final. There can be no retreat from criticism, not in the spirit of reductionism that strips the text of its meaning, but in the spirit of a criticism that prevents destructive misreadings and also opens the door to deeper penetration of the text. In this respect, the contributions of historical criticism in depicting the context for Peter's confession and lapse in Jesus' ministry and in the early church, form and redaction criticism in noting the particular theological usage (or nonusage!) of these texts by the different Gospel writers, and ideology critique in alerting us to the way in which vested interests shape interpretation— all of these represent gains in understanding the passage. Nevertheless, their partial insights do not replace one's holistic interpretation of what the text means as another hermeneutical act of understanding that draws on all the resources of methodology and makes difficult judgments in the midst of the conflict of interpretations. Ricoeur has sometimes called this last "moment" in the hermeneutical spiral a "second" or "postcritical" naivete, which avoids being stuck in the "desert of criticism" that never allows one to appropriate the text in an authentically believing or religious way.[37] In the complexity of interpretation, one can forget *why* one is attempting to understand in the first place!

The text is not *replaced* by interpretation; it is *illuminated* by interpretation. An analogy would be the relationship of a movie critic's work to a movie. One would never think of substituting the criticism for the movie! Nevertheless, the criticism may enable one to understand and appreciate the movie in a deeper way. There is a spiral that circles back to the text. Ricoeur argued that texts such as Scripture are first-order language, and are revelatory or disclosive in a primal way. The reflection of interpretation, theology, or philosophy then does not begin from the Cartesian idea of an independent, autonomous ego so much prized by modernity. Rather, such reflection is second-order language dependent upon prior language closer to life. First-order language "gives rise to thought," in the words of Ricoeur;[38] it, however, cannot be replaced. One must return again and again to the text.

To return to Peter's predicament, Peter himself exemplified this hermeneutical dynamic, one that often figures in a Christian's pilgrimage. Peter moved to a deeper insight into his first understanding through his confession of Jesus as the Messiah.[39] Then Jesus Himself challenged Peter to move further still, a challenge that embroiled Peter in a troubling conflict of interpretations. Peter presumably could have refused to grapple with a revision of his conception of the Messiah, or he could have remained caught in a confusion that prohibited any conviction. Both of these options in a myriad of ways are all too often the false paths of contemporary as well as ancient discipleship. Jesus, however, prodded Peter towards a new understanding that, despite the critical distance towards traditional messianic conceptions embedded within it, meant not less but more conviction; in short, a deeper discipleship. Having to take a second critical look at one's convictions is not always, therefore, a temptation to be resisted but can be the path to a more adequate and mature faith.

Ricoeur's hermeneutical spiral with its regular return to the text with renewed questions and insights points to his view of the richness of meaning that at least classic texts engender. One might ask, though, especially in a time that often revels in the variety of interpretations: Are there any constraints on the production of meaning? Ricoeur's view is that a text is "a limited field of possible constructions."[40] This means that it is not a blank slate on which anything can be written. Some interpretations are clearly and objectively better than others. Usually the standards are "better" or "worse," however, rather than simply "true" or "false." It is difficult to limit a text to a definitive, once-for-all meaning. Ricoeur offered a "principle of plenitude" in this regard: a text "means all that it can mean."[41] A word of caution is important: he did not say that a text means anything and everything. Actually, Ricoeur's principle is a modern reaffirmation of an insight discovered over and over again by students of Scripture, namely, a text's meaning can rarely be thoroughly plumbed. Peter's rejection of Jesus' suffering had a particular meaning in its original context for Peter, for Jesus, and for the other disciples who were present. It had a particular meaning for those early Christians who suffered; and it had a particular meaning in those early congregations in its striking contrast with the great affirmation of Peter, as Matthew, my exegesis (and sermon), but not Luke, stressed. This principle implies also that one sermon can seldom plumb the meaning and implications of a text. This is certainly true for the sermon that follows!

The center of gravity for Ricoeur is the text itself. Ricoeur opposed Romantic hermeneutics (to reexperience what the author experienced), many critical approaches (to discern the prehistory of the text, which Ricoeur terms the "world behind the text"), and the tendency of scholasticism of all kinds to replace the text with its own extrabiblical formulations. Ricoeur stressed that the text offers us a world mediated by the text itself, a world in front of the text. This focus upon the final form of the text is where philosophical hermeneutics makes common cause with other approaches such as canonical criticism and literary criticism.[42] In the above exegesis, the prehistory of the text had its place, but the focus was on the text itself and what was justified by the text. The weight lay on interpreting the challenging message of the canonical and final form of the text rather than on admittedly helping but often more limited questions having to do with the background of the text.[43] Ricoeur said, "To interpret is to explicate the type of being-in-the-world unfolded *in front of* the text."[44]

This formation of the self through the worlds opened up by texts is again in contrast to much of modern thought's assumption of a sovereign self that dominates the object of its knowledge.[45] It is true that grasping the world in front of the text is a creative act of the productive imagination, but such "understanding is quite different from a constitution of which the subject would possess the key. In this respect, it would be more correct to say that the *self* is constituted by the matter of the text.[46] For the Christian, Scripture is the text *par excellence* that forms, or rather transforms, one's life. In this way, Ricoeur makes again Gadamer's point that, in giving oneself to the text, it is possible to understand oneself and reality anew.

With regard to the broader question of grasping Jesus' identity as the Christ with the aid of the Holy Spirit as Peter did, it is clear that no hermeneutical theory can "explain" the working of the Holy Spirit. Hermeneutical philosophy, however, can shed light on some of the issues raised by such an appeal to the Holy Spirit. This philosophical approach certainly calls into question the automatic relegation of such "spiritual insight" to the realm of pure subjectivity, irrationality, and lack of rigor. Elements involved in such discernment such as lack of conclusive external proof, irreducibly personal judgment, pulling together a wide range of factors into a new gestalt, all are seen as inherently involved in every area of life. By themselves, therefore, they do not render a judgment irrational. While people may disagree on whether the Holy Spirit can influence one's judgment, indeed, on whether there is a Holy Spirit at all, these disagreements are themselves "hermeneutical-type" judgments that are not in and of themselves irrational. While recognizing the element of personal insight, there is also the element of appealing to support for one's insight. In the case of Peter, his confession was not just a leap in the dark. After all, he had followed Jesus for some time and had some basis for a judgment. The fact that his own conclusion could still be off the mark in a significant way and that some in his time would never come to agree with him at all, anymore than they do today, does not detract from this element of public support or grounding. Peter's judgment, therefore, could be said to be publicly grounded but not publicly conclusive. Traditionally, the latter aspect would characterize it as lacking rationality. It is precisely this verdict that hermeneutical philosophy challenges since it regards any knowledge claim, at bottom, to suffer from the same defect. Rather than concluding then that everything is irrational or even nihilistic, hermeneutical philosophers extend the range of what is considered rational. In this way, the human sciences are seen in principle just as rational as the hard sciences.

Therefore, there is no philosophical reason to regard biblical exegesis as somehow less rational than other disciplines. There is no philosophical reason to rule out beforehand the legitimacy of a judgment that Jesus is the Christ, nor the appeal to the illumination of the Holy Spirit as an aid to the discernment of that claim. The philosophical theory does not mean in itself that such claims *are* consequently rational or true. It does open the door, a door that has largely been slammed tightly shut in philosophy and often in the general public, to such claims having a legitimate possibility of being rational and of being true. Whether they are or not is finally a matter of hermeneutical judgment, aided perhaps by texts such as we have considered here and—according to this passage and traditional Christian belief—by the Holy Spirit.

The Sermon

Confessing the Savior

Text: Matthew 16:33-23

For a kid who wasn't too big, and admittedly not much of a fighter, it was a ticklish situation. I was in the third grade, and my best friend was itching for a fight. Even at that tender age, the disagreement was over the affections of a girl. Still, I was not inclined to fight over the matter, but not so my friend, who was known as the best fighter around. In the midst of this standoff came a surprise; another classmate, apparently perturbed as I was by the mismatch, suddenly stepped in, and in the next moment they were rolling on the ground. I stared at the melee before me, stupefied and quite a bit embarrassed that someone else was taking my lumps for me. Fortunately, the fight did not last long, as the teacher predictably intervened, but it left me with much to think about. How was it that my best friend could suddenly turn on me, which had never happened before? And how was it that this other classmate, whom I certainly knew as a classmate but not particularly as a close friend, would come to my defense in what seemed to me at the time to be a heroic gesture! I thought I knew both of them, but I really didn't; or at least I was forced to "re-know" them.

It was this kind of shock, intensified to its highest degree, that Peter ironically experienced at Caesarea Philippi, ironic because it was preceded perhaps by Peter's greatest moment of insight and penetration into Jesus' identity. Peter, who often is characterized by rapid swings in the Gospels, soared to the heights but almost as quickly plummeted to the depths.

Amid the welter of claims and counterclaims, charges and countercharges, the disciples had withdrawn with Jesus far to the north at Caesarea away from the draining press of the crowds and the controversies. The questions they had been facing about who Jesus was and what He was doing challenged them not only from without but also from within. After all, they were the ones who made a radical commitment to Jesus, leaving home and business to follow Him in the hope—and confidence—that He was One worth following. Were they sure they knew exactly what that meant? Did they really understand who He was?

The Confession

Now Jesus, too, was asking: "Who do men say that the Son of Man is?" (v. 13, RSV). In stark confrontation with the question, the disciples found themselves still at a loss. They offered some possibilities, attractive in themselves but still far from the mark: "Some say John the Baptist, others say Elijah, and others Jeremiah or one of the prophets" (v. 14, RSV). None ventured to go further and to risk his own opinion. All in all, it was a very unimpressive response from an inner circle of disciples. They had heard Jesus' teaching, they had seen His mighty deeds, they had become familiar with His character, and they were obviously not ignorant of the traditions that provided the clues to Jesus' identity. Surely aware of their perplexity, it is no surprise, then, that Jesus may have thought it was time for a little clarification. Jesus, however, wanted to hear it from them, perhaps looking for the increased precision that comes from having to put tacit, half-formed thoughts into words. Yet He quickly found that the disciples were loathe to stake themselves on a particular answer. Rather, they gave the opinions of the ubiquitous "some." They had staked themselves on Jesus, yes, in impressive ways, but they were apparently not yet sure of their ground.

Except Peter. In a pointed question, Jesus asked, "But who do you say that I am?" (v. 15, RSV). The always-quick-to-respond Peter declared in what is clearly a high point of the Gospel, "You are the Christ [the Messiah], the Son of the living God" (v. 16, RSV). How was Peter able to have this insight in light of the disciples' previous hesitancy? How was he able to crystallize what several had no doubt been inactively thinking and yet were unable to verbalize? Jesus' answer was: "Blessed are you, Simon Bar-Jona! For flesh and blood has not revealed this to you, but my Father who is in heaven" (v. 17, RSV). Only with the aid of the Holy Spirit was Peter enabled to have this insight and to take this step beyond seeing Jesus as an important prophet who was, nevertheless, like many preparatory prophets before Him, to identifying Jesus with the hoped for, longed for Messiah.

For those in the early church who would hear and read this Gospel, for those in the church and for those contemplating being in it, perhaps on the basis of the message of this Gospel, this was surely a key passage. No doubt it would have been heard as confirmation of several things. First and foremost, it would be a confirmation of the identity of Jesus as the Messiah. And second, it would confirm that this was not crystal clear to everyone; in other words, Jesus' identity was and could be disputed. Discerning who Jesus is, and becoming a disciple, involves more than just the "facts"; it requires illumination by the Holy Spirit.

Surely many who heard this Gospel could identify at some point in their lives with the hesitancy and perplexity of the disciples. For some of you today who, like the disciples, live amid claims and counterclaims, charges and counter-charges, about who Jesus is, this also should strike a chord. Jesus' identity is just as debated today. Perhaps the options are different: "He was a good man, a moral teacher, a revolutionary, and so on." "The evidence is uncertain." "The rational position is one of agnosticism." There are many such answers. Even those who might be expected to give a clear answer may, like the disciples, feel more safe uttering what others say rather than their own convictions. Nevertheless, at some point one must face the direct question Jesus posed to Peter, "Who do you say that I am?" (v. 15, RSV). In the midst of the tangle of conflicting views, many people do somehow, like Peter, strike through the maze of possibilities and arrive at a conviction that Jesus of Nazareth is indeed the Son of God.

This passage reminds us both of the possibility of that insight and also how difficult it can be to come by. What can seem clear in terms of one's own perspective can seem doubtful, foolish, or even deranged to others. This passage shows us that convincing others of one's own conviction is not as simple as just giving the facts. There are inescapable elements of personal experience, personal judgment, and the illumination representing the mysterious activity of the Holy Spirit, who blows as does the wind. Perhaps one's stance is not as precarious as Soren Kierkegaard's figure of "being suspended over 40,000 fathoms," but faith is indeed held, as Kierkegaard so powerfully portrayed, "in the midst of objective uncertainty." When conviction reigns, nevertheless, one can surely identify with Peter's ringing confession and with Jesus' equally ringing affirmation.

The Condemnation

What a shock it must have been to hear what happened next! Peter, who had understood so well, did not understand.

The channel for the Holy Spirit had turned into a sounding board for the devil. Thinking of those in the early church who heard this Gospel and this passage read over and over again, what would it have said to them? Perhaps it would have been confusing. It is easy to understand that one outside the church might misunderstand and not recognize Jesus. That person needs to have the illumination of the Holy Spirit recorded in the earlier passage. What is striking here is that such a misunderstanding came from one who understood—indeed, one who understood better than anyone heretofore—and from one who clearly had already been illuminated by the Holy Spirit. How could this be? How can one believe, discern, and yet still not understand? How can one understand so much and yet misunderstand?

For those who heard this story, it would have been a reminder that becoming a follower of the Way, being baptized, and breaking bread with the church does not mean that one cannot seriously—and sincerely—stray. It serves as a reminder that those in the inner circle can nevertheless be drastically wrong. Even if one has clearly been in tune with the Holy Spirit in the past, one can in the next instance represent the opposite. It would have been, and is, a sobering message, calling for humility in the Christian life and for renewed "re-cognition" of Jesus. It is a reminder that, as Paul said, "Now I know in part" (1 Cor. 13:12, RSV), and again, "Not that I have already obtained this or am already perfect; but I press on to make it my own, because Christ Jesus has made me his own" (Phil. 3:12, RSV). It is a stern caution against knowing better than God what God is about! We have difficulty facing this mystery of God. Our dilemma is perhaps captured by the ruminations of a little black Mississippi girl. Apparently she had faced already her share of troubles; so when asked to draw a picture of God, she said, "When I draw the Lord, He'll be a real big man. He has to be to explain the way things are."[47] Sometimes, however, we want to jump in and help things out by explaining things for the Lord ahead of time, but this passage calls for care when we think we know the way it really is. It suggests that whatever insight we may think we have into the nature of God, it is possible that we may be extraordinarily surprised by further revelation. And when it comes to others' claims to know the ways of the Lord, it is an appeal also for us to follow Paul's admonition to "test everything" (1 Thess. 5:21, RSV).

The Consequences

This passage is yet more specific. It addresses one specific way in which we easily misunderstand, namely, in the area of suffering, precisely the same area the little girl was concerned about. Peter could not believe that suffering would come to the Messiah, likely intuiting that, if the Messiah experienced such suffering, it did not bode well for the followers of the Messiah. Ever since, Christians have been tempted, with Peter, to rebuke such an implication. It is clear from the passage immediately following that suffering, however, is not reserved just for the Messiah: "If any man would come after me, let him deny himself and take up his cross and follow me" (16:24, RSV).

It is understandable that we would shrink from suffering. Perhaps that is why Jesus apparently spoke so directly, even harshly, about it. Jesus Himself clearly struggled with it in the garden of Gethsemane, but this passage makes plain that a denial of suffering is inspired by some other source than the Holy Spirit!

As a teenager, I remember being attracted to just such a message, that if one would claim all the resources of being a Christian, one would be free of illness and want. Not only that, one would end up being rich! I will never forget the story one very popular representative of this view told about giving away a small jet and in turn being given a bigger jet. Even at the time, in my credulity, I thought that it probably helped if one started out with a jet! It was attractive to think that following Christ would lead to comfort and prosperity, and I heard this from people who seemed to know Christ better than I. It seemed that, like Peter with his amazing confession, they had an inside track. After all, it was only those with the best and the most faith who could claim such benefits; but I learned that as much as they thought they knew, they really did not know everything. Insofar as I was convinced by their message, I had to come to "re-know" or "re-cognize" Jesus.

The Christian life is one of such continuing reacquaintance with the Christ. Even after an inspired confession that Jesus is the Christ, we need further inspiration and further insight. Moreover, this passage stands as a stern reminder that the swing from the side of God to that of Satan can be stunningly swift. What is encouraging, though, is that we know from the rest of the story that all was not lost for Peter. Jesus' affirmation of Peter as a rock was not premature but predictive, despite the further twists and turns of Peter's discipleship. Jesus did not continue to regard Peter as on the side of Satan, nor did He dismiss Peter as a disciple. All the indications are that His admonition, as sharp as it was, was intended to help and not harm Peter, to be itself a way of calling Peter farther on the way of discipleship. We can absorb from Peter, who continued to have missteps, that a crucial ingredient after such a fall is simply to continue to follow, learning the lesson, to be sure, yet also trusting that Christ will not abandon but will continue to lead.

The story of Peter is surely told as an example, and as one of a salutary warning—lest we be too presumptuous that we are everywhere and always led by the Holy Spirit—so that we might avoid the mistake of Peter. It stands also as a promise that despite such a precipitous fall, from heaven to hell, so to speak, there is hope, there is forgiveness, and there is a future with the One who not only goes to the cross but is also raised on the third day (v. 21).

Conclusion

This text underscores the challenge of grasping the identity of Jesus. It is a frank admission that such an identification is not simple, but it is also encouragement that it is possible. It does this as one of the sharpest warnings in Scripture about the possibility of misunderstanding Christ even as a Christian. The correction of Peter, however, is combined with the promise of what he would become. The Matthean community could confirm discipleship for themselves, thus giving Peter's failure a hopeful prognosis; by extension it provides the same hope to other disciples.

The text poses sharply the problem of interpretation. The text itself must *be* interpreted—not always an easy task—and the subject matter itself *is* interpretation. Interpretation, or hermeneutics, therefore is central on two levels. The philosophical hermeneutics described here, as a philosophical approach centered in the phenomenon of interpretation, offers guidance at both levels.

In concert with other contemporary hermeneutical approaches, it points to a focus on the claims of the canonical text, "the world in front of the text" rather than "the world in back of the text." It suggests that one should take seriously the first, perhaps uncritical, claim of the text, then test this first "naivete" with the help of all critical methodologies that are available. It emphasizes, however, that one should not become mired in the "desert of criticism." Interpretation is not complete until one moves to postcritical naivete, a second, now postcritical appropriation. Such an appropriation, furthermore, while not as objective as the traditional paradigm of knowledge would demand, can in principle be regarded as solidly rational.

The issue of the rationality of an interpretation of a text points to the more significant issue raised by this particular text, namely, the legitimacy of interpreting Jesus as the Messiah, inspired by the Holy Spirit. While being cautious about how much support a philosophical theory can give to such a claim, I suggested that in our culture it helps to open the door for the legitimacy of such a claim. Perhaps it can even encourage consideration of such a claim. One cannot demand more of a philosophical theory, but it has done well if it has done so much. The rest, the coming to a conviction that Jesus is the Christ, the awareness that nevertheless we know in part, and a willingness to suffer, is accomplished better through the preaching of the gospel, through our own "ears to hear" (Matt. 11:15, RSV), and through the mysterious activity of the Holy Spirit.

Notes

1. Frank Stagg, "Matthew," vol. 8 in *The Broadman Bible Commentary* (Nashville: Broadman Press, 1969), 171; and David Hill, *The Gospel of Matthew*, in *New Century Bible* (London: Oliphants, 1972), 259.

2. Stagg, "Matthew," 176.

3. William L. Lane, *The Gospel of Mark*, in *The New London Commentary on the New Testament* (London: Marshall, Morgan, & Scott Publications, 1974), 290.

4. In Matthew 14:2, in fact, Herod says of Jesus, "This is John the Baptist, he has been raised from the dead" (RSV). Since John and Jesus were contemporaries, it is a mystery how one could understand such an assertion!

5. Hill, *The Gospel of Matthew*, 259.

6. Ibid., 260. See also Craig L. Blomberg, *Matthew*, vol. 22 in *The New American Commentary* (Nashville: Broadman Press, 1992), 250.

7. I. Howard Marshall, *I Believe in the Historical Jesus* (London: Hodder and Stoughton, 1977), 233; and Stagg, "Matthew," 53. For the larger, much-disputed question of whether any of the titles go back to Jesus Himself or whether the predictions of His passion and resurrection go back to Him, see Marshall's book as a whole, particularly 230-232. For another extensive discussion, see George R. Beasley-Murray, *Jesus and the Kingdom of God* (Grand Rapids: Wm. B. Eerdmans Publishing Co., 1986), 237-247. As is evident, I see both aspects of this passage as rooted in the historical Jesus, while recognizing, as do these authors, the way the Gospel writers have fashioned their material, much as a preacher does, to have an evangelistic and instructive impact.

8. "Son of Man," *The Oxford Dictionary of the Christian Church* (London: Oxford University Press, 1958), 1271-1272.

9. Lane, *The Gospel of Mark*, 297.

10. George Eldon Ladd, *A Theology of the New Testament* (Grand Rapids: Wm. B. Eerdmans Publishing Co., 1974), 142. See also pp. 159-172 for a discussion of the title *Son of God* in the synoptics and the way in which it differs from the messianic tradition. Although Jesus is called Son of God by Satan in the temptations and by demons, Jesus is pictured as being reluctant to publicly accept this title also, in contrast to speaking of Himself as the Son (see Matt. 11:25-27; compare the attribution of Jesus as Son in His baptism, Matt. 3:17, and in the transfiguration, Matt. 17:5).

11. Randolph V. G. Tasker, *The Gospel According to St. Matthew: An Introduction and Commentary*, in *Black's New Testament Commentaries* (London: Adam and Charles Black, 1960), 149.

12. William F. Albright and C. S. Mann, *Matthew*, in *The Anchor Bible* (Garden City, N.Y.: Doubleday and Co., 1971), 198.

13. Stagg, "Matthew," 176.

14. For an introduction to structural approaches to exegesis, see the

articles in the first volume of *Semeia* 1 (1974), focusing on the interpretation of the parables.

15. It is not the focus of my exegesis, nor is there enough space, to focus
on the vexed meaning of Peter's relationship to the founding of the church
and the meaning of the giving of the keys, not to mention the questions
about the originality of the passage since only Matthew includes it. What is
significant to note is that interpretations on the matter by experts differ
sharply. For example, Stagg's conviction that it has nothing to do with the
Roman Catholic interpretation of Peter as the first pope is matched only by
the conviction of Albright and Mann that it does! Stagg, "Matthew," 172-173;
Albright and Mann, *Matthew*, 195-197. Stagg pointed out, "This is probably
the most controversial passage in the Bible among Christians," 172. See
more recently Blomberg, *Matthew*, 254-256.

16. For example, it is interesting to note that in Matthew, Mark, and
Paul, Mary Magdalene is regarded as the first witness to the resurrection.
Only Luke records Peter as the first witness. For a probing account of the
wider situation in the early church that may lie behind such differences, see
Elisabeth S. Fiorenza, *In Memory of Her: A Feminist Theological Reconstruction of Christian Origins* (New York: Crossroad Books, 1984), 315-334,
especially 332.

17. This need for a "second touch" is reinforced in Mark by the fascinating story of Jesus' giving a blind man a second healing touch that immediately precedes this story (8:22-26). Compare Henry Turlington, "Mark," vol.
8 in *The Broadman Bible Commentary* (Nashville: Broadman Press, 1969),
333; compare James Brooks, *Mark*, vol. 23 in *New American Commentary*
(Nashville: Broadman Press, 1991), 132-133.

18. Frank Stagg, *New Testament Theology* (Nashville: Broadman Press,
1962), 56.

19. The narrative whole is formed between the text and the reader's
reconstruction. See Mary Gerhart, "The Restoration of Biblical Narrative,"
Semeia 46 (1989):16. Compare the view of reader-response theory as a
whole that emphasizes this point. See, for example, Wolfgang Iser, "The
Reading Process: A Phenomenological Approach," in *Reader-Response Criticism: From Formalism to Post-Structuralism*, ed. Jane P. Tompkins (Baltimore: John Hopkins University Press, 1980).

20. See, for example, Acts 1:17; 21:9-14; 1 Corinthians 12—14; Ephesians
4:11; Revelation 2:20. For a fuller discussion, see Fiorenza, *In Memory of
Her*, 294-309.

21. Helpful insights in this regard were gained through discussion with
Ken Brewer, a Drew University doctoral student doing research at the
University of Tubingen, Germany, who graciously consented to read an
earlier draft of this chapter. Our discussion of these issues provided enjoya-
ble confirmation of the virtues of dialogue, described in connection with
Gadamer, below.

22. For a sampling of early biblical hermeneutics, see Karlfried Froelich, ed. and trans., *Biblical Interpretation in the Early Church: Sources of Early Christian Thought* (Philadelphia: Fortress Press, 1984).

23. Paul Ricoeur, "The Task of Hermeneutics," in *Hermeneutics and the Human Sciences: Essays on Language, Action, and Interpretation*, ed. and trans. John B. Thompson (New York: Cambridge University Press, 1981), 44-54.

24. Ricoeur gives a brief summary account of this history of hermeneutics in *Hermeneutics and the Human Sciences*, 44-62. Another helpful introduction is Richard E. Palmer, *Hermeneutics: Interpretation Theory in Schleiermacher, Dilthey, Heidegger, and Gadamer*, in *Northwestern University Studies in Phenomenology and Existential Philosophy* (Evanston, Ill.: Northwestern University Press, 1969). For a detailed introduction to philosophical hermeneutics and its possibilities for biblical hermeneutics from an evangelical perspective, see Anthony C. Thiselton, *The Two Horizons: New Testament Hermeneutics and Philosophical Description with Special Reference to Heidegger, Bultmann, Gadamer, and Wittgenstein* (Grand Rapids, Mich.: Wm. B. Eerdmans Publishing Co., 1980).

25. Martin Heidegger, *Being and Time*, trans. John Macquarrie and Edward Robinson (San Francisco: Harper and Row Publishers, 1962), 183,193.

26. Hans-Georg Gadamer, *Truth and Method*, ed. and trans. Garret Barden and John Cumming (1965; reprint ed., New York: Crossroad Publishing Co., 1975).

27. Ibid., 274.

28. Paul Ricoeur, "The Metaphorical Process as Cognition, Imagination, and Feeling," in *Philosophical Perspectives on Metaphor*, ed. Mark Johnson (Minneapolis: Minnesota University Press, 1981).

29. For his broader treatment of this theme, see Gadamer, *Truth and Method*, 235-274.

30. Ibid., 274.

31. Thiselton, *Two Horizons*, 306.

32. For example, Gadamer, *Truth and Method*, 239: "Methodologically conscious understanding will be concerned not merely to form anticipatory ideas, but to make them conscious, so as to check and thus acquire right understanding from the things themselves."

33. Ibid., 104.

34. See Gadamer, *Dialogue and Dialectic: Eight Hermeneutical Studies on Plato*, trans. P. Christopher Smith (New Haven, Conn.: Yale University Press, 1980).

35. A premier expression of this rigid distinction lies in Krister Stendahl's, "Biblical Theology, Contemporary," vol. 1 in *Interpreter's Dictionary of the Bible* (New York: Abingdon Press, 1962), 419-420.

36. See, for example, Paul Ricoeur, "The Model of the Text: Meaningful Action Considered as a Text," in *Hermeneutics and the Human Sciences*,

197-221; and idem., *Interpretation Theory: Discourse and the Surplus of Meaning* (Fort Worth: Texas Christian University Press, 1976), 71-88.

37. Ricoeur, *The Symbolism of Evil*, vol. 17 in Religious Perspectives, trans. Emerson Buchanan (New York: Harper and Row Publishers, 1967), 349.

38. Ibid., 352.

39. In a sense, one could say that Jesus, and Peter's horizon of tradition, was the "text" that Peter was called upon to interpret.

40. Ricoeur, "Model," 213.

41. Ricoeur, "Metaphor and the Problem of Hermeneutics," *Hermeneutics*, 176.

42. See chapters 3 and 4 above. Ricoeur's and Gadamer's views lend themselves to canonical approaches but are not exactly identical with them. One could, for example, take one of Jesus' sayings that appears in different contexts in the Gospels, such as Jesus' saying about salt losing its taste (Matt. 5:13; Mark 9:49-50; Luke 14:34-35), and speak of the world in front of that text as an independent pericope apart from its particular placement in a Gospel.

43. The weight, therefore, tends to fall more on understanding the meaning that the early readers might have construed than on what authors might have intended in the secret recesses of their mind. This emphasis is allied philosophically therefore with reader-response theory." See Iser, "Reading Process," and Edgar V. McKnight, *Postmodern Use of the Bible: The Emergence of Reader-Oriented Criticism* (Nashville: Abingdon Press, 1988). Ricoeur made it clear, however, that a text comes from people; that is, it is a human document. Despite the consequent "distantiation" from the inner life of the author, it is appropriate and enlightening to raise questions about the purpose and intent insofar as these are centered in what lies before one in the text or texts rather than in the author's mind. See Ricoeur, "The Hermeneutical Function of Distantiation," *Hermeneutics*, 131-144. In this sense, biblical inspiration presents no problem in that it obviously occurs in people but does not stop there; it leads to texts.

44. Ibid., 141.

45. Ricoeur, "Appropriation," *Hermeneutics*, 190-193.

46. Ricoeur, "Distantiation," 143-144.

47. Robert Coles, *The Spiritual Life of Children* (Boston: Houghton Mifflin Co., 1990), xiv.

7

A THEOLOGICAL APPROACH

Raymond Bailey

Where does one gain input for theological, homiletical decisions? The historicists believed that only a rational, empirical analysis of objective data should guide human decision making. The Romanticists turned to human experience; the literary critics sought meaning in the narrative. Theological hermeneuts look not behind the text, in the text, or in front of the text, but above the text.

Theological hermeneutics de-emphasizes anthropological insights and skills. Revelation is rather understood as a self-authenticating act of God. Revelation transcends the form of the message and the receiver. How and where God makes God's self known is understood differently by different theologians. Various interpreters identify different keys to revelation. Meaning imposes itself on the listener.

Jürgen Moltmann called his method of interpretation political hermeneutics, and with it he has profoundly influenced liberation and contextual hermeneutics. Moltmann stressed God's concern for the poor and oppressed and their vulnerability to the Word of God. His presuppositions are in essence theological. God creates hope for those in despair. Hope for the oppressed is born through faith in the resurrection of Jesus Christ and anticipation of their own resurrection. The good news of that event leaps time to transform those who receive the message.

Wolfhart Pannenberg was early associated with the theology of hope, but his hermeneutical method is more developed than that of Moltmann. It is distinctive from other theologians in identifying the sphere of revelation. Pannenberg expanded the sphere of revelation beyond the church and salvation history. He believed that revelation is neither contained in history nor in the language that records it. Revelation, according to Pannenberg, occurs *as* history and not just the history of a religion or religions. The *kerygma* is the declaration of God's mighty acts that lies behind the text. Events are meaningful. The most meaningful is the resurrection of Jesus, which was a novel and unrepeatable event accessible to anyone who has eyes to see. Pannenberg synthesized reason and faith.

Pannenberg used Gadamer's fusion of horizons, but with a special twist. He began with the assumption that the events making up the matter of the text are distinct from the text. The confrontation of the experience of the interpreter with the biblical world opens the interpreter to the revelatory event. E. Frank Tupper interpreted Pannenberg's intention this way:

> The attempt to formulate a comprehensive horizon compels the interpreter to project a conception of reality as a whole; moreover, the essential historical differentiation between the text and the interpreter requires the projection of a concept of reality as history, that is, universal history.[1]

Event is more than linguistic; it is a self-disclosing act of God. Jesus' resurrection is the proleptic revelation of the future. The revelatory power of the resurrection lies in its uniqueness and its place in universal history.

Karl Barth was without question one of the most influential theologians of the twentieth century and the most radical of the theological hermeneuts in his insistence on God's initiative and control of revelation. According to Barth, God can only be known through God's self-disclosure. Barth appeared on the preworld war scene to declare a pox on the houses of both the historical positivists and the psychological hermeneuts. He stormed the stage of biblical theology and called Christians back to "The Strange New World Within the Bible."[2] The subject matter attested in Scripture is unique and, therefore, not subject to the hermeneutics applied to ordinary literature. Ordinary hermeneutics could be used but not to disclose the reality of God's presence. Barth used historical criticism and treated it as an important tool of exegesis but inadequate for the comprehension of God's self-disclosure. Barth argued that human attempts to appropriate the meaning of Scripture were futile. The meaning of Scripture could be appropriated only through faith as the grace of God's revelation.

Barth began his theology with the doctrine of the Word of God. His basic presupposition was that God is Ultimate Being who in absolute freedom elects when, how, and to whom God will reveal God's self. Where revelation occurs as God's act, there is the Word of God. "Word of God" is used in three senses: Jesus Christ, the Bible, and in Christian preaching.

The Bible as Witness

Barth differentiated between the word of witness and "the Word." The Bible is not identical to the revelation of God consummated with Jesus Christ; rather, it is an inspired witness which proclaims and affirms that revelation. Barth contended that Scripture does not claim absolute authority for itself as revelation but points beyond the text to a superior authority. The Bible declares that there is a "Word of God" but that it cannot be encased in language. The preacher with the church points to Holy Scripture which points to the Christ through whom God is known.

David Mueller noted Barth's insistence that the witness of human authors of Scripture is not identical to God's revelation; therefore, "the Bible in and of itself cannot be equated with the Word of God which it attests."[3] This does not mean, however, that the Word of God is found apart from the witness of Scripture: "The Word of God cannot be known apart from engagement with Holy Scripture through which his Word is made known to faith."[4] All Christian proclamation must begin with the Bible.

The only way in which Scripture asserts its own authority is the fact that it focuses on God's disclosure of God's self in Jesus Christ. It stands or falls with the reality of Jesus Christ as the incarnate Word of God: "It cannot independently reveal, but only attest, the revelation which did and does take place in the humanity of Jesus Christ."[5]

The importance of Scripture is not lessened by its character as inspired human witness. It is a vehicle through which God provides for the appropriation of His Word to and for us; that is, "it has become for us an actual presence and event."[6] The Bible is not just a testimony of a past event; it is a means of a new saving event. The reader is warned that the sign must not be confused with what it signifies. Scripture should be encountered with an awareness of its limitations as human language and its limitlessness as revelation. Revelation is always an act of God over which humans exercise no control. The Holy Spirit is the activating power that generates a revelatory experience through the witness of Holy Scripture. God not only spoke in times past but also speaks in every age.

The writers of Scripture did their work as obedient response to the will of God. Only *miracle* can explain how the human word becomes divine in the Bible. Barth's understanding of inspiration is based on his exegesis of 1 Timothy 3:14-17 and 2 Peter 1:19-21. His amplification of verse 16 of the Timothy passage elaborated the meaning of *theopneustia*: "given and filled and ruled by the Spirit of God."[7] He stated that the Holy Spirit is the "real" author of the content of the Bible. However, he did not allow for the possibility of any kind of mystical manipulation of the minds of the biblical writers: "*Theopneustia* in the bounds of biblical thinking cannot mean anything but the special attitude of obedience in those who are elected and called to this obviously special service."[8] In other words, the human witnesses wrote as inspired, sensitive hearers in the context of their own personalities. Barth perceived the writers of Scripture as "holy" only in function, that is, in the exercise of their office.[9] They acted in faith, and God's message through them is open only to readers of faith.

Barth urged the interpreter to focus on the content proclaimed rather than on the form or those who shaped the form. He cautioned against an approach to Scripture limited to the historical situation and/or the historical figures with their literary form.[10] Barth stated that there is no special hermeneutic for biblical studies. Scriptural analysis is not unlike any other literary analysis. The uniqueness of Scripture lies in its relation to revelation; that is, in the fact that "the Spirit of God is before and above and in scripture."[11] The work of the interpreter must be obedient response in the same sense that the writer's work was obedient response. The Holy Spirit who inspired the original testimony inspires the interpretation of the canonical text in different ages and cultures.

Barth proposed that we come to the critical study of the Bible without fear that it will be unable to stand examination. Extrabiblical sources and methods must always be subordinated to the Scripture itself. Historical and philological tools are servants of the text rather than managers of the content. The technical problems surrounding a pericope must not become normative for the exposition of the text. Barth said that only those trained in theology should preach and that the minister should use every critical tool at his or her disposal to exegete the Scriptures: "Academic exegetical work is demanded, exact philological and historical study."[12] The best methods and great knowledge of theology, however, will not make God's Word available on demand: "The relation between preaching and revelation cannot be seen as a feature that can be conferred or produced by any technique."[13]

How then does one hear the "Word" contained in the "words"? Exegesis is dependent on a true hearing of the content of Scripture. The Word of God is controlled neither by the literary form of the material nor by the intellectual capacity of the reader. Barth contended that serious exegesis is possible only when the exegete is properly related to the object of the biblical account. Understanding is a result of a proper relationship between the sender and the receiver. Barth insisted that an attempt at objectivity in reading Scripture is "comical." The Word has freedom in the speaker and hearer alike. Again we encounter the circular relationship between the sender, the channel, and the receiver:

We have to know the mystery of the substance if we are really to meet it, if we are really to be open and ready, really to give

ourselves to it, when we are told it, that it may really meet us
in the substance.[14]

Faith speaks to faith. Mueller summarized Barth's thesis on
the role of the Holy Spirit as follows: "Only through God's
initiative in his historical revelation fulfilled in Jesus Christ,
attested in Scripture and continually made alive through Scripture in the present through his Holy Spirit, does knowledge of
God become actual for us."[15] We come to the "word" knowing it
is the "Word" because of our enlightenment by the Holy Spirit.

The truth of God contained in the Bible is hidden from
sinful humans. Sin blinds humans to the reality of God's
revelation. Thus meaningful exegesis requires the mysterious
work of the Spirit. When one approaches Scripture with confidence in human reason, one is inclined to impose human
intelligence onto the Word. God's hiddenness within the biblical words and forms challenges the human interpreter to see
that understanding is gift appropriated through faith—the
gracious act of God. Faithful readers come to Scripture in
humility, aware of the dangers inherent in relying on human
reason and skill. It is not so much a matter of our understanding as it is a matter of being understood. It is not that we
know, but that we are known. Instead of reaching out with
grasping hands and minds, we open up to receive the gift.

Revelation: The Work of the Holy Spirit

Revelation is from God to us; God's gracious presence in
history. The miracle which took place when the testimony of
the prophets, apostles, and evangelists was given literary
form must happen again. The reader's understanding and
reception of the Word must be a response to the call of God.
Scripture's meaning does not depend upon the composition of
the material or the perceptiveness of the reader. It is mediated
by the Holy Spirit. The Holy Spirit is no less the author of our
contemporary experience than it was the author of the writings themselves. Barth saw biblical *theopneustia* as a continuing phenomenon that occurs for us and in us. The essential

Word, Jesus Christ, is revealed in the Bible by the work of the Holy Spirit:

> The Witness of Holy Scripture is therefore the witness of the Holy Spirit. He is indeed the power of the matter of Holy Scripture. By Him it became Holy Scripture; by Him and only by Him it speaks as such. In doing so it mediates revelation.[16]

How does Barth's theology affect the preparation of the preacher to undertake the awesome task of proclamation? Barth's emphasis on the Christ event demands a text centered on the historical revelation. What follows is an attempt to exegete a Christological text using Barth's principles and then to construct a sermon true to the theology implicit in the text.

Like Whom? (Phil. 2:5-11)

This passage has engaged biblical exegetes and theologians for centuries. Much of the attention has focused on *kenosis*, the "self-emptying" of God. It has been interpreted as foundation for a high Christology and as the foundation for the "God is dead" theology that flashed across the American scene in the sixties. The focus of the passage, however, is not on the nature of God or salvation but on ethics—the impact of Christ on believers.

The tone of the first chapters of this epistle is warm and personal. The reader senses a special relationship between Paul and the community at Philippi. Paul wrote to his friends from prison with unselfish concern for the factionalism that had arisen in the congregation. The text is about being Christian in the world. It appears to have been prompted by the failure of Christians to live at peace within the faith community itself. Paul urged the Philippians to find the basis for their life together in Christ Jesus. The rendering of verse 5 in *The New English Bible* may best capture the thrust of the passage: "Let your bearing towards one another arise out of your life in Christ Jesus." This use of "in" does not refer to the thought or internal feelings of Jesus.[17] A recurring theme in

Paul's letter is life "*in* Christ." The sense is that of Galatians 2:20, "It is no longer I who live, but Christ who lives in me" (RSV). Barth noted that "*En Christo Iesou* designates in point of fact the reality, the place, the area in which the people exist."[18] This is a startling notion to the modern mind. Here is mystery that defies the rationalist and the empiricist. This is truth that is greater than the ordinary language that expresses it. Life in Christ is no ordinary existence and is the means of overcoming "selfishness or conceit" (2:3, RSV). This is a truth that propels itself across the ages and lays claim on Christians in all places at all times.

Paul's admonition opens a new dimension that no historical analysis or psychological insight will naturally produce. Here is a moment of revelation that explodes from the strange claim of the God-human. The nature of Christ is presented, not in metaphysical terms, but in the will to incarnation. No philosophical explanation of how God can become human is offered. We are rather told what God did.

The ethos of Christ is perceived through His saving acts. Verses 6-8 have, to the modern mind, the ring of myth. The idea of God taking the form of any human being is incomprehensible to persons living among the scientific and technical marvels of the end of the twentieth century. How can any human be "equal" to God? There is no hint of adoptionism or earned status. The writer does not explain but only reports. This he declares is what was and is.

The mystery of the Trinity pushes the mind further from normal perceptions. If Jesus was in the "form of God" *(morphē)*, was He merely like God ("created in the image") in some attributes? This would not necessarily imply oneness or even kinship. *Morphē* does infer "substance." *Morphē* can suggest "form which corresponds to the underlying reality."[19] Paul pushed the sense with a clear declaration that Jesus is *to einai isa theō*, "equal with God." Philosophical speculation is not invited as to the nature of the equality. This relationship was not something sought or obtained. It was (and is). This is significant when we recall the temptation presented to Eve in the Eden story: "You will be like God" (Gen. 3:5, RSV). The people originally addressed and those of us addressed today are inclined to look after our own interests (Gen 3:6). Jesus had by His nature and being those things which many seek and yet willingly, consciously gave it up. He had no need to prove His identity. "He is so much God's equal that he does not by any means have to make of his equality a thing to be asserted . . . not because he could also give it up, but because his possession of it . . . is beyond dispute."[20] Insecurity—self-doubt—compels humans to go to great lengths to demonstrate knowledge, power, masculinity, femininity, or whatever. The security of the inward dwelling Christ can free us of that stress and striving.

He (*heauton*, "himself") "emptied himself" and took on the "form"—substance—of humanity:

> Elsewhere in the New Testament, the verb and its cognates have a uniformly bad sense. The adjective means "empty-handed," "vain," "useless"; and the verb "to empty of significance," "to make worthless or vain" (Rom. iv. 14:1 Cor. i. 17; etc.). Here the sense is equivalent to he "beggared himself," "became as poor as a beggar" of 2 Chron. viii. 9. He lays aside the insignia of majesty and glory.[21]

It is incomprehensible to sophisticated moderns that a human, let alone a divine being, would become a "servant" or "slave" like others. Not all humans are servants in the sense of waiting on others; therefore, the implication must be greater than that. Jesus took upon Himself the bondage of sin, human impulses, the struggles of time, space, and the flesh. He experienced all the anguish that is a part of the human experience. In this form, His divinity was shielded from ordinary human perception. Only the eyes of faith looking through the lens of the Holy Spirit can see God in the form of flesh. Modern believers tend to be too harsh in judging the people of Jesus' day for not recognizing His divinity. Those closest to Him had difficulty penetrating His human form to see that He was "God with us." It is not easy for one not conditioned to believe in the resurrection to see in the simple Nazarene carpenter the glory of God. Jesus "exists in such a way that to any direct, immediate way of regarding him—e.g., to the historical and psychological approach—he does not present the picture of his proper, original, divine being."[22]

"He humbled himself" (Phil. 2:8, RSV). Jesus was not humiliated by circumstances or persons. No one had power over Him. He was not the blind victim of historical forces beyond His preexistent control. Jesus *surrendered* power and majesty. Jesus did not even assume a position of human honor. God did not come as a prince or as a person of wealth, social status, or physical strength. "He humbled himself, and became obedient unto death" (v. 8, RSV). It is a mistake to compare the martyrdom of Jesus to that of those followers who met a similar but not replicable experience.

Christ's humility and servanthood were appealed to as examples for the Philippians and for us. Likewise, Christ's *obedience* is an example for us. Jesus was obedient to His nature and to His mission. His obedience on behalf of believers makes a demand for obedience on our part. This passage thunders the paradox of the gospel—gift and demand. Jesus is the Source of power for living as a Christian in the world, and He is the mirror that reflects how one in the image of God can be true to that identity.

The exaltation of Christ is not a reward for obedience; it is the revelation of God. Here is the seal of the truth of this narrative. God could not remain hidden. Not even the blindness of sin will forever conceal the glory that indicts fallen humanity. The One on the cross did not *become* the exalted Lord; He *was* the exalted Lord who could not be seen in His glory except on the cross. Glory and authority were not things He had to earn, nor qualities to be grasped. Sin is a curtain that obscures our vision of God until it is pierced by the resurrection of the humble Servant on the cross. The true scandals of the gospel which challenge human reason in this proclamation are incarnation and resurrection. We are apprehended by this truth stranger than human fiction.

Analysis of Exposition

Theological hermeneutics stresses perpendicular as opposed to horizontal authority. God speaks from above the text. The Holy Spirit who inspired the original writer must inspire the contemporary reader/listener. Barth said that the interpreter should not be absorbed in detailed philosophical issues or historical criticism of the narrative. The questions regarding the place and time of Paul's imprisonment when he wrote the letter are interesting but have little impact on the *meaning* of the text. Whether the passage is in the form of a hymn, pre-Pauline or otherwise, does not alter the message. The force and vividness of the poetic can contribute to its power to open the windows of our minds but will not determine meaning.

The temporal and cultural discontinuity creates a remoteness that can jar us to open our eyes to see and our ears to hear. The interpreter immerses himself or herself in the text to think after the author and identify with the author's obedient response to the revelation. This identification is not to share the author's thoughts or feelings but to share the author's experience of revelation. The God who spoke, speaks. The revelation is not directly accessible but is prompted by the divine gift of faith which allows the interpreter imaginatively to enter the textual situation. The contemporary reader/listener personally responds to the transcendent Word contained in the words that bear witness through incredulous possibilities. We do not share the cosmological perspective of the Philippians, but we do share the shock of the bizarre possibilities presented in the text.

This text does not tell us about God, but God presents God's self through the text. "One can only believe ... Or not believe. There is no third way."[23]

The Sermon

Turn Your Eyes Upon Jesus

Text: Philippians 2:5-11

"Turn your eyes upon Jesus," we sing. "Look full in his wonderful face."[24] When you turn your eyes upon Jesus, who do you see? Or what do you see? When you turn your eyes upon

Jesus, do you see the plump, well-fed baby with blue eyes, the country-looking child that appears in so many Dutch paintings? When you turn your eyes upon Jesus, do you see the willowy Jesus, the thin and bony Jesus so popular with Spanish artists? When you turn your eyes upon Jesus, do you see the meek and mild Nazarene, the saccharin Christ featured in Sunday School art? Do you see a person who is dressed in clothes from a long time ago, someone who's just a figment of the far past, another time, another place, with little to do with our lives? When you turn your eyes upon Jesus, whom do you see?

Do you see a God who is distant from us? When you turn your eyes upon Jesus, do you think of a Jesus who stands ready to zap you if you step out of line, a Jesus who is just waiting for you to fail, a Jesus who is far away and so high above you that there is no way you could ever be a part of Jesus or let Jesus be a part of you?

Jesus the Man

Most Christians today are comfortable with the distant deity of Christ. We're very comfortable with the idea that Jesus was, as the Scriptures tell us and as historical theology has affirmed for us, God. We are comfortable with the divine Christ, high and lifted up.

We are not so comfortable, however, with the Christ affirmed in Scripture who is "son of man." Christ is "very God," but He is also "very man." The notion that Christ "emptied himself" and was born in the likeness of a human disturbs us. The Scriptures say that He suffered everything that we suffer; He was tempted in all ways even as we are tempted. Are we comfortable with that Jesus?

Are we more comfortable with the Jesus who lived long ago and far away or more comfortable with a Jesus who is living today? One New Testament theologian has suggested that we ought not to be so concerned about who Jesus *was* as we are about who Jesus *is*. Why are we more comfortable with Jesus "very God" than we are with Jesus "very man"?

The humanity of Christ places the greatest demand upon

us. The God who "humbled himself," became a servant, and was "obedient unto death," is the one who intimidates us. The human Jesus, the Jesus who walked this earth, who experienced all the things that we experience, the Jesus who had to live in a family that didn't understand Him, and was rejected—that Jesus lays claim to our lives. Not a single member of Jesus' own family followed Him until after His death. Mother Mary and brothers and sisters discouraged His ministry. They came and said, "Hey, boy, you've lost your mind. You're embarrassing us. You're going to get hurt. Jesus, stop all this foolishness, and come home."

Jesus knew what it was to have friends, followers, and persons under His supervision who didn't understand Him, who gave all the wrong answers every time He gave a test. Jesus understood what it was like to be out of step with His culture, to be mocked, and to be ridiculed. Jesus was not in the political majority anymore than He was in the religious majority; He was a Man without a country, a Man without a people.

Jesus is portrayed in the Gospels as One who knew what it was to be tired and hungry. The human Jesus knew what it was to laugh and to cry. He knew what it was to sweat, to ache, and to face long days and longer nights.

Sin is missing the mark. Sin is a failure to hit the target, failure to achieve the end or purpose for which we were created. We talk a lot about missing the mark, but who is the mark? Paul said that we should have the mind of Christ. Our conduct is to reflect our relationship to Him.

"Male and female, created He them, in His own image" (AT), the writer of Genesis said. Created in the image of God—what a beautiful idea. What does that mean?

What does it mean to be created in the image of God? The believers at Philippi couldn't even get along with one another. They were operating out of selfish motives, and Paul pointed them toward the mark. Jesus not only came to reveal to us who God is, but also He came to reveal to us who we should be. He is the full revelation of God—none of us would question that—but He is also the full revelation of One created in the image of God. Because we are created in the image of God, Paul could write to us in Romans 8:28 that we are predestined to conform to the image of Christ. Turn your eyes on Jesus and see who you are supposed to be. Turn your eyes upon the life of Jesus to see how one created in the image of God should behave.

We are not comfortable with the humanity of Jesus because of the demand implicit in that identity. To admit His humanity is to destroy our common excuse for failing. If we fail in some way in our Christian lives and Christian experience, what do we say? "After all, we're only human." If we say He was human too, there goes our excuse.

We interpret the Sermon on the Mount as Jesus' ethic beyond human capacity. It doesn't apply to us because we are "only human." It was just an ideal. He really didn't expect us to live it. It was an interim ethic, short term measures for first century believers who thought Jesus was coming quickly. Jesus didn't really expect us to be "Jesus people," "Kingdom people," living in the twentieth century. Turn your eyes upon Jesus, and see who and what you are supposed to be.

Jon Sabrino, a Spanish theologian, has observed that "in his historical life Jesus gave to us many concrete demands but none greater than the demand that we reproduce in our behavior and in ourselves the life of Christ."[25] If there is one theme that runs through all the writings of Paul, it is what some have called Christ mysticism. When Paul talked about Christ "in me" and me in Christ, what does that mean? He said we should have our mind *in* Christ (Phil. 2:5). What would it mean for me to give Christ full rein in my life?

Jesus the Example

How does the life of Jesus in the likeness of humanity address us? Some will respond that Jesus is an excellent model for professional ministers and—maybe—the leaders of the church but not for ordinary people like us. Jesus was a layperson; that was part of His trouble. Jesus had no formal theological training. Jesus was a layperson. He was neither Pharisee nor Sadducee. He was called "Rabbi" because He

taught with wisdom and because of what He did, not because
of any formal authority that had been put upon Him.

Jesus—carpenter Jesus—from Nazareth. I don't know where
it is in your state or hometown, but in every state there is
some place that no one wants to be from. Nazareth was that
kind of place. Here came Jesus from Nazareth. He began His
ministry in the wrong part of the country; everybody knew
that the great preachers, the "real" prophets, did their work in
Judea. Jesus began His ministry in Galilee and spent most of
His time there. That was the wrong place. He was a man from
the wrong place, from the wrong kind of parentage, with the
wrong training, beginning His ministry in the wrong place,
this Jesus. He *emptied* Himself and took the form of a servant.
Jesus "though he was in the form of God, did not count equality with God a thing to be grasped, but emptied himself" (vv.
6-7, RSV).

Jesus emptied Himself, gave up everything for the love of
others. To empty oneself is as repulsive in our time as it was in
the time of Jesus. Our emphasis today is on self-actualization
rather than self-denial. Jesus emptied Himself to enter our
lives, and some self-emptying is required to make room for
Him in our lives today. It is we who need to do the emptying.

A young Buddhist once called on a spiritual master to teach
him everything so that he could become a master himself. The
wise teacher ordered tea for the young student. When it arrived, he began to pour the beverage into the young disciple's
cup. Soon the liquid overflowed the cup, over the saucer onto
the feet of the visitor. "The cup," the young man cried, "is full!
It will hold no more." "Ah," responded the teacher, "as you are
so full of yourself that there is no room for wisdom." Self-
assured, successful moderns are often so full of themselves
that there is no room for the Christ. Turn your eyes upon
Jesus, and see how to empty yourself for the love of God.

One of the hard questions for us is: Could Jesus have failed
in His mission? I believe that in human form He could have.
Had He listened when the tempter whispered, "Climb up on
the highest peak," what would have happened? It's really a
very modern technique. The tempter says, "Look, there's an

easy way to do this. You climb up on the highest peak of the temple; we'll call CNN, NBC, CBS, and ABC, and get them all over there. When we get all the press there, the crowds gathered, and the cameras rolling, You jump off. The angels will come and bear You up and so the whole world will see that You really are who You say You are. If You do it this way, it will be easy." What would have happened? I believe that if Jesus had, in disobedience to the Father, leaped from the temple that He would have been crushed on the rocks below and died, even as He died on the cross of Calvary. It was in obedience that God confirmed Jesus in His role as Son of God and God's servant. Jesus was obedient through continuing contact with His Commander. He spoke often to the Father,... and He listened to the Father.

Turn your eyes upon Jesus and see how to relate to persons. Paul's Letter to the Philippians was prompted by competition and conflict in the church. Competition is a way of life in America. We are taught to be winners and to look out for our own interests. Living together in the church should equip us to live in the world.

A few years ago, I wrote an article in which I said that the church is not God's home. The world is God's house, and the church is only the servant in God's house. I received a nasty letter from a good layman who wrote to point out that I didn't understand my Bible. He noted that God doesn't care about the world: God cares only about the church. I wrote back and asked, "Sir, can you tell me what John 3:16 means?" For God so loved what? The church? A few chosen people? Was not that where Israel missed the boat in misunderstanding that they were called to serve? Go back to Genesis 12 and discover that when Abraham was called he was told, "You will be a blessing" to all nations or "families of the earth" (v. 2, RSV). When you turn your eyes upon Jesus, you see One who demonstrated what it means to be a humble, obedient servant.

The disciples had difficulty understanding a Messiah who came to be a Suffering Servant. Twentieth century disciples still struggle with Jesus, the Lord who serves and who calls them to serve. Turn your eyes upon Jesus to see how to serve.

Jesus gave to those who had nothing to give in return. He showed us how to gain all by giving all. His way confounds all logic. Any sensible person knows that it is better to be served than to serve, but what if God really did become a servant? Then all human logic is shattered, and human values melt in the light.

Jesus the Invitation

T. S. Eliot's play, *The Cocktail Party,* explores empty lives of people living out the delusions of the good life. These people spend their lives in pursuit of pleasure, but realize only despair. They go from relationship to relationship, happy hour to happy hour, psychologist to psychologist. One young woman discovers the secret of Jesus, self-emptying and serving. She disappears from the social whirl, and after only two years the word comes that she has died: crucified on an ant hill on a faraway island where she had been nursing plague-infested natives who would have died anyway. Her friends sip their drinks and murmur, "What a waste!" Sometimes, it is hard to find even twelve who turn their eyes upon Jesus and follow Him.

Jesus came to us in a form we could understand. He stripped Himself so He would not offend us. He came to us, and He sends us to others. He went to them by the seashore, He went to them in the marketplace. Paul wrote the Letter to the Philippians in a prison cell from which he had been witnessing to his guards about Christ.

We make a difference in the world by going to where the people are. We create moments for God to show Himself when we give a cup of water in Jesus' name or a piece of bread in Jesus' name. We enflesh God's love when we go into the inner city, into the apartment house complexes, and into the great learning and intellectual centers. Servants of Christ go to all kinds of people in all kinds of places, all kinds of work, doing all kinds of different things, following the example of Jesus.

Turn your eyes upon Jesus, but He may not fit your ideas of the perfect God.

Jesus is the mirror that reflects reality. We look longingly to see in Him a reflection of ourselves. "Mirror, mirror on the wall, who's the fairest of them all," we ask. "Jesus" is the reply; and we know the anguish of the rich young ruler, for we, too, have much to which we cling.

When we sum it all up, we see in Jesus one who found fulfillment in life by not seeking those things that others seek—political, personal security. We see the humble One who showed us what it means to be exalted in humility. Jesus found fulfillment by giving Himself away. He showed us what it means to be created in the image of God and live out that reality.

I am told that the third best religious seller of all times—behind only the Bible and *Pilgrim's Progress*—is a book entitled *In His Steps* by Charles Sheldon. Charles Sheldon was a Congregational pastor, and the book is a series of sermons he preached on Sunday nights and then published. He never obtained a copyright, so this book produced no royalties for the author. The story begins as a beggar confronts a preacher in worship. The pastor had delivered an erudite, esoteric sermon on what it meant to be a Christian when the beggar appeared and confronted him. Nothing was done for the beggar. The beggar died, and the pastor was forced to examine his theology and ethics. In subsequent sermons, he challenged the congregation to consider every action in light of "What would Jesus do?" Only a small band responded. They bonded together and pledged that for one year—in all of their dealings, in their businesses, in their families, in the community, and in the church—before they did anything, they would ask, "What would Jesus do?" It turned their lives upside down. It turned the church upside down. It turned the city upside down.

What a difference it would make if a band like us, just those of us who are gathered here today, committed ourselves for even one year to ask ourselves, "What would Jesus do?" and then did what Jesus showed us how to do. He didn't just tell us; He showed us how to do. What kind of difference would it make in our lives and the lives of others? What if we turned our eyes on Jesus?

Robert Browning wrote: "Only one life, twill soon be passed; Only what's done for Christ will last."

Only what's done for Christ, in Christ, and with Christ will last. When we are called to be Christians, we are called to be like Christ:

> Have this mind among yourselves, which is yours in Christ Jesus, who, though he was in the form of God, did not count equality with God a thing to be grasped, but emptied himself, taking the form of a servant,... And being found in human form he humbled himself and became obedient unto death (Phil. 2:5-8, RSV).

Conclusion

The message of this passage and of this sermon has little appeal to a success-oriented society. The thought of God-man boggles the mind and strains imagination, let alone logic. The notion of a God who hides in the form of a servant is repulsive to a generation reared on desire for bigger and better. How can we see an exalted Lord through the disgrace of an unjust death in the most barbaric of fashions? Thomas Merton wrote that Jesus made the ordinary, extraordinary, but this is too ordinary, too extraordinary. The foolishness of the cross is too bizarre for enlightened moderns. It is the strangeness of it all, the bizarre character of the tale that breaks through our smugness. Only faith can apprehend truth that is stranger than fiction.

God encounters us in His Word—Jesus Christ who transcends human words, human philosophy, and human psychology. The truth of Scripture is experienced rather than understood. God reveals Himself through the arena of the Scriptures. We are arrested, astonished by God meeting us in His Word:

> The Holy Scriptures will interpret themselves in spite of all our human limitations. We need only dare to follow this drive, this spirit, this river, to grow out beyond ourselves toward the highest answer. This daring is faith; and we read the Bible rightly, not when we do so with false modesty, restraint, and

attempted sobriety, for these are passive qualities, but when we read it in faith.[26]

Barth saw in Scripture the means of our becoming aware of the human sinful condition and of establishing a point of contact between Creator and creature. It is only through such contact that we may hope for the recovery of the *imago Dei* (the image of God). When God speaks and humanity hears, God's freedom and omnipotence are affirmed: "The Bible tells us not how we should talk with God but what he says to us; not how we find the way to him, but how he has sought and found the way to us."[27]

Barth understood preaching as an act ordained of God as a vehicle for God's declaration of *yes* to sinners: "The point of the event of preaching is God's own speaking."[28]

NOTES

1. E. Frank Tupper, *The Theology of Wolfhart Pannenberg* (Philadelphia: The Westminster Press, 1973), 117.

2. Karl Barth, *The Word of God and the Word of Man* (London: Hodder and Stoughton, 1928), 28-50.

3. David Mueller, "The Contributions and Weaknesses of Karl Barth's View of the Bible," *The Proceedings of the Conference on Biblical Inerrancy, 1987* (Nashville: Broadman Press, 1987), 425.

4. Ibid., 429.

5. Karl Barth, *The Doctrine of the Word of God*, vol. 2 in *Church Dogmatics I* (Edinburgh: T. and T. Clark, 1955), 518.

6. Ibid., 463.

7. Ibid., 504.

8. Ibid., 505.

9. Ibid., 491.

10. Ibid., 494.

11. Ibid., 504.

12. Karl Barth, *Homiletics*, trans. Geoffrey Bromiley and Donald Daniels (Louisville: Westminster-John Knox Press, 1991), 77.

13. Ibid., 56.

14. Barth, *Church Dogmatics*, 470.

15. Mueller, "The Contributions and Weaknesses of Karl Barth's View of the Bible," 431.

16. Barth, *Church Dogmatics*, 538.

17. Francis W. Beare, *A Commentary on the Epistles to the Philippians* (New York: Harper and Row, 1959), 73-85; compare Richard R. Melick, Jr.,

Philippians, Colossians, Philemon, vol. 32 in *The New American Commentary* (Nashville: Broadman Press, 1991), 95-109.

18. Karl Barth, *The Epistle to the Philippians* (Richmond: John Knox Press, 1962), 58-65.

19. Beare, *A Commentary on the Epistle to the Philippians*, 79.

20. Barth, *The Epistle to the Philippians*, 62.

21. Beare, *A Commentary on the Epistle to the Philippians*, 81.

22. Barth, *The Epistle to the Philippians*, 63.

23. Barth, *The Word of God*, 41.

24. Helen H. Lemmel, "Turn Your Eyes upon Jesus," *Baptist Hymnal* (Nashville: Convention Press, 1975), 198. Used by permission.

25. Jon Sabrino, *Christology at the Crossroads* (Maryknoll, N.Y.: Orbis Books, 1978), 15.

26. Karl Barth, *Evangelical Theology: An Introduction* (New York: Holt, Rinehart, and Winston, 1963), 34.

27. Barth, *The Word of God*, 43.

28. Barth, *Homiletics*, 47.

BIBLIOGRAPHY

Alter, Robert. *The Art of Biblical Narrative*. New York: Basic Books, 1981.

Auerbach, Erich. *Mimesis: The Representation of Reality in Western Literature*. Translated by Willard R. Trask. Princeton: Princeton University Press, 1953.

Barth, Karl. *Church Dogmatics I*. Volumes 1-2. Edinburgh: T and T Clark, 1955.

——————. *The Epistle to the Philippians*. Richmond: John Knox Press, 1947.

——————. *Evangelical Theology: An Introduction*. New York: Holt, Rinehart and Winston, 1963.

——————. *The Word of God and the Word of Man*. London: Hodder and Stoughton, 1928.

Barthes, Roland. "The Struggle with the Angel: Textual Analysis of Gen. 32:22-32." *Image-Music-Text*. Translated by Stephen Heath. New York: Hill and Wang/Farrar, Strauss and Giroux, 1977.

Beardslee, William A. *Literary Criticism of the New Testament*. Guides to Biblical Scholarship Series. Philadelphia: Fortress Press, 1970.

Beasley-Murray, George R. *Jesus and the Kingdom of God*. Grand Rapids: Wm. B. Eerdmans Publishing Co., 1986.

Bell, Bernard W. *The Afro-American Novel and Its Tradition*. Amherst, Mass.: University of Massachusetts, 1987.

Belo, Fernando. *A Materialist Reading of the Gospel of Mark*. Maryknoll, N.Y.: Orbis Books, 1981.

Berger, Peter L. *Facing Up to Modernity*. New York: Basic Books, 1977.

Betz, Hans D. "The Origin and Nature of Christian Faith According to the Emmaus Legend." *Interpretation* 23 (1969):36.

Bleicher, Josef. *Contemporary Hermeneutics: Hermeneutics as Method, Philosophy and Critique*. Boston: Routledge and Kegan Paul, 1980.

——————. *The Hermeneutic Imagination*. New York: Methuen, 1982.

Blenkinsopp, Joseph. *Prophecy and Canon: A Contribution to the Study of Jewish Origins*. Notre Dame: University of Notre Dame Press, 1977.

Bloom, Harold. *Deconstruction and Criticism*. New York: Continuum Publishing Corp., 1984.

Bloomfield, Morton W. "Allegory as Interpretation." *New Literary History* 3 (1972):301-317.

Booth, Wayne. *Critical Understanding.* Chicago: University of Chicago Press, 1979.

——————. *The Rhetoric of Fiction.* Chicago: University of Chicago Press, 1961, 1983.

Braaten, Carl E. *History and Hermeneutics.* New Directions in Theology Today. Volume 2. Philadelphia: Westminster Press, 1966.

Brooks, Cleanth. *The Well-Wrought Urn: Studies in the Structure of Poetry.* New York: Harcourt, Brace and World, 1947.

——————, and Warren, Robert P. *Understanding Fiction.* 1943. Reprint. New York: Appleton-Century-Crofts, 1959.

Brown, Frank B. *Transfiguration.* Chapel Hill, N.C.: University of North Carolina Press, 1983.

Brown, Raymond E. "Parable and Allegory Reconsidered." *Novum Testamentum* 5 (1962):36-45.

Bruce, Frederick F. *Biblical Exegesis in the Qumran Texts.* Grand Rapids: Wm. B. Eerdmans Publishing Co., 1960.

Brueggemann, Walter. *In Man We Trust: The Neglected Side of Biblical Faith.* Richmond: John Knox Press, 1973.

Bultmann, Rudolf. "New Testament and Mythology." *Kerygma and Myth.* Edited by Hans Werner Bartsch. Translated by Reginald H. Fuller. London: The Society for Promoting Christian Knowledge, 1954.

Burke, Kenneth. *A Grammar of Motives.* 1945. Reprint. Berkeley: University of California Press, 1969.

——————. *The Philosophy of Literary Form: Studies in Symbolic Action.* 2d ed. Baton Rouge: Louisiana State University Press, 1967.

——————. *A Rhetoric of Motives.* 1950. Reprint. Berkeley: University of California Press, 1969.

——————. *The Rhetoric of Religion: Studies in Logology.* 1961. Reprint. Berkeley: University of California Press, 1970.

——————. "Rhetoric—Old and New." *The Journal of General Education* 5 (1951):203.

Buss, Martin J., ed. *Encounter with the Text: Form and History in the Hebrew Bible.* Philadelphia: Fortress Press, 1979.

Buttrick, David. *Homiletic: Moves and Structures.* Philadelphia: Fortress Press, 1987.

Caird, G. B. *The Language and Imagery of the Bible.* Philadelphia: Westminster Press, 1980.

Callahan, John C. *Four Views of Time in Ancient Philosophy.* Cambridge, Mass.: Harvard University Press, 1948.

Cambridge History of the Bible. 3 Volumes. Edited by Peter R. Ackroyd, et al. New York: Cambridge University Press, 1963-1970.

Chatman, Seymour. *Story and Discourse: Narrative Structure in Fiction and Film.* Ithaca: Cornell University Press, 1978.

Childs, B. S. *Biblical Theology in Crisis*. Philadelphia: Westminster Press, 1970.

──────. *The Book of Exodus: A Critical Theological Commentary*. Philadelphia: Westminster Press, 1974.

Coats, George W., and Long, Burke O., eds. *Canon and Authority*. Philadelphia: Fortress Press, 1977.

Cotterell, Peter, and Turner, Max. *Linguistics and Biblical Interpretation*. Downers Grove, Ill.: Inter-Varsity Press, 1989.

Crossan, John D. *In Parables: The Challenge of the Historical Jesus*. San Francisco: Harper and Row Publishers, 1973.

──────. *The Dark Interval: Towards a Theology of Story*. Allen, Tex.: Argus Communications, 1975.

──────. *Raid on the Articulate: Comic Eschatology in Jesus and Borges*. San Francisco: Harper and Row Publishers, 1976.

──────. "Waking the Bible." *Interpretation* 32 (1978):269-285.

──────. *Cliffs of Fall: Paradox and Polyvalence in the Parables of Jesus*. New York: Seabury Press, 1980.

Culpepper, R. Alan. *Anatomy of the Fourth Gospel*. Philadelphia: Fortress Press, 1983.

Dewey, Joanna. *Markan Public Debate: Literary Technique, Concentric Structure and Theology in Mark 2:1-3:6*. Atlanta: Scholars Press, 1980.

Dillon, Richard J. *From Eye-Witnesses to Ministers of the Word: Tradition and Composition in Luke 24*. Rome: Biblical Institute Press, 1978.

Dilthey, Wilhelm. *Essence of Philosophy*. 1907. Reprint in English of German. New York: AMS Press, 1954.

──────. *Introduction to Human Sciences*. 1883. Reprint in English of German. Detroit: Wayne State University Press, 1988.

Dockery, David S. *Biblical Interpretation Then and Now*. Grand Rapids: Baker Book House, 1992.

Eagleton, Terry. *Literary Theory: An Introduction*. Oxford: Basil Blackwell, 1983.

Ebeling, Gerhard. "God and Word." *The Interpretation of Texts*. Volume 1 in *Hermeneutical Inquiry*. Edited by David E. Klemm. Atlanta: Scholars Press, 1986.

Epp, Eldon J. "Paul's Diverse Imageries of the Human Situation and His Unifying Theme of Freedom." *Unity and Diversity in New Testament Theology: Essays in Honor of George Eldon Ladd*. Edited by Robert A. Guelich. Grand Rapids: Wm. B. Eerdmans Publishing Co., 1978.

Fee, Gordon D. *New Testament Exegesis: A Handbook for Students and Pastors*. Philadelphia: Westminster Press, 1983.

Ferguson, Duncan S. *Biblical Hermeneutics*. Atlanta: John Knox Press, 1986.

Fiorenza, Elizabeth S. *In Memory of Her: A Feminist Theological Reconstruction of Christian Origins*. New York: Crossroad Publishing Co., 1984.

Fish, Stanley E. *Is There a Text in the Class?* Cambridge, Mass.: Harvard University Press, 1980.

Fishbane, Michael. *Text and Texture: Close Readings of Selected Biblical Texts.* New York: Schocken Books, 1979.

Fokkelman, J. P. *Narrative Art in Genesis.* Assen, The Netherlands: Van Gorcum, 1975.

—————. *Narrative Art and Poetry in the Books of Samuel.* King David. Volume 1. Assen, The Netherlands: Van Gorcum, 1981.

Fosdick, Harry E. *The Modern Use of the Bible.* New York: Macmillan Publishing Co., 1925.

Fowler, Robert. *Loaves and Fishes: The Function of the Feeding Stories in the Gospel of Mark.* Atlanta: Scholars Press, 1981.

Frei, Hans. *The Eclipse of Biblical Narrative.* New Haven, Conn.: Yale University Press, 1947.

—————. *The Identity of Jesus Christ.* Philadelphia: Fortress Press, 1974.

Froehlich, Karlfried, ed. and trans. *Biblical Interpretation in the Early Church: Sources of Early Christian Thought.* Philadelphia: Fortress Press, 1984.

Frye, Northrop. *The Great Code: The Bible and Literature.* New York: Harcourt Brace Jovanovich, 1982.

Funk, Robert W. *Language, Hermeneutic, and the Word of God:* New York: Harper and Row Publishers, 1966.

—————. *Poetics and the Narrative Text.* Sonoma: Polebridge Press, 1992.

Gadamer, Hans-Georg. *Dialogue and Dialectic: Eight Hermeneutical Studies on Plato.* Translated by P. Christopher Smith. New Haven, Conn.: Yale University Press, 1980.

—————. *Truth and Method.* Translated and edited by Garret Barden and John Cumming. 1965. Reprint in English from German. New York: Crossroad Publishing Co., 1975.

Geertz, Clifford. *The Interpretation of Cultures.* New York: Basic Books, 1973.

Genette, Gerard. *Narrative Discourse: An Essay in Method.* Translated by Jane E. Lewin. Ithaca: Cornell University Press, 1979.

Gerhart, Mary. "The Restoration of Biblical Narrative." *Semeia* 46 (1989):16.

Grant, Robert M., and Tracy, David. *A Short History of the Interpretation of the Bible.* 2d ed. Philadelphia: Fortress Press, 1984.

Green, G. *Scriptural Authority and Narrative Interpretation.* Philadelphia: Fortress Press, 1987.

Gregory, Joel C. "Interpretation in Preaching." *Southwestern Journal of Theology* 27 (1985):8-18.

Gunn, Giles. *The Interpretation of Otherness.* New York: Oxford University Press, 1979.

Hartman, Geoffrey H. *Criticism in the Wilderness.* New Haven, Conn.: Yale University Press, 1980.

Hayes, John H., and Holladay, Carl R. *Biblical Exegesis*. Atlanta: John Knox Press, 1982.

Heidegger, Martin. *Being and Time*. 1935-1949. Translated by John Macquarrie and Edward Robinson. Reprint in English of German. San Francisco: Harper and Row Publishers, 1962.

Hesselgrave, David J. *Communicating Christ Cross-Culturally*. Grand Rapids: Zondervan Publishing House, 1978.

Hill, David. *The Gospel of Matthew*. New Century Bible. London: Oliphants, 1972.

Hirsch, Eric D., Jr. *Aims of Interpretation*. Chicago: University of Chicago Press, 1978.

——————. *The Philosophy of Composition*. Chicago: University of Chicago Press, 1981.

——————. *Validity in Interpretation*. New Haven, Conn.: Yale University Press, 1973.

Holland, L. Virginia. "Kenneth Burke's Dramatistic Approach in Speech Criticism." *Critical Responses to Kenneth Burke, 1924-1966*. Edited by William H. Rueckert. Minneapolis: University of Minnesota Press, 1969.

Howard, Roy, J. *Three Faces of Hermeneutics: An Introduction to Current Theories of Understanding*. Berkeley: University of California Press, 1982.

Johnson, A. M., Jr. *Structuralism and Biblical Hermeneutics*. Pittsburgh Theological Monograph Series, no. 27. Pittsburgh: Pittsburgh Theological Seminary, 1979.

——————. *The New Testament and Structuralism*. Pittsburgh Theological Monograph Series, no. 11. Pittsburgh: Pittsburgh Theological Seminary, 1976.

Johnson, Barbara. *The Critical Difference: Essays in the Contemporary Rhetoric of Reading*. Baltimore: Johns Hopkins University Press, 1980.

Johnson, Joseph A., Jr. *Proclamation Theology*. Shreveport, La.: Fourth Episcopal District Press, 1977.

Kaiser, Otto, and Kummel, Werner G. *Exegetical Method: A Student's Handbook*. New York: Seabury Press, 1963.

Kaiser, Walter C., Jr. "Legitimate Hermeneutics." *Inerrancy*. Edited by Norman L. Geisler. Grand Rapids: Zondervan Publishing House, 1979.

——————. *Toward an Exegetical Theology*. Grand Rapids: Baker Book House, 1981.

Keck, Leander. *The Bible in the Pulpit: The Renewal of Biblical Preaching*. Nashville: Abingdon Press, 1978.

Kee, H. C. *Community of the New Age*. Philadelphia: Westminster Press, 1977.

Kelber, Werner H. *The Kingdom in Mark: A New Place and a New Time*. Philadelphia: Fortress Press, 1974.

——————, ed. *Mark's Story of Jesus*. Philadelphia: Fortress Press, 1979.

—————, ed. *The Passion in Mark*. Philadelphia: Fortress Press, 1976.

Kermode, Frank. *The Classic: Literary Images of Permanence and Change.* Cambridge, Mass.: Harvard University Press, 1979.

—————. *The Genesis of Secrecy: On the Interpretation of Narrative.* Cambridge, Mass: Harvard University Press, 1979.

Klemm, David E. *Hermeneutical Inquiry.* 2 Volumes. Atlanta: Scholars Press, 1986.

Koester, Craig R. "Messianic Exegesis and the Call of Nathanael (John 1:45-51)." *Journal for the Study of the New Testament* 39 (1990):23-34.

Ladd, George Eldon. *A Theology of the New Testament.* Grand Rapids: Wm. B. Eerdmans Publishing Co., 1974.

Lane, William L. *The Gospel of Mark.* The New London Commentary on the New Testament. London: Marshall, Morgan and Scott Publications, 1974.

Leach, Edmund. *Genesis as Myth and Other Essays.* London: Jonathan Cape, 1969.

—————, and Aycock, D. Alan. *Structuralist Interpretations of Biblical Myth.* New York: Cambridge University Press, 1983.

Leiman, Sid. *Canonization of Hebrew Scripture: The Talmudic and Midrashic Evidence.* Hamden, Conn.: Shoe String Press, 1976.

Lewalski, Barbara K. *Protestant Poetics and the Seventeenth Century Religious Lyric.* Princeton: Princeton University Press, 1979.

Louis, Kenneth Grds, et al. *Literary Interpretation of Biblical Narratives.* Nashville: Abingdon Press, 1974.

—————. *Literary Interpretation of Biblical Narratives.* Volume 2. Nashville: Abingdon Press, 1982.

Lundin, Roger; Thiselton, Anthony; and Walhout, Clarence. *The Responsibility of Hermeneutics.* Grand Rapids: Wm. B. Eerdmans Publishing Co., 1985.

McFague, Sallie. *Metaphorical Theology: Models of God in Religious Language.* Philadelphia: Fortress Press, 1982.

McKnight, Edgar V. *The Bible and the Reader: An Introduction to Literary Criticism.* Philadelphia: Fortress Press, 1985.

—————. *Postmodern Use of the Bible: The Emergence of Reader-Oriented Criticism.* Nashville: Abingdon Press, 1988.

—————. *Speaking in Parables: A Study in Metaphor and Theology.* Philadelphia: Fortress Press, 1975.

Marshall, I. Howard. *I Believe in the Historical Jesus.* London: Hodder and Stoughton, 1977.

—————. *The Gospel of Luke: A Commentary on the Greek Text.* Exeter: The Paternoster Press, 1978.

—————, ed. *New Testament Interpretation: Essays on Principles and Methods.* Grand Rapids: Wm. B. Eerdmans Publishing Co., 1977.

Martin, Wallace. *Recent Theories of Narrative.* Ithaca: Cornell University Press, 1986.

Mitchell, Henry H. *Black Preaching: The Recovery of a Powerful Art.* 1970. Reprint. Nashville: Abingdon Press, 1990.

——————. *Celebration and Experience in Preaching.* Nashville: Abingdon Press, 1990.

——————. *The Recovery of Preaching.* The Lyman Beecher Lectures, 1974. San Francisco: Harper and Row Publishers, 1977.

Moyd, Olin P. *Redemption in Black Theology.* Valley Forge: Judson Press, 1979.

Mueller-Vollmer, Kurt, ed. *The Hermeneutics Reader: Texts of the German Tradition from the Enlightenment to the Present.* New York: Continuum Publishing Corp., 1985.

Osborne, George. *Meaning and Significance.* Downers Grove, Ill.: Inter-Varsity Press, 1991.

Palmer, Richard E. *Hermeneutics: Interpretation Theory in Schleiermacher, Dilthey, Heidegger and Gadamer.* Northwestern University Studies in Phenomenology and Existential Philosophy. Evanston, Ill.: Northwestern University Press, 1969.

Patte, Daniel, ed. *Semiology and the Parables.* Pittsburgh Theological Monographs. Number 9. Allison Park, Pa.: Pickwick Press, 1976.

——————. *What Is Structural Exegesis?* Guides to Biblical Scholarship Series. Philadelphia: Fortress Press, 1976.

Perrin, Norman. *Jesus and the Language of the Kingdom.* Philadelphia: Fortress Press, 1976.

Petersen, Norman. *Literary Criticism for New Testament Critics.* Philadelphia: Fortress Press, 1978.

——————. "'Point of View' in Mark's Narrative." *Semeia* 12 (1978):97-121.

Phillips, John B. *Your God Is Too Small.* New York: Macmillan Publishing Co., 1961.

Polzin, Robert M. *Biblical Structuralism: Method and Subjectivity in the Study of Ancient Texts.* Atlanta: Scholars Press, 1977.

Powell, Mark A. *What Is Narrative Criticism?* Guides to Biblical Scholarship Series. Minneapolis: Augsburg Publishing House, 1990.

Prince, George. *Narratology: The Form and Function of Narrative.* New York: Mouton/Walter de Gruyter, 1982.

Resseguie, James L. "Reader Response Criticism and the Synoptic Gospels." *Journal of the American Academy of Religion* 52 (1984):307-324.

Rhoads, David, and Michie, Donald. *Mark as Story: An Introduction to the Narrative of a Gospel.* Philadelphia: Fortress Press, 1982.

——————. "Narrative Criticism and the Gospel of Mark." *Journal of the American Academy of Religion* 50 (1982):411-434.

Ricoeur, Paul. *The Conflict of Interpretations: Essays on Hermeneutics.* Edited by D. Ihde. Evanston: Northwestern University Press, 1974.

——————. *Essays on Biblical Interpretation.* Philadelphia: Fortress Press, 1980.

—————. *Hermeneutics and the Human Sciences: Essays on Language, Action, and Interpretation.* Translated and edited by J. B. Thompson. New York: Cambridge University Press, 1981.

—————. *Interpretation Theory: Discourse and the Surplus of Meaning.* Fort Worth: Texas Christian University Press, 1976.

—————. "The Metaphorical Process as Cognition, Imagination, and Feeling." *Philosophical Perspectives on Metaphor.* Edited by Mark Johnson. Minneapolis: Minnesota University Press, 1981.

—————. *The Rule of Metaphor: Multi-Disciplinary Studies of the Creation of Meaning in Language.* Toronto: University of Toronto Press, 1977.

—————. *The Symbolism of Evil.* Translated by E. Buchanan. Religious Perspectives, Volume 17. New York: Harper and Row Publishers, 1967.

—————. *Time and Narrative.* 3 Volumes. Chicago: University of Chicago Press, 1984-1988.

Rimmon-Kenan, Shlomith. *Narrative Fiction: Contemporary Poetics.* London: Methuen, 1983.

Robinson, Haddon. *Biblical Preaching.* Grand Rapids: Baker Book House, 1980.

Robinson, James H. *Adventurous Preaching.* The Lyman Beecher Lectures, 1955. Great Neck, N.Y.: Channel Press, 1955.

Rueckert, William H. *Kenneth Burke and the Drama of Human Relations.* 2d ed. Berkeley: University of California Press, 1982.

Sanders, J. A. "Hermeneutics." *Interpreter's Dictionary of the Bible.* Supplementary volume. Nashville: Abingdon Press, 1976.

—————. *Torah and Canon.* 2d ed. Philadelphia: Fortress Press, 1972.

Schleiermacher, Friedrich D. *Hermeneutics: The Handwritten Manuscripts.* Edited by H. Kimmerle. Translated by J. Duke and H. J. Forstman. Missoula, Mont.: Scholars Press, 1977.

Schweizer, Eduard. *The Good News According to Luke.* Translated by David E. Green. Atlanta: John Knox Press, 1984.

Selden, Raman. *A Reader's Guide to Contemporary Literary Theory.* Lexington: University of Kentucky Press, 1985.

Smith, Alfred G. "Entropy and Synopsis." *Communication: Concepts and Perspectives.* Edited by Lee Thayer. Washington, D.C.: Spartan Books, 1967.

Smith, Kelly Miller. *Social Crisis Preaching.* The Lyman Beecher Lectures, 1983. Macon, Ga.: Mercer University Press, 1984.

Stagg, Frank. *Matthew-Mark.* The Broadman Bible Commentary. Volume 8. Nashville: Broadman Press, 1969.

Sternberg, Meir. *The Poetics of Biblical Narrative: Ideological Literature and the Drama of Reading.* Bloomington: Indiana University Press, 1985.

Stott, John R. W. *Between Two Worlds: The Art of Preaching in the Twentieth Century.* Grand Rapids: Wm. B. Eerdmans Publishing Co., 1982.

Suleiman, Susan R., and Crosman, Inge. *The Reader in the Text: Essays on Audience and Interpretation.* Princeton, N.J.: Princeton University Press, 1980.

Sundberg, A. C., Jr. *The Old Testament in the Early Church.* Harvard Theological Studies. Volume 20. Cambridge, Mass.: Harvard University Press, 1964.

Tannehill, Robert C. "The Disciples in Mark: The Function of a Narrative Role." *Journal of Religion* 57 (1977):386-405.

——————. *The Narrative Unity of Luke-Acts: A Literary Interpretation.* Philadelphia: Fortress Press, 1986.

Taylor, Gardner C. *How Shall They Preach.* The Lyman Beecher Lectures, 1976. Elgin, Ill.: Progressive Baptist Publishing House, 1977.

Thiselton, Anthony C. *The Two Horizons: New Testament Hermeneutics and Philosophical Description with Special Reference to Heidegger, Bultmann, Gadamer, and Wittgenstein.* Grand Rapids: Wm. B. Eerdmans Publishing Co., 1980.

Todorov, Tzvetan. *The Poetics of Prose.* Oxford: Basil Blackwell, 1977.

Tompkins, Jane P., ed. *Reader-Response Criticism: From Formalism to Post-Structuralism.* Baltimore: Johns Hopkins University Press, 1980.

Uspensky, Boris. *The Poetics of Composition: Structure of the Poetic Text and the Typology of Compositional Forms.* Translated by Valentina Zavarin and Susan Wittig. Berkeley: University of California Press, 1973.

Via, Dan O., Jr. *The Parables: Their World and Existential Dimension.* Philadelphia: Fortress Press, 1975.

——————. *Kerygma and Comedy in the New Testament.* Philadelphia: Fortress Press, 1975.

Von Rad, Gerhard. *Theology of the Old Testament.* 2 Volumes.Translated by D. M. G. Stalker. New York: Harper and Row Publishers, 1962, 1965.

Waters, David M. "David Tracy and Theological Conversation: A Hermeneutic for Sermon Development in the Pastoral Context." Ph.D. dissertation, The Southern Baptist Theological Seminary, 1991.

Wilder, Amos N. *The Language of the Gospel: Early Christian Rhetoric.* 1964. Reprinted as *Early Christian Rhetoric: The Language of the Gospel.* Cambridge, Mass.: Harvard University Press, 1971.